T. S. ELIOT

A MEMOIR

T. S. ELIOT
A MEMOIR

By ROBERT SENCOURT

Edited by Donald Adamson

Illustrated with photographs

DODD, MEAD & COMPANY

NEW YORK

ISBN: 0-396-06347-0
Library of Congress Catalog Card Number: 79-169732

Printed in the United States of America

Foreword

We rejoice for one
Whose heart a midsummer's long winter,
Though ashen-skied and droughtful, could not harden
Against the melting of midwinter spring,
When the gate into the rose garden
Opening at last permitted him to enter
Where wise man becomes child, child plays at king.

A presence, playful yet austere,
Courteously stooping, slips into my mind
Like a most elegant allusion clinching
An argument. Eyes attentive, lined
Forehead—"Thus and thus runs," he makes it clear,
"The poet's rule. No slackening, no infringing
Must compromise it."[1]

In these lines Mr. Cecil Day Lewis has celebrated the memory of T. S. Eliot; and it would hardly have been possible to convey in fewer or more striking words the appearance of the man, the subtlety of his personality, and the deep happiness of his second marriage. It is the purpose of this book to open up other perspectives, and throw light on the years of Eliot's greatest creative maturity.

On Robert Sencourt's death in May 1969, the typescript of his memoir remained unfinished. Eliot and he first met in the late spring of 1927, only five years after the publication of *The Waste Land* and three years before the appearance of *Ash-Wednesday;* both men were expatriates who preferred England to their countries of origin. They shared a deep interest in the religious and metaphysical literature of the seventeenth century (Sencourt's *Outflying Philosophy,* of 1924, had dealt with Donne, Vaughan and Sir Thomas Browne; Eliot was writing essays on Robert Southwell and Lancelot Andrewes for *The Times Literary Supplement*). Sencourt was also a major influence in Eliot's conversion to Anglicanism,[2] and arranged for him to meet Charles, Lord Halifax, who until his death in 1934 was the leader of the Anglo-Catholic laity in England. Sencourt and Eliot became firm friends, and so remained until Eliot's death on 4 January 1965. It seemed imperative to complete and publish this memoir—so different in character from Mr. Day Lewis's tribute, but no less valuable—for through such books as these our enjoyment of the poetry to which we pay tribute may actually be enhanced.[3]

What Sencourt has handed down to us is the record of his own recollections and impressions, both of the man and the writer. His book is a memoir, rather than a biography; this is a fact which cannot be too strongly emphasized. Much time will need to elapse before an objective and definitive biography of Eliot can be written. Indeed, like Meredith, the poet is said to have expressed the wish that there should be no official biography of himself.[4] Similarly, he expressed the wish that his original version of *The Waste Land* might never appear in print;[5] yet such is the importance of the document that its publication is both likely and desirable. It was to comply with this wish, however, that Mrs. T. S. Eliot felt unable to assist me by waiving her control over the copyrights. Readers will therefore, I hope, forgive Robert Sencourt (and myself) for any gaps or inadequacies in the book. Much more would have been said about Eliot's poetry, plays and miscellaneous writings,[6] had it been possible to quote freely from both published and unpublished sources; but it seems most unlikely that any release from these restrictions will be forthcoming in the near future.

Enough remains of Sencourt's original typescript for the publication of a personal memoir to seem justified.[7] Apart from their thirty-seven years' friendship, the two men had common acquaintances in England, the United States, Italy and Switzerland. In 1965 Sencourt (in America at the time of Eliot's death) gathered much fresh material from the poet's relations and friends. On his return to England he heard other reminiscences. But over and above these various reasons for writing a memoir, there was one reason of paramount importance: Robert Sencourt had known the poet's first wife, and in January 1965 must have been one of the few remaining people to have stayed with Tom and Vivienne Eliot at 68 Clarence Gate Gardens.

It is becoming a critical truism to state that, without a knowledge of Eliot's first tragic marriage, a complete appreciation of his poems is totally impossible—whatever Flaubert, Valéry and Eliot may have said about the objective impersonality of art. In particular, it is impossible to take in the full, heart-rending meaning of *The Waste Land* and *Ash-Wednesday* without this knowledge. Eliot himself was well aware of this. He made no attempt to deny that Vivienne was the quix-otic, elemental spirit who had quickened the poetic impulse within him. On the flyleaf of her personal copy of *Poems, 1909–1925* he wrote in the latter year: "For my dearest Vivien,[8] this book, which no one else will quite understand." His *Dante* (of 1929) bears the inscription: "For Vivienne, with love from her devoted husband." On the flyleaf of the first Mrs. Eliot's *Ezra Pound: Selected Poems* we find: "For Vivienne, in mem-ory of many happy days with Ezra and Dorothy Pound."[9]

It would, of course, have been an intrusion into the Eliots' domestic life and the tragedy of their separation if Sencourt had dwelt unduly upon his memories of Divonne-les-Bains and Clarence Gate Gardens. But one of the disadvantages of public men is that their lives become public property to the extent that they are of general interest. Sooner or later, the facts of Eliot's first marriage must be revealed at least in the degree to which they shed light upon his poetry. Already the late Ber-trand Russell has published his impression (dating back to November 1915) that Vivienne was "a person who lives on a knife-edge, and will end as a criminal or a saint";[10] he further disclosed that, on Eliot's own admission, she might well have died in 1916 but for Russell's solicitous concern.[11] This book fills in the outline of a portrait already sketched by Russell. Indeed, considering his long intimacy with the Eliots, Sencourt is understandably laconic concerning the symptoms and aeti-ology of Vivienne's illness.

If, however, Eliot is to be remembered in centuries to come, it will be as the author of *Four Quartets* and *Murder in the Cathedral*, not because of the personal tragedy to which Russell and Sencourt have drawn attention. Even more so than Pound, Eliot was the originator of a vigorous poetic style, as far-

reaching in its influence upon the poets of today as it is discon-
certing in its juxtaposition of the commonplace and the
sublime. No poet of the twentieth century has more success-
fully awakened men to the sublime triteness of their condition.
(It is no coincidence that Eliot so avidly read the *Pensées*.)
But the triteness in Eliot's verse is never merely banal. On the
contrary, it serves to underline the benevolent completeness
of a universe which, without man and all man's follies, would
be meaninglessly incomplete. Imitating Jules Laforgue and Tris-
tan Corbiere, Eliot is as much an innovator in his style as he is
basically a traditionalist in his humanism. His plays, apart from
The Family Reunion, have the supreme merit—intentionally
lacking in the poems—of avoiding the abstruse and esoteric and
thus appealing to a wider public. But their apparent effort-
lessness conceals immense application to the craft of drama,
and not even the engaging conversational tone of the secular
plays can blind us to the fact that a deep message—Eliot's
message—lies beneath. Besides the poems and plays, yet another
major contribution to English literature is Eliot's criticism.
Whatever contradictions we may discern between his earlier
and later thought (as, for instance, in his attitudes towards
Milton[12] and Yeats[13]), whatever blind spots he may secretly,
or not so secretly, have harboured (as, for instance, in his
antipathy to Shelley[14] and Gerald Manley Hopkins[15]), it is
virtually undeniable that here is the most thought-provoking
literary critic of his and the succeeding generation. Add to this
the early venture into Idealist philosophy, together with his
social criticism, his interest in Eastern thought and his far-
ranging speculations on religion generally, and—even allowing
for his avoidance of the novel-form—we surely have one of
the most universal of modern writers and thinkers. Robert

Sencourt has sought to portray each of these aspects of Eliot's genius as painstakingly as he has recorded his memories of the poet's life. No one, indeed, was better qualified than he to narrate and assess Eliot's churchmanship.

It is perhaps true that no one can view a friend with "roughnesses, pimples, warts, and everything" (as Cromwell desired Lely to portray him). Yet, bearing in mind the comparatively recent date of Eliot's death, I believe that Robert Sencourt's memoir is a reasonably objective presentation of the facts. It is certainly the tribute of one very remarkable man to another.

DONALD ADAMSON

Contents

Illustrations

T. S. ELIOT

A MEMOIR

CHAPTER

1

An American Childhood

IN 1831[1] William Greenleaf Eliot, a New Englander then aged twenty, decided that he would leave Harvard Divinity School and travel down to Washington to complete his education. There he fell passionately in love with a splendid girl a year or two younger than himself. Given the idealism they shared, they decided they would found a Unitarian mission at St. Louis in what was still the western frontier of the United States. St. Louis remained the foremost city along the frontier until the very end of W. G. Eliot's life, when Chicago finally overtook it. Placed on the confluence of the Mississippi and the Missouri, the capital city of Missouri was strongly marked by four currents of immigration: the French, the Southerners, the constant stream flowing in from New England, and the solidly respectable German element, who were frequently Catholic.

The enterprising young Eliot was not only a Puritan pioneer among a large majority of Catholics and Southerners, he was a cultivated man among many rough frontiersmen. Predominantly influenced by the conduct of their Southern neighbors,

Missourians of that day believed in owning slaves; they gambled, they drank, they even settled their quarrels by duelling. Some of these immigrants had come to St. Louis because they sought an unconventional and exciting life, but the great majority, as W. G. Eliot duly noted, had already made money their god—whereas he wanted them to turn away from Mammon towards culture and Unitarianism.

He had not been three years engaged in this enterprise before he was able to return to Washington to bring back his beautiful bride as an ally in his struggle against the men of fortune who surrounded him.

It was the year when, across the Atlantic in England, the young Victoria had risen from bed to find the Archbishop of Canterbury kneeling before her to tell her she was queen. She gave to the century a tone not unlike that which the young bride and bridegroom aimed to give St. Louis. To found a church for his Unitarians was not his only creative enterprise, for the Eliots were to have no less than fourteen children.

By 1849 he was coping with the town's misfortunes. St. Louis had met with disaster from both flood and fire and from this resulted an epidemic of cholera which killed over six thousand inhabitants. Everywhere the Protestant pastor ministered to the infected thousands. Nor did his work end with what little he could do for the sick and dying. In the fifteen years they had been married, the Eliots had begotten six or seven children of their final fourteen; to these they now added twenty-six orphans.

From this sort of philanthropy they turned to nursing and education. During the Civil War they organized a service for the wounded which anticipated the work of the Red Cross. In 1856 William Greenleaf Eliot established a free mission school.

In the following year he founded a university, Washington University of St. Louis. To prepare young men for this university he also opened a preparatory school, Smith Academy, to which his grandsons would go. He added a girls' school, the Mary Institute, built on ground beside his own house. In 1872 he became President of Washington University, a position in which he remained until his death in 1887.

Of his fourteen children, only four sons and one daughter survived. Two of his sons became Unitarian ministers. His second son, Henry Ware Eliot, was born in 1843 and educated at the institutions his father had founded, graduating from Washington University in 1863 to go into business. He began with wholesale groceries, but on the failure of this business transferred after a while to a brickmaking firm. By the age of thirty he was already in a comfortable position as its secretary; he later rose to be chairman, and a man of considerable means —for the growth of St. Louis was to be excelled only by that of Chicago. Although he did not enter the Unitarian ministry, he practised and inculcated the family religion. Henry Ware Eliot had his father's charming way with children: he used to draw faces on their eggshells and had other knacks of keeping them amused; he also played an excellent game of chess.

In 1869, at the age of twenty-six, he married a girl who, like his own Greenleaf grandmother, belonged to an established Massachusetts family, and who was yet more gifted than himself. Charlotte Champe Eliot was to prove herself both as a writer and a reformer. Her father-in-law's decrees, as President of Washington University, were issued like the tables of the law with thunder and lightning from Mount Sinai. From her marriage to his death eighteen years later, Charlotte Eliot lived in his shadow. With his impressive and handsome wife,

William Greenleaf Eliot towered over his family as over his congregation. His descendants admired him as a hero, they worshipped him as a saint, and they loved him for the fine old gentleman he was. After he died, Charlotte set to work to write his life.[2]

Soon after their bereavement, she and her husband found that they were expecting another child. The youngest of their surviving children was already eight, and this meant that they would have to start up a nursery again. A child born to demand this sort of enterprise from its parents often proves to be more interesting than the brothers and sisters who have preceded him, but it could hardly have occurred to Charlotte Eliot that the boy to whom she gave birth in the early fall of 1888, on 26 September, would carry the name of Eliot far beyond the realm of the patriarch who had just died.

Charlotte nurtured his delicacy and filled him with sympathy for those who were less fortunate than he. For she had a special vocation to deal with young delinquents. Her work with them anticipated the Boys Towns and Borstals of our time. At the same time, she brought up her own family—four girls and two boys—to be cultured, correct and able. Nevertheless as her own children grew up they realized that she was also giving her attention to those who were the very opposite of themselves. This was to have a penetrating effect on her youngest child, the future poet.

Henry Ware Eliot, her elder son, was born in 1879 into a family of four sisters, and went on from Washington University to Harvard College, graduating in 1902. He soon set to work to accumulate a sufficient fortune, and married a young lady of exceptional charm and taste who very many years later was to add so much to my own visit to Eliot House in

Harvard. With Therese Garrett Eliot he settled, after attaining middle age, at Prescott Street in Cambridge, only a few minutes' walk from the Harvard Yard. From the beginning he took a devoted interest in the brother nine years younger than himself who was proving his brilliance from the first.

The Eliots were a gay family, living according to the stern principles of their patriarch but full of fun among themselves. They were a household enjoying cultured ease and every social advantage. Every summer vacation they left the oppressive heat of St. Louis for the house that Henry Ware Eliot Senior had built in 1897 on the Massachusetts shore.

As a child young Tom suffered from a hernia and so was rather coddled—for these were still the days of high infant mortality—and he had to be looked after. He had an Irish nurse who frequently talked to him about God, even when he was quite a small boy. He went on to enter Smith Academy, but owing to his hernia, he could not take part in many games and instead exercised his enterprise in fancies and words.

In his poem *Animula*[3] he has given us the sketch of childhood from the dawn of consciousness. Some of it is his own: the awareness of lights and noises, of dry and damp, of warm and cold, the first walks between table-legs and chair, the clutch of toys, the love of kisses, the alternations of shyness and reassurance, the pattern made by the sunlight on the floor, stags running in the pattern of a silver tray, the Christmas tree's fragrant brilliance. And some of it, no doubt, is imaginary or borrowed from others' experience. When he had learned to read, he would often curl up in the window seat behind an enormous book, setting the drug of dreams against the pain of living.

There was also the great river, and the constant companionship it gave him, as it had given to Mark Twain. Like the Atlantic on the Massachusetts shore in summer, it was a powerful presence continually impinging upon his life, watching for its chance to show itself stronger than the men who had to work on it. He could hear its flow as he lay in bed at night or as he sat with his family under the gaslight in the window recess, smelling the grapes in autumn and the delicate keen scent of the April ailantus in the yard which opened onto the girls' school beside his home and which he found a chance to look round after the girls had gone away. He seemed to be the only boy who ever invaded these precincts: when he came back as an elderly man, he told them with a laugh that for this reason he was the school's only alumnus.

Sometimes his nurse would take him out to see the river in flood. The Mississippi was swelled by the confluence of the Missouri which gave its name to the state in which Tom was born. He soon looked on them as a mysterious force reminding men of the unseen powers which they chose to forget. For who could calculate on a river? The Mississippi was a dictator, wilful and treacherous. Sometimes it was so sluggish that one could hardly sail up it, still less believe in the hundreds of miles it had been flowing down from Minnesota. At other times it made traffic easy, as grainboats from the prairies navigated its upper reaches and paddle steamers bustled to and fro between St. Louis and Memphis.

Tom quickly became an admirer of Mark Twain's two great stories of the Mississippi, *Tom Sawyer* and *Huckleberry Finn*. The heroes of Mark Twain's stories have always been keenly admired and equally keenly detested by other boys. They are lucky enough to obtain jobs aboard steamers (almost every boy's ambition in old St. Louis), and come on shore and talk about St. Louey like an old citizen going back to the French tradition. They have money and hair oil, silver watches and showy brass watch chains; no girl can withstand their charms.

Such youths Tom had known not only in the pages of Mark Twain but at the school founded by his grandfather, Smith Academy, where he mingled with a cross-section of the town. They gave a turn to Tom's humour which remained with him till his dying day. The St. Louis of the 1890s had scarcely altered since the days of Tom Sawyer and Huck Finn. There was still the religious tone, the lawlessness; and the same droll social distinctions still persisted except, of course, for the fact that slave-holding had been abolished in the intervening thirty years. For a sight of the wilder West you would now have to go beyond Omaha. But already Tom's imagination took him much further than that. He set his two schoolboy stories in the Pacific,[4] which had suddenly grown more real to Americans after they had acquired the Hawaiian Islands. The first of these contributions to *Smith Academy Record* was *A Tale of a Whale:* a sort of mingling of *Moby Dick* with the travels of Robert Louis Stevenson. Tom's little story tells how mariners arrived at Tanzatatapoo—and since he had already learned to sail on the shore of Gloucester, Massachusetts, he uses his nautical terms with great precision. The sailors catch sight of a whale and chase it, while the harpooner jumps into a gig; on being harpooned, the whale hurls the gig seventy-three feet into the air. Undaunted, three of the crew land on the whale's back and capture as food flying fish that beat against them as they stand on their precarious foothold. When they fail to catch fish, they make sponge cake out of the sponges growing on the whale's bottom. Finally, they sail away to the new possession of Honolulu.

Tom's second story was *The Man Who Was King*. In this a Captain Jimmy Magruder finds his vessel smashed up by a storm and lands at Matahiva, which is said to be one of the Paumotu Islands, and where the natives accept him as their king—until he is eventually about to be deposed, and sails to Tahiti.

The Pacific was not the only subject that appealed to Tom's schoolboy imagination. In *Smith Academy Record* we also find a rollicking poem entitled *A Fable for Feasters*.[5] In unashamed doggerel, it relates how friars used to let themselves go at Christmas time. But a ghost haunted their monastery and once set the prior on a steeple, to everyone's astonishment. As Christmas approached, the Abbot soused all the monastery's eatables in holy water mixed with the relics of a Spanish saint. To keep off the naughty spirits while he and his friars had their feast, he even bolted and barred the doors, but still the ghost managed to creep in and whisked the old man up the chimney before anyone could cry: "O jiminy!"

Those of us who knew Tom Eliot well in the days of his worldwide fame know that he never lost this boyish American humour, nor the fondness for practical jokes which made him delight, in his days of universal renown and mystical elevation, in placing beneath the seat of a solemn colleague a cushion which when sat on gave forth a noise such as caused one courtier to be banished forever from the court of the first Queen Elizabeth.

The river, majestic and magnificent, rolling its mile-wide tide along, shining in the sun below the dense forests on the opposite bank, presented young Tom Eliot with one sense of mysterious power. His Irish nurse gave him another sense of the numinous when she occasionally took him with her to something very different from that Church of the Messiah founded by his grandfather. For an impressionable child the Irishwoman's church had an atmosphere all its own. It belonged to the Catholicism which embraced half of Christianity and more than half of the population of a town which had long ago been given the name of a Catholic saint. For the city of St. Louis was not a town like the cities of Massachusetts, created and guided by Puritans who had been seeking freedom to worship God in ways different from those of the established Church of England. St. Louis was a Catholic town which, forty years before Tom was born, already had a Catholic archbishop. When in later years Eliot considered the phenomenon of religion, he was to believe that in Catholicism there was something far more generally and pervadingly Christian and historic than in the prim moralizing Unitarianism which he had learned at home as the religion of a model grandfather.

Against this must be set the business man's interpretation of Unitarianism: success in this world was the principal aim of life, and to attain success one must cultivate thrift and intelligence; if to these was added a prudent regard for social convention, success was assured. Such was Henry Ware Eliot's ideal. And the duty of the successful man was to serve his Church, his City and the University. The church which H. W. Eliot had in mind was, of course, the Church of the Messiah, built in Locust Street, a few blocks from where he lived. As for the city, its furthest outskirts touched on the Forest Park terminus of the Olive Street tramway, which seemed to young Tom Eliot like the beginning of the Wild West. The university which H. W. Eliot felt it was his duty to serve was the one he himself had attended, and which had been founded by his own father. When Tom considered all these things, he realized how good a beginning it had been to be brought up to put religion and education of the community above any selfish inclinations of his own. His father's principles rather neatly combined social duty with practical success, both of which seemed to advance effortlessly like a well-trained pair of horses. For Henry Ware Eliot, things were either black or white.

Such was one strong imprint on his first sixteen years; these years, he afterwards said, were the most important in his whole life. It seems that in general he profited from Smith Academy, until at the age of sixteen he went on to Milton Academy, one of the select preparatory schools of New England. Milton, which was to Unitarians what Groton and St. Paul's were to Episcopalians, was a place of renown and privilege, an American Eton or Winchester, a school which provides a recognized introduction to good society.

There is a photograph taken of Eliot at Milton which shows a young man with unkempt hair and wild eye, keen with youth and impulse in the excitement of youth's flowering. An earlier one, taken when he was twelve, shows the confident happy boy, secure in the awareness that he was already a success. It was his friend Marianne Moore who first showed me her copy of this photograph. Under it he had written: "My best portrait." At Milton he did not study English, but concentrated on history, Latin and physics. He even tried chemistry, only to realize that he was always three or four experiments behind and could never manage a compound that would explode. Explosiveness was no part of his programme until he joined with an American, Ezra Pound, in a Gunpowder Plot in the Parliament of English literature, and (much later in life) set "crackers" under the chairs of solemn colleagues at board meetings.

The summer trip to the Massachusetts coast was always a pleasant escape from the heat of the Mississippi valley. As Tom grew up, his father became more comfortably off. The Hydraulic Brick Company had done a profitable business in the growing city; and with this increase in profits came greater prosperity for the company's president, whose investments rose in value with the boom that followed the recent invention of the combustion engine. Coal, railroads, and iron and steel had made one series of fortunes; now came the oil companies and motor businesses. America's population increased as never before, offering success to tens of millions of immigrants. The shrewd business mind of Henry Ware Eliot Senior profited from all these developments. Tom grew to manhood in the elegant surroundings of a "man of property," who in Tom's tenth year added to the roomy house at St. Louis another almost equally spacious one situated in a little seaport town in Massachusetts known as Gloucester. This holiday home did not stand directly on the seashore, since the craze for sea-bathing came in later years, but looked out to sea from a crest of elevated moorland. To the south was a long expanse of shore, and to the west, Gloucester harbour. It was a wooden colonial style building but with the fireplaces and chimneys of a man who dealt amply in bricks. Bare rock protruded from the garden and out as far as the sea. Out in the sea a cluster of rocks stood out, on which many ships had been wrecked in stormy weather: dangerous rocks which are known even today as the Dry Salvages.

Lying about a mile east–northeast of Straitsmouth Island off Cape Ann, these rocks are a bare ledge about fifteen feet above the water at high tide. Parallel to these, and about five hundred yards to the west of them, are the Little Salvages, a reef that is only bare at low tide. Half a mile further west is Flat Ground, a ledge of rock eight hundred yards long, which comes near the surface at low water and is therefore dangerous to small vessels. When an easterly gale churns up the sea, the whole group of rocks becomes a mass of seething foam in the breaking and roar of high waves. Even in calm weather, the rocks are carefully noted by sailors rounding Cape Ann, when they help to steer the boat's course; in stormy weather (and storms can blow up very suddenly near Cape Ann), boats are very liable to be wrecked on them.

Henry Ware Eliot Junior, Tom's elder brother by nine years, had been taught to sail by an old salt of Gloucester and passed on his lessons to Tom. They often used to talk with fishermen and sailors and knew among others James B. B. Connolly, a man of Irish descent who wrote a little book *Out of Gloucester*.[6] They used to read about an Eliot who they imagined belonged to their family, the minister Andrew Eliot who, with Anthony Thacher, was shipwrecked on that coast in 1635. They thought of him as a lineal ancestor; but their seventh cousin Admiral Samuel Eliot Morison has since discovered that Henry and Tom Eliot were mistaken. The Andrew Eliot from whom all three of them are descended did not come over from East Coker, Somerset, until 1669.

Admiral Morison, as an extremely experienced sailor who has tracked the whole course of Columbus in a vessel of similar size to that in which the discoverer sailed from Barcelona, is well qualified to speak of the young Eliots' sailing holidays at Gloucester. He writes that "Tom was not only steeped in the lore of Cape Ann; he became familiar with the encompassing ocean. Cruising in college days with his friend Harold Peters, the Dry Salvages was the last seamark they passed outward bound, and the first they picked up homeward bound. Approaching or departing in a fog, they listened for the mournful moans of the 'groaner,' the whistling buoy east of Thacher Island, and the 'wailing warning' of the diaphone on Thacher's itself. They doubtless learned to allow an extra quarter point for set of current when sailing from the Maine coast to Cape Ann, as insurance against running onto the Salvages.

"These waters off Cape Ann are a real test of seamanship for sailors of small boats. There are numerous rocky passages that you can thread if you are 'acquainted,' and the *Coast Pilot* warns you to sheer off if you are not; big ships do well to keep outside the entire collection of reefs. The Dry Salvages, as Eliot writes, is always a seamark to lay a course by. . . . The Eliot brothers learned that when sailing down East, after turning Thacher's, you must either steer north–northeast to clear the Dry Salvages, or due north to pass between Avery Ledge and Flat Ground."[7]

One of the things that most impressed Tom Eliot (for it haunted his mind for thirty years) was the howl and yelp of the sea wind whistling and almost wailing from Cape Ann and what he called "the distant rote in the granite teeth." The word "rote," sometimes spelled "rut," is hardly heard outside New England. It means, says Admiral Morison, the "distant, continuous roar made by waves dashing on a long rocky coast. Often have I heard a Maine man say, 'Sea's making up. Hear that rote!' It may be ten miles distant, but you can distinguish it from traffic noises, jet planes or any other sound."[8] Tom could hear it from his home during the calm after a storm, or when swells from the ocean began crashing against the granite teeth of Cape Ann before the storm actually broke on them.

Thirty years later these rocks were still haunting the poet's memory, and mixed with his reflections on the complexity of stress, anguish and religion, led him to compare the rocks and sea around Cape Ann to the infinite vastness and movement of human life.

Tom was happier in the new house in sight of the sea than at his earliest home in St. Louis. At Gloucester he could commune with nature and all that it has to offer to body, soul and spirit. Sailing was a sport with which a hernia did not interfere; he had mastered it early in life with characteristic efficiency. When he went to Harvard, a friend there noted how he could manage and handle a sail with the best in Gloucester harbour. He kept up his sailing all the time he was at Harvard: there is a photograph of him in his third summer there (1909) wearing a soft white cap as he sails in his brother's yacht, *Elsa*. His parents are with him.

So through the years he remained at home with what Longfellow recollected from a far earlier decade on that shore—"the beauty and mystery of the ships and the peril of the sea." This imprint seems to be as strong as any on his youth: to be at home with the sea both in its companionship and in the intimacy of its danger.

He has told us, too, how curious were his sensations when, looking into a pool on the shore one day, he saw a sea anemone. Another time he noted frail forms of seaweed. There were all kinds of wonders in the sea, not only the living water itself but what men had lost in that water—lobster pots, broken oars and torn fishing-nets. Another time he caught sight of the backbone of a whale, or watched the horseshoe crab scuttling about between the pools, or gazed fascinated at the starfish.[9] As the waves played and broke, they tossed the relics of life before men appeared on the earth a mere 2,000,000 years ago.

"I want to know what it says, the sea," had been Paul Dombey's cry. Tom listened, too, to its many voices and felt that if the Mississippi was a strong brown god, here on the verge of the Atlantic there were many gods who kept company with the mermaids and the black and white of the waves when the wind was strong. This sea haunted him for years. He was to write of it many times and in lines which are among his very finest achievements. Over it, ships traced their routes towards Paris and London—London which was to provide him with his two wives, which was to be his place of work and the background of his fame, and which was later to strangle him with the incurable effects of emphysema.

At Gloucester he discovered that, in spite of the St. Louis drawl which at Harvard was to make his voice sound odd among the young Easterners, his family still cherished the standards and ideals of New England. Indeed, he painfully realized that, just as he had been reckoned a New Englander on the Mississippi, so (partly through drawl and partly through other affinities) in New England he was thought of as something between a midwesterner and a Southerner. Here he was haunted by memories of things he had noticed and loved as a boy in St. Louis: the high cliffs above the river, the flaming cardinal birds, and with them the curious insinuating scent of ailantus flowers in spring. Above all, there was and always remained the long dark river with its multitudinous changes. Conversely, the schoolboy returning to Smith Academy from his summer holiday had been haunted by the things of Massachusetts, the tang of the sea, the red granite cliffs and an ocean as blue as the Mediterranean. The earliest of the stories he wrote at school is replete with the exactitude of one who had learned to sail beside the Dry Salvages.

2

Undergraduate Years at Harvard

WHEN Tom went from Milton to Harvard just after his eighteenth birthday in 1906, he found himself in thoroughly congenial surroundings. Many have called that time Harvard's golden age. William James, author of *The Varieties of Religious Experience*, held the chair of philosophy there until 1907, and Tom, as a freshman, may even have attended some of his lectures. Even after his retirement William James remained a dominating presence at Harvard, as also did Charles Eliot Norton, who was Professor of the History of Fine Arts and translator of Dante who lived in Cambridge ten years after his retirement in 1898.

Harvard, at the height of its eminence, radiated distinction; it was then the essence of American culture. The life of the University was centered in that gathered collection of spaces and buildings which elsewhere in America would be called a campus, but here was proudly known as Harvard Yard. This extension of Boston bore the significant name of Cambridge; like England's city of the same name, it was a finishing school for able and privileged young men.

It was also the stronghold of Protestant and, indeed, Unitarian religion. Its president for twenty-five years had been a third cousin once removed of William Greenleaf Eliot: Charles William Eliot, whose policy and ambition was to make Harvard the great fountain of intellectual power in America. It was to produce a governing class for the United States in the way Oxford and Cambridge (and especially Jowett's Balliol) produced one for the British Empire. He hoped that Harvard University would attract large numbers and endue them with an efficiency that was both scholarly and practical; and indeed, thousands of students came to Harvard and found an institution adequate to meet their needs. Some people thought that C. W. Eliot commercialized the University: he let undergraduates choose their own courses, believing that through the work that suited their own particular interests they would take their part in the happiest age the world had known, while as food for their souls they were plied with what he called the "religion of the future."

This religion of the future was the fulfilment of the practical Unitarianism of the late nineteenth century. It was to capture much of America in the twentieth. Catholics, and even Evangelicals in critical mood, might well have described it as benevolent materialism.

The religion of the future, as envisaged by C. W. Eliot, would be neither gloomy nor ascetic. It would snap its fingers at authority, whether of bishops or of the Bible. It would not personify nature, and would cease to use anthropomorphic terms in thinking of a Supreme Being. It found the idea of sin irrelevant, and therefore that of redemption still more so. It would sweep away the idea of universal sacrifice. It would disdain such an expression as "the Holy Spirit" no less forcefully than that other abhorred expression, "the Mother of

God": it wanted nothing of the cross or passion of the Kingly Redeemer. No curses, no sadness, no sacrament, no saving of souls would arrest its steady forceful push towards the progress, comfort, efficiency and well-being of Americans. It would concentrate on people's safety and welfare by service to progress and contributions to the common good.

On 22 July 1909, just as Tom had completed his undergraduate course at Harvard, President Eliot summed up his views on metaphysics, saying that among other things the "religion of the future" would: believe in one God indwelling the entire Creation; seek to prevent illness and disease; lead to universal goodwill; cultivate love and hope; and would harmonize the teachings of Jesus Christ with democracy, individualism, social idealism, zeal for education, research in preventive medicine, advances in business ethics, and welcomes to change and invention.

All this was a pretty shrewd assessment of the trend of America from then till now. C. W. Eliot gave a charter for the material progress of the United States. Besides all the material changes of the twentieth century, philanthropic and educational endowments and organizations would increase in number, all of them aided by personal effort. But still in the background would be the entrenched wealth of Boston and the social position of those ruling families, in which the Eliots took an eminent place.

The life of these Bostonians had its gracious side. Admiral Morison has described in *One Boy's Boston* just the sort of place Boston was for a boy born into the easygoing broadminded aristocracy of Beacon Hill.[1] But that was an atmosphere foreign both to Henry W. Eliot of St. Louis and to Charles W. Eliot of Harvard.

Besides, even Henry James had forsaken Boston. Early and

subtle associations had also nurtured in Tom Eliot an instinct for European culture. Suppose that in the sensitiveness of the heart and the intensity of intellectual ability there is a need for inner communion with the spirit and wisdom of the universe. Young men with such appetites would reject what is proffered by self-satisfied elders. Arriving from Unitarian Milton at Unitarian Harvard to study classics and philosophy, Tom felt rather irritated and resentful at what President Eliot took from the past to depict the "religion of the future."

Rejecting the religion of the American future, young Tom Eliot also swept out of consideration one of the most distinguished figures Massachusetts had produced in the world of nineteenth century literature. Nobody had ever made such an impression on Cambridge as Henry Wadsworth Longfellow. Not only was he the much-travelled scholar, not only did his popular verses reach throughout the English-speaking world in accents of the heart; in Cambridge he enjoyed the added prestige of the *grand seigneur*. After marrying an heiress, he lived in the sumptuous colonial house where George Washington himself had lived. This house in which Longfellow's daughter Alice was still living when Tom went to Harvard in 1906, had a garden which actually touched that of his Hinkley cousins in Berkeley Street. So much prestige did Alice Longfellow inherit from her father that in some houses she was actually given precedence over any other guest. To write of the turn of the twentieth century in Massachusetts and leave out any mention of Longfellow would be to ignore a poet as revered then as he is forgotten now. When Tom took lodgings in Auburn Street, Cambridge, the houses of both Longfellow and the Hinkleys were close by.

But Longfellow was not the only American whom he rejected. He believed that American literature from 1900 to 1910 was a complete blank, chose to forget Henry James, and though he did confess to me that Edith Wharton's *Ethan Frome* was a masterpiece, does not seem to have mentioned this opinion to anyone else or noticed anything else by Edith Wharton. I once quoted to Tom her verse on heart-failure:

> Death touched me where your heart had lain.
> What other spot could he have found
> So tender to receive a wound,
> So versed in all the arts of pain?[2]

After I had finished reading this following a discussion with him and Vivienne in Clarence Gate Gardens, his only comment was: "Dead as a dead fish."

What the young men of Harvard did read were the English poets of the 1800s. They were the basis of Tom's education in the Middle West. He thought that Smith Academy was a good school because of the thorough grounding he had received from its masters at the turn of the century. In his boyhood he enjoyed *The Lays of Ancient Rome*, and in his early teens came the immense excitement of Shelley, Matthew Arnold and Tennyson. He read all these with more enthusiasm than he ever at that time read Shakespeare. Tom, in fact, complained that one of his masters gave him a distaste for Shakespeare which lasted well into his maturity.

Of all the poets whose acquaintance he made at Harvard, Dante was to have the deepest and most abiding influence. The *Divina Commedia* was more consistently studied at Harvard than at any other English-speaking university, and this may well have been Tom's first introduction to the poet whom he was later to study in still greater depth at the Sorbonne.

Perhaps the most unlikely intellectual influence of Harvard was the knowledge he acquired there of Oriental philosophy and religion: strange in that Eastern mysticism seemed so much at variance with the philosophy of Harvard's president. I once told him that I had been brought up among devotees of theosophy: "It has saved you years of research into Indian religion," was his reply. In the Graduate School of Harvard University (1911-1914), Tom did these years of research. A lecturer named James Woods plunged him into the mazes of Patanjali's metaphysics; he studied Sanskrit under Charles Lenman, one of the greatest authorities on the subject in modern times. Though all this left him in what he later called a state of enlightened mystification,[3] he had become aware that the *Bhagavad Gita* was a classic of the mystical life which for many years he preferred to St. Paul's Epistles; and throughout the years he returned as often to Arjuna as to Dante. But every time he went back during these undergraduate years to join in his family's Sunday worship, he found it an increasingly stifling ritual, and was never more satirical than in the verses entitled *Spleen*[4] and (a few years later) *Mr. Eliot's Sunday Morning Service*.[5]

Should we want a more inward picture of his mind at Harvard, we must remember how much of himself he put into the poem first published in 1917, *The Love Song of J. Alfred Prufrock*.[6] Undoubtedly it tells us more than anything else of his outlook as an undergraduate. It is overhung by the immanence of a tremendous question, but we must not ask what this question is. With the disarming confidence of a child, he makes a plain confession of his inability to unravel his own complexities. He attempts to show the connection between ices and crisis, between revisions and visions. And inevitably perhaps, at his age, he fails. Was Tom then another Hamlet with a query whether life was worth continuing? Less than that. Yet how cleverly his rhymes weave together his doubts and claims and how cunningly devices exploited by Browning and Tennyson express his wit, lassitude and cynicism.

Beneath Eliot's enjoyment of his competence, one detects (as elsewhere in his writings) a struggle between the inhibitions of his Puritan training, the reticences bred by caution, and his desire to be more normally passionate than he really was. It was an age when the conventions of position were ruthlessly enforced, and clan counted for more than it was worth. Four elder sisters kept a watchful eye on him as a young boy: his game was to dodge them, and clutch—at what?

Though Eliot was fascinated by the masterpieces he read as a boy (and those who knew him had plenty of evidence that he knew most of them by heart), he also shared the taste of younger poets to get away from models and conventions to direct expression. In the 1890s Ernest Dowson had given one example of this in his poem *Non Sum Qualis Eram*. Eliot was far more impressed by two realistic poems written by Scotsmen. One was *The City of Dreadful Night*, the nineteenth-century James Thomson's masterpiece written in highly coloured and elaborate direness; the other was not actually a classic, but most vigorous in its expressions: it was *Thirty Bob a Week*, by John Davidson, and it haunted him almost continually. Eliot found inspiration in the contents of this poem, for he too had a good many dingy urban images to reveal. What one notices most about John Davidson is his vivid handling of harsh experience:

> They say it daily up and down the land
> As easy as you take a drink, it's true;

But the difficultest go to understand,
And the difficultest job a man can do,
Is to come it brave and meek with thirty bob a week,
And feel that that's the proper thing for you.[7]

Behind this harsh and seemingly inequitable experience was
the mystery of a universe in which somewhere presumably
there was a Providence guiding the affairs of men. Davidson
stated a problem which was in perfect accord with the temper
of Tom's mind even when at Milton; this same problem remained with him at Harvard and on into his mature life. John
Davidson had summed it up in two stanzas: [8]

But I don't allow it's luck and all a toss;
There's no such thing as being starred and crossed;
It's just the power of some to be a boss,
And the bally power of others to be bossed:
I face the music, sir; you bet I ain't a cur;
Strike me lucky if I don't believe I'm lost!

I didn't mean your pocket, Mr, no:
I mean that having children and a wife,
With thirty bob on which to come and go,
Isn't dancing to the tabor and the fife:
When it doesn't make you drink, by Heaven! it
makes you think,
And notice curious items about life.

Such observations as these formed a background to Eliot's
academic course, as he read and reread them in the intervals of
classics and philosophy. He was coming to grips with the
savageness of life (or, as Davidson ironically puts it, noticing
its "curious items"), and at the same time imbibing the
thoughts of certain professors and lecturers, and writing his
own verses.

He rapidly became a contributor to the students' magazine, *The Harvard Advocate*, in which John Hall Wheelock and Van Wyck Brooks had also begun to publish. It was at that time printing the work of two of Eliot's friends, W. G. Tinckom-Fernandez and Conrad Aiken. Eliot's contributions began on 24 May 1907 with a poem very conventional in tone and strongly reminiscent of Tennyson.[9] It was followed on 3 June by a beautifully written lyric which he had already published in somewhat different form when at school in St. Louis.[10] It is an adroit adaptation of the stanza of *In Memoriam*, and was the finest of Eliot's poems to be published in *The Harvard Advocate*. Exquisite in feeling, it also shows enterprise in workmanship.

His fourth poem contained an element of horror.[11] The flowers around Circe's palace had petals fanged and red; springing from the limbs of dead men, they were marked by hideous streaks. Beside them were panthers and a python. There was even in the flow of the fountain an echo of the voices of men in pain. Elements of exoticism and disillusionment had clearly come into Tom's life during those first terms at Harvard. Far from looking forward, like President Eliot, to the "religion of the future," he preferred to write of flowers; and even when engaged in that, he was more aware of their withering in the dawn than of their freshness. Exactly the same mood of shattered leaves before the mellowing year was conveyed in another early poem, published in *The Harvard Advocate* on 26 January 1909.[12]

Was this sense of early withering due to low vitality, or was it partly due to the petty rivalries and frequent internal wranglings which, as another student wrote at that time, were threatening the prestige of Harvard as the leading university of America? Or was it perhaps due to Tom's fading Unitarian faith, a loss of faith which caused him to be bitter towards all worship? The reasons for an attitude more in keeping with age than youth (though youth itself is acutely aware of "beauty that must die") are deep and complex, and beyond the scope of this memoir. But whereas most young people's despair arises from a sense of the transitoriness of things, contrasted with the radiance of the present, his arose principally from a loss of faith—a state of mind from which he was only completely emerging when I first met him in 1927. Such was the undercurrent of his life at Harvard, a life which in other respects followed the pattern of his comrades, as he kept up with his lectures, indulged in athletic exercise and—though shyer than most young men—attended dances and parties at which his enormous sense of fun was keenly relished. The view of the world expressed in *The Harvard Advocate* poems and *Prufrock and Other Observations* was still only a "veil'd Melancholy," an undercurrent waiting to come up to the surface: waiting for literary friends to guide his powers of expression and for his poetic sensibility to mature.

3

The Emerging Scholar

WHILE still an undergraduate at Harvard, Tom Eliot had read *The Symbolist Movement in Literature*, by Arthur Symons,[1] and found a gate opening into a new world. Symons began by taking up the conclusion of *Sartor Resartus* that the path to the supernatural ran along the external world. "It is in and through *Symbols*," Carlyle had written, "that man, consciously or unconsciously, lives, works, and has his being."[2] A symbol is a representation, but does not aim to be a reproduction: it denotes an idea or form; the seen points to the unseen. "In a Symbol," said Carlyle (or rather, his spokesman Teufelsdröckh), "there is concealment and yet revelation: hence therefore, by Silence and by Speech acting together, comes a double significance. . . . In the Symbol proper, what we can call a Symbol, there is ever, more or less distinctly and directly, some embodiment and revelation of the Infinite."[3]

In the mid-nineteenth century this metaphysical vision had swept consciously into French literature, at first through Baudelaire and later through the poets Verlaine and Mallarmé. Now, in the elegant precision of Arthur Symons' book, Eliot became familiar with Rimbaud, Verlaine, Mallarmé, Maeterlinck and Huysmans.

But Symons led the young undergraduates of Harvard past these better-known names to introduce them to a much lesser known poet, Jules Laforgue: and here *The Symbolist Movement in Literature* sketched a mentality curiously resembling that of Tom Eliot himself. Laforgue was born in Uruguay in 1860. He had gone to France as a boy and at the age of twenty was living in Paris, a young man of cultivated tastes and with a remnant of fortune. There he dressed in the English style, with high collars and dark ties and often carrying an umbrella under his arm. The face of this young dandy of the Third Republic gave no hint of his inner feelings; he published no indiscretions. "We know nothing about Laforgue," wrote Symons,[4] "which his work is not better able to tell us." He died in 1887 four days after his twenty-seventh birthday, in the year before Tom Eliot was born.

Here was the man on whom Tom would model himself, the man who wrote letters of an almost virginal naiveté to the girl whom he was about to marry and finally did marry in the same Anglican church in Kensington where, seventy years later, Tom himself was to marry his second wife. Into his *Imitation de Notre-Dame la Lune* and other works Laforgue did not hesitate to introduce slang, technical terms and colloquialisms. He noted in rapid strokes what others would describe with meticulous exactness. His verse achieved sheer excellence by its mockery of prose. He banished the cadences, eloquence and high sensuousness of traditional poetry to prick his readers into shocked and surprised awareness of the banal. As Tom read these verses at Harvard in 1909–1910, the verses of a young man who had died in Paris in the year he himself had been conceived in St. Louis, it almost seemed to him that in his body the soul of Laforgue had sought a reincarnation. Indeed, Eliot described his feeling for Laforgue as one of profound kinship, or rather of peculiar personal intimacy. Seized by this surprise of an unimagined affinity, he was transformed within a few weeks. Like meeting a friend in the flesh, this meeting through the medium of verse brought a new development to Eliot's personality. He himself told me that the impact of this encounter was basic. He did not imitate Laforgue; he was changed in his personality, and from now on, his verse was that of a changed man. The messenger of a new poetic technique, he began to give America a new form of poetry which was not that of America but of Paris. And Paris did not relax its hold on him for over twenty years.

At every point Laforgue fulfilled the young poet's poetic instincts: the instinct to welcome the commonplace things of life into poetry; the instinct to throw wildly dissimilar things together and the instinct to recognize beyond the paraphernalia of Catholicism the stress of pervading mystery.

Eliot found in Laforgue more of a model than any poet he had ever read. Here was someone as far removed as possible from the hard intellectual searching of metaphysics and logic, a mind troubled by many things but not troubled by philosophy. For while, on the one hand, Eliot demanded the hard process of the logical mind dryly expressed, he was equally aware that life is always escaping from logic into the involvements of feeling and experience.

It was this realization which led not only to two early poems in the style of Laforgue, published in *The Harvard Advocate* on 12 and 26 January 1910,[5] but to thorough disillusionment with the type of religion meted out to him by his father and mother. In *Spleen*, the poem of 26 January 1910, he gives a vivid picture of the Unitarian worship of his relatives: we are shown a procession of upper-class Americans on their way to church on Sunday morning, the men wearing their top hats, the women their bonnets, and all wearing a dignified Sunday expression. The family reach the church porch: suits and ties punctiliously correct, hats and gloves in hand, they wait, fastidious, bland and yet impatient, at the threshold of the Divine. It is a picture drawn with a vigor beyond any that Laforgue commanded, only matched in forcefulness of expression by Baudelaire.

So much for the impact of Paris before Tom had even crossed the Atlantic. But now (1910) his undergraduate and master's days were over,[6] and, having been taught by Symons to prefer Paris to London, he decided to spend a year at the Sorbonne. His family opposed the move. What, at the turn of the century, did the name of Paris suggest to the virtuous élite of Massachusetts? It was the place of Émile Zola and the yellow-backed novels which good Americans thought unsuitable to have on their bookshelves. It was the place of the Moulin Rouge where girls wearing next to nothing danced before men. It was not a place where clean-limbed Americans would be likely to remain as unsullied as they came. Look what had happened to "The American" of Henry James. Besides the licentiousness of its entertainment, Paris offered the agnosticism of its intellectuals. A place less affected by Puritan traditions was hardly to be found.

To Tom, however, as to many young Americans, it was the centre of elegance, intellectual brilliance and of all that was highest, most interesting and most stimulating in the new movements of the mind. It meant the legacy of Laforgue and

Baudelaire. When Tom arrived there, these standards were being vigorously upheld by old and young. André Gide and others had founded the *Nouvelle Revue Française* in the previous year, and one of its earliest collaborators was a brilliant youth from Bordeaux, Jacques Rivière. Rivière's brother-in-law, Alain-Fournier, who was then at work on a classic novel of adolescence, *Le Grand Meaulnes*, actually taught French to the young Harvard graduate.

Tom came, moreover, not only to the city of Laforgue and Corbière but to where Anatole France was delighting his readers with gentle cynicism, a brightly polished style and an eye for effects that were vivid, comic and sensuous. Paul Bourget's novels provided the upper classes with dramatic narrative and keen psychological insight. Against the background of a country which still turned its eyes from the thought of war, Maurice Barrès wrote a French which exquisites praised, while Charles Maurras, in a French that was equally classic but more earnest, insisted on the maintenance of a traditional order in society: an order of which the symbols were the altar and the throne. He suggested, in fact, that the altar was the apanage, and to some extent the substitute, of a throne which no longer existed. The more Catholic tendencies of his work were already being developed by Henri Massis. The names of new poets, such as Vildrac, were already on young lips, suggesting that the poetic secret had not died with Verlaine and Mallarmé.

Eliot's tendency to criticize was at last overcome by something that compelled him to admire. He was dazzled, enlightened and transformed.

Such was the beginning of Eliot's intimacy with Paris, a theme which has been the subject of many disquisitions and

one large tome. Next to the influence of England, the Paris
of Eliot's stay vied with Dante in its power to make the American cosmopolitan. He remained in close relationship with the
Nouvelle Revue Française. Every fortnight Eliot bought one
of the *Cahiers de la Quinzaine*, every month the *Nouvelle
Revue Française*, in its grey paper cover. Every week he
visited the Collège de France, where Bergson delivered his
philosophy lectures to a crowded auditorium. Tom found that
if he wanted a seat, he had to arrive there a quarter of an hour
beforehand. At the Sorbonne he regularly attended lectures
on Dante. He bought the latest work of Gide or Claudel on
the day it came out. He used to see Anatole France walking in
his black cloak along the Seine embankment. Sometimes Paris
seemed to him the whole of the past, sometimes the whole of
the future, and these two combined to make the perfect
present.

It was also a source of friendship. The friend whose memory
lingered longest with him was a medical student, Jean Verdenal, who in a life tragically cut short at Gallipoli also found
time to be a poet. In letters at the Houghton Library, Harvard,
I found the record of this affinity of hearts.[7]

But Eliot saw the vicious side of the city as well. He has
given convincing evidence of this in what he wrote of a book
about a young procurer called *Bubu de Montparnasse*, by
Charles-Louis Philippe.[8] This book is no masterpiece, but it
tells much about the underworld of prostitution in Paris at the
time. Bubu pursued that business as a pastrycook might sell
brioches. Everything he did was set down by the author with
simple directness. Philippe did not wallow in pornography,
but he was never held back by scruple or distaste from telling
just what was always happening in well-known areas of Paris—

how girls sold themselves not simply to their customers, but with the help of partners who shared their profits.

The book dealt plainly with a traffic that was universal. Scrupulous as he was, Tom would never deny the existence of sex instinct either in himself or anybody else. If anything he longed at times to get away from correctness and expand in warmth; he found an opportunity to do this in the sympathy with which he read this sordid book. He was convinced that it was not pornography but simply a picture of the lust of which few young men are ignorant. And so he praised it as a masterpiece, even as a moral tract. It should bring every reader to humility, and if it did that, it would be more effective than a powerful sermon.

Much later, in 1937, in his preface to *Nightwood* by Djuna Barnes,[9] he elaborated this idea. He spoke of the Puritan morality, with its emphasis on thrift and success. He referred to the later view that financial hardship was the product of social maladjustment. But these views, he felt, were too much alike. Evil comes when we attach ourselves to created things. If we regard the people in *Nightwood* or *Bubu de Montparnasse* as a sideshow of horrid freaks, we miss both the writer's point and the moral lesson independent of the writer. It is wrong to pass judgment on morbid and sinful people. If we are thankful that we are not as other men are, what is that but Pharisaism? More than ever after his year in Paris, Tom recognized the limitations of his family.

In other ways, too, the stay in Paris had deeply affected the subtle elegant of Harvard. When the time came, in the summer of 1911, for him to return to his University and begin academic research in earnest, Conrad Aiken—his friend of undergraduate days—noticed that he was a changed man. Perhaps the most striking difference was a wider, more tolerant outlook on the world. Who would have imagined, eighteen months earlier, that he would bring back with him from his travels a nude by Gauguin, and proudly display it in his new rooms in Ash Street?

He still maintained, of course, the social habits and connections of his first three years at Harvard: dancing, visiting his cousins the Hinkleys, and attending theatres and parties. And he still went in for more strenuous exercise. At his Boston gymnasium he would "swarm with passion up the rope" (as he expressed it to Conrad Aiken), and he took boxing lessons with an Irish tough who rivalled those he had met on the shore at Gloucester and who reminded him how ubiquitous in the neighbourhood of Boston this type was: it was a type he was later to caricature as Sweeney, sometimes in a disreputable quarter of Boston, sometimes naked in his bath, sometimes with cynical humour among the nightingales.

His closest friend and confidant was still Conrad Aiken, to whom he would put the question: should one ultimately settle in Paris, or even London? At other times he would read aloud to Aiken from a work which has since disappeared: it was a kind of supplement to *Prufrock* and was called *The Bird Song of San Sebastian*, but he does not seem to have completed it until rather later in life, when it was felt to be too intellectual. Tom, however, had not returned to Harvard to write playful poetry, but to study philosophy; and this was to be his main intellectual work during the next three years (1911–1914). In the Harvard Graduate School he read for a Ph.D. in philosophy, and also studied Sanskrit and Pali. The subject of his dissertation was the epistemology of F. H. Bradley, and its original title was *Meinong's Gegenstandstheorie considered in relation to Bradley's Theory of Knowledge.* (It has since been published as *Knowledge and Experience in the Philosophy of F. H. Bradley.*[10]) In a preliminary examination Tom was required to translate both French and German philosophers.

What drew Eliot to F. H. Bradley, and what was he seeking to establish in his dissertation? For the subject of a thesis that would demand at least three years concentrated study, he sought a mind more transcendental, more sinewy and elastic than any of the mentors of his undergraduate days. Of these, Irving Babbitt had peremptorily denounced Romanticism, stressing the superiority in literature of logic and continuity. The arbiters of French literature were to be Racine and Boileau; the monster who had perverted all who followed him was Rousseau, Father of the French Revolution. And indeed, this demand that neither personality nor temperament should count in the assessment or creation of literature, this denial of Burke's dictum that our passions instruct our reason, fitted in exceedingly well with that combination of strenuous intellect and low physical vitality which, from beginning to end, played a major part in Eliot's psychology, and which always took charge when he left the three things which gave him his personal charm: his modesty, his warmth of heart, and his humour. Among family and friends, these personal qualities governed his life; in philosophy and criticism his other side, moulded by Babbitt, asserted itself. Yet Babbitt was not of sufficient intellectual stature to mould the thought of a dissertation in philosophy—as Eliot was only too keenly aware.

His other undergraduate mentor, William James, had a mind much fuller and richer than Babbitt's. He is a philosopher in his own right, comparable in stature with Schelling, J. S. Mill or Bergson. But there was some quality in James's thought which Eliot found definitely antipathetical. Was it his insistence that metaphysical assertions are non-verifiable and therefore meaningless, and that our notions of truth and right are entirely grounded on expediency? In any case Eliot did not feel drawn to write an academic thesis on *The Principles of Psychology*, *A Pluralistic Universe*, and *Pragmatism*.

With F. H. Bradley, on the other hand, he had an intuitive sense of personal communion. Here was a man who had thought long and deeply on the relation of appearance to reality, and of experience to truth: a mind which realized that truth, though a metaphysical ultimate, has many sides and that one apprehension of this ultimate cannot rule out another, provided that the inquiry is vigorous and honest. Such tolerance and urbanity must have been partly responsible for attracting Eliot towards Absolute Idealism. Bradley as a metaphysician would never have been so arrogant as to claim that only such a method as his could arrive at truth. He was searching for the Absolute, but that did not mean he excluded the idea of God as a supreme Reality not to be confused with the total universe: beyond that there is always another Reality, to which such human limitations as are connoted by the term "Personality" do not apply.

Yet besides tolerant urbanity there was also undeviating firmness on metaphysical essentials; and it was the unique blend of both which constituted Bradley's particular appeal: the fact that, despite all his diffidence in matters of technique, he based his philosophical outlook on the strong conviction of an Absolute towards which the fragmentary, independent and finite existence of the phenomenal world is inevitably tending.[11] Eliot was far from having attained to religious belief, but he was equally far from James's pragmatism. He was later to confess that what drove him away from philosophy was its divorce (since the Middle Ages) from theology.[12] What led him to Bradley was the compatibility of Idealism and religion.

The dissertation itself is concerned with problems of human knowledge, and in particular the subject matter of psychology.[13] According to Bradley, there is an inceptive fusion of the processes of knowing, feeling and willing, named by him "Immediate Experience" and such that the act of knowing and the object of knowledge are one, in exactly the same way that the acts and objects of sensation and volition are coterminous. This "Immediate Experience" is reducible into the two classes of Subject and Object, though whether temporally or logically is left unclear. When this reduction into Subject and Object ("I" and "non-I") has been made, is anything left over to the mind which could appropriately be termed "mental content"? For, if there were such a thing, this would automatically become the subject matter of psychology.

To Eliot, however, mental content was a mere epiphenomenon: neither the cause nor the effect of any apprehension of reality. Whereas Bradley believed that mental presentations do exist on a practical, as distinct from a strictly philosophical, level and that the function of psychology is to study such phenomena without reference to their meaning, Eliot asserts on the contrary that, however objective the awareness in observer A that "B hopes to become an air hostess," Immediate Experience itself is neither objective nor subjective: in other words, both A and B may be convinced as to the substantive existence of hopes of becoming an air hostess, but at the metaphysical level which is the special prerogative of philosophy, Subject and Object are indistinguishable. It is a persuasive argument, and would have been still more persuasive if Eliot had developed it in the direction of sensationalism.

So Eliot pursued his philosophical speculations during the

three years immediately preceding the First World War. It was a long and daunting task, even for a brilliant metaphysician, so much so that in the year before his death Eliot was to confess he no longer understood his dissertation.[14] How much, if anything, he had managed to write of his thesis by 1914, when Harvard awarded him a Sheldon Travelling Fellowship for one year's study at Oxford, we do not know. In all probability, he was partway through the writing when he arrived in England. But meanwhile he had undergone an even more valuable philosophical experience than Bradley's *Theory of Knowledge*, and at the same time made a lasting friendship.

Soon after Eliot arrived back at Harvard from France, Bertrand Russell (with Wittgenstein, the most brilliant philosopher of his generation) came over to Harvard and was much discussed. Eliot attended some of his seminars. It has been asserted that Russell found Eliot the most brilliant of his American pupils.[15] This, as Russell himself has told me, is quite without foundation.[16] The co-author of *Principia Mathematica* had not so much as noticed Eliot's presence when symbolic logic was under discussion. Yet Eliot had managed to attract Russell's attention when the talk was on Heraclitus. The young man came out with the unexpected remark that Heraclitus always reminded him of Villon! Russell, who was both a metaphysician and an inflammable heart, was fascinated by the idea of the philosopher of fire and change having affinities with a poet whose theme is passion. This remark, therefore, fixed Eliot in his memory and caused them to become intimate in the first years of Eliot's life in England.[17]

So the three years of academic research in America drew to a close, and the time came to take up the Sheldon Fellowship and embark for Europe again. Tom did not proceed directly to Oxford, however. His Department insisted that he should attend lectures by Rudolf Eucken at Marburg University. He left Harvard soon after the end of Trinity Term, renewed his links with Paris during the earlier part of the summer vacation, and then went on to the Bavarian town which, of all German towns, I feel has most of the elegance of Paris; he intended to stay at Marburg for one or two months. Eight years afterwards the memories of its Hofgarten, of the neighbouring *Starnbergersee* and of a Lithuanian girl whom he met there were still with him: in spite of her Russian nationality, she claimed (to his amused surprise) that she was a real German, "echt deutsch," and so was to take a place in the most complex and cosmopolitan of all his poems.[18]

As for Eucken, he was a man filled with a conviction of the role of spirit in life, and deeply absorbed in explaining the relationship of man and spirit. But hardly had Eliot gone on from Munich to Marburg than he became aware that philosophy was but a remote voice in the Europe of August and September 1914. His arrival in Germany had almost coincided with the murder at Sarajevo (28 June 1914) of the Archduke Ferdinand, heir to the thrones of Austria and Hungary. The classic music of Germany, with the concerts and quartets that Tom loved, was exchanged for the beat of drums, the blast of trumpets, and the roar of new machines of death.

The effect on Marburg was like the fall of a thunderbolt. Eliot had not been there a fortnight before it was decided that he must leave it and proceed to Oxford.[19] On reaching London, he remembered that Conrad Aiken had given him an introduction to a poet from Idaho who was then living in Kensington. This man, only three years older than himself, was Ezra Pound.

4

Eliot at Oxford

ONE afternoon in mid September 1914 Tom went through the quiet garden which is still sheltered by the Church of St. Mary Abbot, Kensington, and there at the corner of a tiny street he found the man for whom he was looking. It was a small dark flat in the corner house which I found being pulled down in 1965. At the head of a steep and narrow staircase one came to a gaslit room where Pound did his cooking; a smaller room looked on to a quiet street with a garden beside it, and it was into this room that Eliot was led by a man who could not sit still.

As I look back, it seems to me very odd that I had met Ezra a whole year before Tom did. There was, of course, a literary society in my Oxford college, St. John's. In 1913 its leading spirit was an undergraduate whose brother was T. E. Lawrence. He had been brought up as a pious Protestant by parents who had not married because the father had been unable to obtain a divorce from a poor woman who was out of her mind. But this the Lawrence boys naturally never guessed: they never imagined that the mother who, ostensibly as Mrs.

Lawrence, had brought them up in the New Testament was legally Miss Shaw.

Young Lawrence decided at one point that the best man he could get to talk to his society was the boisterous American master of the Vorticists. Pound came and addressed the society, and indeed my own rooms in College were used for the meeting.[1]

Born in 1885, some two hundred miles north of Salt Lake City, and educated at the University of Pennsylvania and Hamilton College, New York State, Pound had decided that even the eastern coast of the United States was stifling: he needed to enrich his hot blood with the cool air of Europe. In 1908 he appeared in London, with little money but much self-confidence; he was a robustious innovator in whom fifty years later expert critics were to detect the inaugurator of a giant movement. He had just published *A Lume Spento* in Venice. After various wanderings in America, France, Italy and Germany, he returned to England in 1911. In 1914 he became a contributor to an avant-garde literary periodical, *Blast*, presided over by the artist Wyndham Lewis, to whom Pound soon decided to introduce his new friend.

"Of these three friends of mine (Joyce, Pound and Eliot), Eliot was the second to swim into my ken," Lewis writes,[2] "—some years later than Ezra Pound, very much earlier than James Joyce. But he *slid* there rather than swam, as I recall the event, into my half-awakened consciousness." Lewis noted in the new Amreican visitor a graceful neck and a smile which, like Conrad Aiken, he could compare with that of Mona Lisa. Though he had that enigmatic air of knowing much, he looked young and attractive.

Here was the young man of whom Pound had been boasting

as the author of *The Love Song of J. Alfred Prufrock*. To tell
the truth, this *was* Prufrock, for the poem, afterwards so de-
servedly famous, was nevertheless a series of personal reactions,
jests, skits and confessions. Until now, Pound had set before
Lewis a variety of preposterous creatures at whom the painter
had been apt to gaze with a stony stare. But this young man,
from whom his host's gaze would not wander for long, was
both brilliant and engaging. Tea was served in the diminutive
triangular sitting-room by Pound's wife.

This tea party in Ezra's rooms was the first of many literary
introductions from which Tom benefitted in London. Pound
could not allow so notable a find to pass unadmired and un-
envied by a writer whose literary and financial position was so
much more comfortable than his own. This writer was Ford
Madox Ford whose house, South Lodge, stood at the foot of
Notting Hill. For young Eliot, this house was the gateway to
a wider literary world.

From Notting Hill he was to go east to that charming part
of London between the Strand and the Thames where elegant
houses were built in King George III's reign by the Adam
brothers who appropriately called these buildings the Adelphi.
In one of them lived a little Quaker lady, Miss Harriet Shaw
Weaver, who looked as chaste, as classic and as demure as the
Adelphi houses themselves. But her aspect was deceptive.
Through the literary journal, *The Egoist*, of which she was
patron, she was as active in fomenting literary revolution as
the wild, woolly westerner who took Eliot to see her. In *The
Egoist* Eliot was to be given an opportunity of publishing
reviews and articles which would secure a wider public in his
native country through an American literary journal, *The
Dial*. After *Smith Academy Record* in St. Louis and *The Har-*

vard Advocate, this was the next step in his literary progress.

Already Pound's literary introductions were taking him far. But there were other tracks into English life for the urbane invader from Massachusetts. Not only was Pound in touch with Wyndham Lewis and Ford Madox Ford, he also knew other men of established names, including Laurence Binyon, Osbert Sitwell and Edmund Gosse. But these contacts had to be stored up until after Tom's year at Oxford.

Meanwhile, even during the fortnight before Michaelmas term began at Oxford in 1914, there was Ezra, breaking into the literary world of London in a way that sometimes reminded one of a bison, and sometimes of a grizzly bear. London, which always welcomes sensations and novelties, especially if imported from abroad, made as large a place as could possibly be expected for the impecunious westerner. Apart from the hurtling tempest of his judgments, he fired volley upon volley of astonishing verse. But what did Eliot himself think of this verse? Twenty or so years after first meeting Pound, he claimed, in a mood of uncharacteristic hyperbole, that here was the shrewdest literary critic of the twentieth century. At the time of their first meeting, however, Eliot confessed to Conrad Aiken that he thought Pound incompetent as a poet. But it was not long before he looked to him as a master, firmly denying that he himself was the greater man.

It was now the beginning of October 1914. Neutral Americans, whether in London or elsewhere, were watching the countries of Europe slaughter their finest youth in a tournament of mutual ruin. Turning his eyes from that grim sight, Pound indulged himself in divers antics of his own. But Eliot remained the model of caution and correctness. He passed in an hour's journey from this whirlpool of literary experimentation in London to an Oxford college bordered on one side by a secluded street paved with cobblestones and on the other by the trees and open spaces of Christ Church meadow. In the damp, grey chill of Oxford's Michaelmas term, and with Harold Joachim as his tutor, Tom settled down to his work on metaphysics at Merton College.

When Americans come over from Harvard to take their first taste of Oxford as the fall of the year descends upon it, they feel little glamour and much disillusionment. It is true even today, but was much truer in 1914, that the collection of buildings which made up Oxford University was something far finer than could be seen at Harvard or Princeton: the spires and towers of central Oxford had been making their captives for many hundreds of years and Wordsworth, coming to them some ninety years earlier, had said that their presence overpowered the soberness of reason. But what an American was apt to notice was that even in the presence of towers and spires, one felt above all that they were a dull grey. Moreover, around that central and historic Oxford was the sheer sordidness of slum which covers acre after acre of practically every English town, new or old. This stifling monotony takes most Americans entirely by surprise. They have seen many photographs of English country houses, beautiful castles, cathedrals and gardens all shining in the rarity of summer light. But they have been given no inkling of how much of an English town is mean and sordid streets. Tom, of course, had felt the same sort of thing about Boston and Cambridge, but Oxford was no better.

It was also a most unpleasant surprise to an American to find his college gates shut at nine o'clock, that there was no central heating in any college, no showers and even most of the hot baths far away from one's own rooms. When I first came into my own college in 1911, three years before Eliot, the only means of having a bath was to have a tub put in one's own chilly room, with water that itself was never hot. In the college life of those days there were, on the other hand, one or two amenities which now, like everything that goes with plenty of servants, have been discarded. The greatest comfort was to have a large coal fire burning in one's room, and of course, the college servants (or scouts, as they were called) brought in breakfast, lunch and tea which one could eat either alone or with one's own choice of company.

It was during this year that Tom more or less completed his thesis on F. H. Bradley under the guidance of Bradley's most distinguished pupil, Harold Joachim. Joachim at that time was a Fellow of Merton College, teaching philosophy to all Merton men reading in the school of *Literae Humaniores* or, as it was more popularly called, "Greats." This course of study demanded a thorough knowledge of the chief works of Greek and Latin literature, and not only their poets and playwrights but also their philosophers. Naturally, like any other college, Merton also had a certain number of research students, men who had already obtained their bachelor's degrees and were now specialising in some particular academic discipline. Eliot was one of them and it is easy to see why he chose to belong to Merton, where the teacher of philosophy was Bradley's most gifted exponent. In 1919 Joachim was appointed to the Wykeham Professorship of Logic at New College, Oxford, and so left Merton and the teaching of undergraduates. For when he became a professor Joachim's duties consisted merely in lecturing to the University and in supervising research.

Eliot seems to have shown the same intellectual versatility at
Merton as he had already shown at the Harvard Graduate
School. Just as, in his first three years of research, he had
studied Sanskrit and Pali as well as attending to his academic
dissertation, so at Oxford he found time for a careful study of
Aristotle besides putting the finishing touches to his work on
Bradley's epistemology. He owed much to Joachim. Particularly exciting was his exposition of *The Nicomachean Ethics*,
the fullest of Aristotle's writings on human conduct, but how
many unsuspected lines of thought Joachim could also reveal
in, for example, the *Posterior Analytics*, where the placement
of the slightest comma can denote a change of meaning. Tom
was later to confess to me that he had learned more from
Joachim about the writing of good English than from any
teacher of literature.

So *Knowledge and Experience in the Philosophy of F. H.
Bradley* drew finally to a close. The carefully polished text
was despatched to Harvard and read by his examiners. In due
course, Tom had the satisfaction of learning that it had been
accepted. Tom referred to his dissertation as being "unread-
able," but the opinion at Harvard was that it was a masterly
exposition of one aspect of Bradley's philosophy. Not that this
meant he was now a doctor of philosophy, for there remained
some final examinations at Harvard before the doctorate could
be conferred.

Life at Merton was not all study, however. Tom made new
friends among the undergraduates of the College, and did not
neglect his athletic pursuits. In a letter to Mr. R. H. C. Davis
dated 24 June 1963,[4] he recalls some of his Oxford friends: a
Frenchman named André Vagliano who left the College in
1915 to serve with the Cuirassiers, and who was to become

thirty years later the Amateur Open Golf Champion of France; a Yorkshireman named F. C. Westgarth whose vocation was to the Church of England; and above all, Karl Henry Culpin, almost five years his junior, with whom he shared one of the deepest friendships of his life.

Karl had come up to Oxford from Doncaster Grammar School in 1912 and was in his third and final year when Tom met him. Defective eyesight had prevented him from enlisting in the army. He was of darkish complexion and normal physique. Of course, he had to wear glasses, but the eyes that shone behind them twinkled with the combination of a warm heart and an endearing humour. As soon as Tom and Karl started talking to each other, each knew that he had found an ideal companian. The Yorkshireman's brain was brilliant enough to keep pace with the American's, and this exercise was the more stimulating because it was not centred on philosophy or literature but history and economics. Tom, who never forgot that he was a businessman's son, was more than at home with Karl's subjects; he actually welcomed them. Karl was just as aware of the best in literature. Keen as he was on Samuel Butler and Meredith (both of whom were of great importance at that time to the elect of Oxford), he had the discernment to relish *Prufrock* from the moment when his American friend placed this volume in his hands. Like Ezra Pound, Culpin immediately felt that here was the great new poet of the age, a man who far outshone such poets as Masefield. In *The Daffodil Field* and *The Everlasting Mercy* Masefield had brought the working man and his language within the scope of acceptable poetic treatment, but he had not depicted either youth's disillusioned hopelessness or the exact environment of town lives. Tom was beginning to strike these new chords, and Karl appreciated his enterprising initiatives. For with a German Christian name and a German mother, Karl Culpin's feelings were not so English as to immure him within that inner wall which kept the average English youth from either liking or being liked by Americans. He died on 15 May 1917, of wounds received in action near Fresnois.[5]

Besides friendship, sport helped to beguile Tom's leisure hours at Merton. But now it was no longer boxing or gymnastics. The River Isis added its allurements to the Mississippi and the Missouri, and the Massachusetts seaboard. Tom took up rowing, and though he never graduated to the Boat Race did at least represent his College in the reduced size of crew which the War made necessary. Tom stroked the Merton four-oar and even led it to victory in one of the intercollege boatraces. As a reward for his prowess, he was given a pewter mug on which the names of the winning contestants had been engraved, and he jealously guarded this trophy for many years until eventually, after a household removal, he found that the precious trophy had been stolen.

5

The First Years of Marriage

WHEN the Christmas vacation came, Tom may have gone back to see Pound in Kensington. In any case he spent much of his six weeks' holiday at Swanage, in Dorset. There he was with two other young Americans one of whom, Brand Blanshard, I met at Yale not long ago after Eliot's death. "It was astonishing to me," said Blanshard, "that he became famous as a poet. All his talk to us was in the realm of philosophy." He was absorbed in Bertrand Russell's *Principia Mathematica*, the most abstruse of the philosopher's materpieces. Professor Blanshard recalls his sitting hour after hour at the dining-table of their little cottage with one of the volumes of this work propped up before him. "He was regarded by his fellow students as an able and promising young philosopher, but none of us had any idea of his past or his future on the literary side."[1] With *Principia Mathematica* and symbolic logic in his mnd, he went back to concentrated work on his thesis at Merton and so continued throughout the Lent term.

But when the summer term began, with its alternations of chill and flowering, he met a girl at Oxford with whom he was often to be seen dancing. At Cambridge, Massachusetts, I was shown a letter he wrote on 26 April 1915 mentioning her name, Vivienne.[2]

She was not only a graceful dancer but witty and good-looking. She attracted him by a combination of melancholy, disillusionment, fragility and sensitiveness, while sudden lightnings would flash out of her clouded sky and throw light on startling secrets of the mind, and the perversities of human nature. As a girl Vivienne Haigh had been of lithe physique, and a good swimmer and tennis-player. She had taken lessons in ballet dancing, and had even worked in ballet. She and her family often travelled on the Continent. For eight years she had been an only child, until a brother Maurice was born.[3] They issued from a world of culture and elegance where their father was a distinguished painter and etcher of private means. She and her brother were tremendous friends as they grew up. He went to Malvern School and was still there when the war broke out. He at once went to Sandhurst to prepare for a commission and, by the time his sister had met Tom, was already a subaltern in the Manchester Regiment.

The intellectual world had always held a great attraction for Vivienne. At Montana-Vermala, during a holiday with her parents in Switzerland, she had made friends with an American girl, Lucy Thayer, who had come over from Connecticut with a taste for contemporary literature. Like Lucy Thayer and a friend of Lucy's named Butler-Thwing, Vivienne was sensitive to novelties in poetry; she combined her delicate vitality with a quick and intense mind, avid of communion with "the best that is known and thought in the world." Besides these attributes, she was overflowing with fun and gaiety, and found an outlet for the tension of her mind in abundant physical energy.

For the next seventeen years of Tom's life, this attachment was the insoluble enigma and enduring drama of his life; it met the thousand hidden instincts of the warm sensitive eagerness that underlay his Puritan upbringing, classical discipline and inherent austerity. Now, when they were both twenty-six, and as his dissertation on experience in relation to reality exhausted his energy for abstraction and analysis, he suddenly found himself in need of company, relaxation and romance.

The weeks of spring rushed by in mounting exhilaration: the Oxford term led on to its "high Midsummer pomps." As soon as it was over, he went down to a humble street in Soho and took lodgings there,[4] while Vivienne arranged with her friend Lucy Thayer that Tom and she should be married on 26 June at a registry office near her home in Hampstead. Without a word of warning to his parents, with no one to share his secret but the one new friend to whom he had opened his heart at Merton, and with Lucy Thayer and another friend of Vivienne's as witnesses, he went to Hampstead Registry Office and vows were exchanged. Even at the registry office the law knew of no marriage which was not a life contract, even though that contract dispensed with religious sanctions and heavenly blessing. By this contract they entered into married intimacy, only to find how much adjustment it requires.

Thus both husband and wife faced their relatives with a *fait accompli*. Vivienne's parents were staying at a hotel in Lincolnshire, where Maurice's regiment was quartered, when they received a telegram announcing the news. It came as a surprise, particularly as there had been no formal engagement— a thing almost unheard of then in families of their position. Yet, despite their initial shock, their one wish was for the young couple's happiness. Maurice Haigh has described to me just how they felt: "My father was a kindly and simple man and my mother a very loving mother, and both very quickly recognized Tom's sincerity and high character and they took him to their hearts as a son-in-law." As for Maurice himself, he and Tom made friends at once and remained on the best of terms for fifty years, even after Tom and Vivienne's judicial separation, her death and her husband's remarriage. Indeed, Tom even consulted Maurice about a possible separation, and it was Maurice (via John Hayward) who told him of her death and who drove with him to her funeral. So much for speculations about any disapproval of Tom on Vivienne's side of the family.

But what of his own parents in Massachusetts? As soon as they were told of the marriage, they insisted upon seeing their son. Eliot's return to Gloucester in the late summer of 1915 was one of the most tense and important moments in his life. And it was a crisis he had to face alone, for Vivienne remained behind in England.[5] No record remains of Eliot's confrontation with his parents. But what he had to do was explain to them that he made up his mind to break with the whole of his past life, and almost all its connections, renounce the prospect of an academic career which his masterly dissertation now opened up, and go back to some dim prospects in London.

Even today this seems a puzzling, indeed almost disquieting, decision. Why give up the opportunity of an academic career after eight years of careful preparation? The seemingly obvious course for Eliot in 1915 was to return to America and become a lecturer in comparative religion. He did not wish to do so. Then, as later in his life, the academic analysis of religion and the actual practise of the religious life seemed to him to be almost antithetical. He preferred, as always, to adopt the non-academic point of view. Besides, despite all his study, there was something in Indian philosophy he did not quite under-stand—and never would. It was a matter of temperament.

To his parents it all seemed inexplicable. Nine months in Europe had culminated in what was none other than a clandes-tine marriage. That in itself ran counter to every convention of a family established in the Eliots' milieu. For them, it was essential that a wedding should be a social occasion. To rush to a registry office with two witnesses whom he hardly knew appeared to them not only precipitous and unbecoming but almost scandalous. Why had he done it? Why this suddenness? What would be the outcome of it all?

It is not surprising that such questions filled his family with misgiving. He had been a young man of perfect manners and very regular ways, naturally careful and cautious. Admittedly, he had given up their religion—but without making open pro-fession of the fact. They had not particularly liked the idea of his going to France in 1910, but still he had finally left Har-vard with the honour of a Sheldon Travelling Fellowship to complete his dissertation in philosophy. This dissertation was now about to be submitted, but instead of making it the début into a brilliant academic career to bring still more lustre to the family name, he had chosen to abandon them and peaceful America—for the sake of what? A problematical future and a bride they had never met. All this was strangely out of charac-ter, contrary to the prudence on which they had always prided themselves.[6] Business people in a position of social and moral leadership, they could not but be aghast at this alarming turn of events.

His father refused to continue his allowance. He had main-tained this son until the age of twenty-six, but he could not give encouragement to what looked not only like caprice but obstinate determination to return to wartime England, with all its strain and scarcities. The position had been put very clearly to Tom during this family reunion by a man of great kindliness and business acumen. Father and son parted bitterly. Defying practically all that both his family and America had given him, Tom said he doubted whether he would even bother to take the oral examination for his Harvard doctorate.[7] He sailed back again across a grey Atlantic to rejoin his bride— and to immerse himself in war-torn London in whatever job he could pick up. He was never to see his father again (though his mother and sisters did visit England in the early 1920s). Yet the future seemed bright to him as he returned, joyfully and impatiently, to resume married life, but at a cost he was almost immediately to discover.

Since he had no resources, Tom's return to England was inevitably inauspicious. He had to earn his living in a number of ways. But on his return from the "family reunion," the warmest welcome to himself and his bride came from Karl Culpin and Culpin's sister Mary. Mary had first met Tom in his favourite Soho, at a small restaurant called "Au Petit Savoyard" where a Frenchwoman served a cheap appetizing meal. The young bridegroom discovered that Mary had an ear for music, and later took her to hear Dolmetsch play. This was a taste they shared with Pound, who had a harpsichord in his tiny flat behind St. Mary Abbot. Pound even invited them once to a little concert consisting entirely of his own compositions. Mary Culpin told me that Tom then played the piano, not the harpsichord, and could even tackle Beethoven sonatas; the example of Beethoven haunted his mind throughout the years. Some months after his return from America, and when he and Vivienne had ceased to be the guests of Bertrand Russell, Mary Culpin helped them to move into 18 Crawford Mansions, a little flat in Crawford Street off Edgware Road—a vulgar quarter where their rough, crude charwoman talked boldly of abortions, and so went down into literary history as Lou in *The Waste Land*.

From the Culpins I learned more of Vivienne as she was at that time, twelve years before I met her. Essential to her vivacious nature was her mingling of sparkle and sensitiveness with the sardonic and playful. This was the secret of her undeniable seductiveness, a quality which was felt by at least two of the most brilliant minds of the time (Tom Eliot and Bertrand Russell). It is normal for a woman to enjoy her power to play upon the strings and nerves of manhood till they hasten the throbbing pulse with sensations of peculiar pleasure. Of this normal femininity in Vivienne all who knew her at all well were deeply aware. It was not surprising if impressionable men who saw much of her came under the spell of her fragile, mercurial vivacity. Her bridegroom was probably the first of these; he may not have been the last, but no other man could offer her what he did: the combination of personal attractiveness and a mastery of verse, a skill in defining new impressions, which was the acme of brilliance and originality. None of his admirers was keener than she, for none was so tender, mischievous and intimate; yet it was this appreciation which was soon to provide him with his severest trial. Her wit added to her insinuating femininity. As she met Tom's sallies with her own, the fun of their company was at its height. It was as the gay American that he most delighted her, and she returned the delight by turning her own disillusionment into a frolic of cynicism.

To occupy himself with something that would bring him in
some kind of income, the obvious thing to do was to apply for
a teaching post in a school. There happened to be a vacancy at
£140 a year in a fine old grammar school at High Wycombe,
some twenty-eight miles from London. Already in 1914 it was
a position of dignity under a remarkable headmaster, George
Arnison, who lived on until Eliot's last years. His portrait in
the school hall shows a man with keen blue eyes that could
pierce the secret recesses of boys' characters. His personality
was commanding enough to ensure discipline. Severities, therefore, were very rare, but hardly had Tom arrived at the school
than the exceeding naughtiness of one of his pupils produced
one of those melodramas which occasionally enlivened school
life. But the offence of this particular boy at High Wycombe
was something different from that. All Mr. H. C. T. Briden
could remember of the incident was that he had done something "very, very naughty." So he was thrashed before Tom
and the whole class.

Mr. Briden, who later became a chartered accountant working in London Wall, told me that the boys liked the American
master and hardly noticed he was not English. He taught
French and history in that form below the fifth which was
then known as the Shell. These thirteen weeks of teaching at
Wycombe Grammar School were an essential element in
Tom's life. He thus entered into direct contact with boys
brought up against the English background of class and religion. The stamp which this type of education gives was
something he had escaped at both Smith Academy and Milton:
it was to lead him to a post in another school where the Church
tradition was more marked.

While spending the autumn term of 1915 at this fine Elizabethan grammar school, Tom and Vivienne lived in London as guests of Bertrand Russell.

We have already seen how Tom and Bertrand Russell first had occasion to meet at Harvard in the previous year. As chance would have it, Tom soon ran into him again within a month of his arrival in London from Marburg. Russell relates how one day in October 1914 he met Eliot in New Oxford Street.[8] Tom differed from Russell in that he was not a pacifist, yet despite the fact that Russell was prepared to go to prison for his pacifist beliefs they remained friendly. We do not know whether Tom renewed contact with Russell during his three terms at Merton, but within a fortnight of the Eliots' wedding day the eminent mathematician had been invited to dine with the young couple.[9] Russell informs us that, from the secretive way in which Tom had divulged his marriage, he expected the bride to be "terrible,"[10] but it turned out that she was quite different from the woman he imagined: lighthearted, animated, vivacious, a perfect contrast (so he thought) to Tom, with his listless refinement. After the bridegroom's return from America, Russell suggested that they should move into his flat,[11] in which he was lucky enough to have two bedrooms. It was from this flat that Tom made the daily journeys to High Wycombe.

At this time Russell was involved in a double crisis. The first had come after his separation in 1911 from Alys, his first wife, who had been born a Pearsall Smith in Philadelphia. I often used to meet Alys Russell at the home of Lord and Lady Sanderson and she struck me as a sweet and congenial, if rather plaintive, type, and I learned later that she had disappointed her husband by being barren. At the time when Tom and Vivienne shared Russell's flat, he was still only separated from her (the divorce did not come until 1921), but this did not prevent him from embarking upon a second drama, as he became associated with two ladies of the aristocracy, Lady Ottoline Morrell and Lady Constance Malleson.

No memoir of the literary history of this period can be complete without a portrait of Lady Ottoline. She was the wife of a member of Parliament and the half-sister of a duke. Her husband, Philip Morrell, was a man of considerable fortune, who had entered the House of Commons as a Liberal in 1906 and shared Russell's pacifist attitude towards the War. Her half-brother, the sixth Duke of Portland, reigned at Welbeck Abbey, where he entertained kings. She was a woman of unusual appearance and daring originality, who had studied English literature under Sir Walter Raleigh before he came to us at Oxford.

When, years later, I met her with the Eliots, I was impressed by her combination of sympathy, generosity and high breeding. Her distinguished bearing was set off by dress unconventionally elaborate. Miss Catherine Gibbs told me how she once met Lady Ottoline at the little Oxfordshire station of Culham. It was a chilly May morning but Lady Ottoline swept along the little platform wearing a flowing muslin dress of white and a picture hat round which curved an arum lily. That was the way in which the mistress of Garsington Manor sallied forth to eclectic gatherings in London where young celebrities mingled with the old nobility.

The iron gateway of Garsington Manor opened on to a little courtyard above which rose its Elizabethan gables. Taking this over from a farmer, Lady Ottoline rapidly transformed it by making its atmosphere as sumptuous and exotic as that of any house in Oxfordshire. Tapestries, satins and brocades stood out against the vivid colours painted on its panels and walls. Along-side it was a hedged path on which peacocks moved the scin-tillating blue of their necks and the array of their outspread tails. The garden led down to a swimming-pool from which naked forms would emerge on to the paths. Lady Ottoline seemed to some of her guests not unlike one of her peacocks as she floated among them in coloured shawls and nurtured genius. Men and women from politics and high society, such as Margot Asquith and Lord Crawford,[12] mingled with her literary discoveries of whom the chief at that time was Lytton Strachey, already busy with the vivid ironies of *Eminent Victorians*.[13] No greater contrast with Crawford Street could have been imagined for Eliot than when he was introduced to this house by Bertrand Russell.

By 1915, however, Russell's four-year affair with Lady Ottoline was becoming little more than a casual friendship. He has recorded that he fairly frequently visited Garsington, but now found Lady Ottoline "comparatively indifferent."[14] Yet it was not until the following year (to be precise, the summer of 1916) that he met, and fell in love with, Lady Con-stance Malleson. Thus, at the time when Tom and Vivienne were his guests, he had slipped out of a relationship with Lady Ottoline and had not yet entered into another. He mentions, too, that for a whole year he was looking for a woman to replace his former mistress, but without success.[15] It was at this time that Russell became particularly close to the Eliots. He was particularly taken with the vivacious and attractive Vivienne.

Yet, however vehement his desire for the solace and vi-brancy of love, it was never the sole passion of Russell's life. This, he has told us,[16] was governed by three passions, simple but overwhelmingly strong: the longing for love, the search for knowledge, and pity for the suffering of mankind. Like great winds, these passions blew him hither and thither, along a wayward course reaching to the very limits of despair.

"I have sought love, first, because it brings ecstasy—ecstasy so great that I would often have sacrificed all the rest of life for a few hours of this joy. I have sought it, next, because it relieves loneliness—that terrible loneliness in which one shivering consciousness looks over the rim of the world into the cold, unfathomable, lifeless abyss. I have sought it, finally, because in the union of love I have seen, in a mystic miniature, the prefiguring vision of the heaven that saints and poets have imagined. This is what I sought, and though it might seem too good for human life, this is what—at last—I have found.

"With equal passion I have sought knowledge. I have wished to understand the hearts of men. I have wished to know why the stars shine. And I have tried to apprehend the Pythagorean power by which number holds sway above the flux. A little of this, but not much, I have achieved.

"Love and knowledge, so far as they were possible, led upward toward the heavens. But always pity brought me back to earth. Echoes of cries of pain reverberate in my heart. Children in famine, victims tortured by oppressors, helpless old people a hated burden to their sons, and the whole world of loneliness, poverty, and pain make a mockery of what human life should be. I long to alleviate the evil, but I cannot, and I too suffer."

Such is the self-portrait of the man who now deeply interested himself in the young couple temporarily living with him.

One afternoon in early November Tom, enjoying a half-holiday from Wycombe Grammar School, came back to the

flat around 3.30.[17] "It is quite funny," Russell noted in a letter
to Lady Ottoline Morrell, "how I have come to love him, as if
he were my son. He is becoming much more of a man. He has
profound and quite unselfish devotion to his wife, and she is
really very fond of him." Vivienne, however, could not help
teasing those she loved. Her special habit was always to be
divining some reason for people's behaviour springing from a
more or less discreditable motive; and this habit she could no
more help applying to her adored husband than to others. It
was a psychological quirk which Russell compared with the
sort of cruelty one finds in Dostoievski's novels. As a man
with considerable experience with women, Russell was in a
position to understand her better even than her husband could.
Tom, by comparison, was a simple American who had lived
with healthy, normal people. In the intervals of his involvements with two ladies of the highest rank and after several
years of married life with a Europeanized American, Russell
was far better equipped to understand Vivienne's unusual
ways. He seems to have divined at once that she was mentally
ill and should be judged accordingly. She was, he wrote, "a
person who lives on a knife-edge."[18] There was something in
her of the saint but there was also a criminal streak, as is the
case with many suffering from psychic illness. He realized that
her condition could only deteriorate as time went on.

A few weeks later (in January 1916), Russell took Vivienne
down to Torquay for a holiday while Eliot remained in London.[19] Vivienne wrote to her husband that Russell had been
an angel to her: it seems that he knew how to handle her. "I
believe we shall owe her life to you, even," wrote Tom, as he
waited in Russell's London flat, well looked after by the housekeeper, Mrs. Saich.

Vivienne was much subtler than her husband. If he was complex, she was infinitely more so. She understood him as none had ever done before. She relished to the full his every gift, and especially his verse. It was the infinity of acuteness in her mind and the complexity of her character which fascinated, and also puzzled, him. For no sooner had she pierced his innermost thoughts than she tantalized him by transcending them. All this was easier for an Englishman like Russell to understand than it could be for any American who had spent his first sixteen years in the Middle West, while Vivienne was leading the sophisticated life of a girl in London. But perhaps no event in the early years of their marriage was to have the lasting effect of Vivienne's brief affair with Russell. It was to alter drastically both her hopes for the future with Tom, and her already fragile grasp on sanity.

Nine years later (21 April 1925) Tom was still confiding in Russell.[20] He admired Vivienne's insight and the cogency of her arguments,[21] but as Russell had feared, her mental health had gone from bad to worse. Her spells of vivacity had become less frequent, her helplessness more apparent. Medicine was less effective in general fifty years ago than it is now and would palliate only at the cost of reducing vitality.[22] This situation, we must remember, is the background of everything that Eliot wrote in verse or prose from 1915 onwards.

It was also the background of his schoolteaching. With the end of the autumn term at High Wycombe in 1915, Tom decided—perhaps on account of the lengthy daily journeys to and fro—that he would do well to transfer to another school. At Highgate, in north London, he found a job which not only demanded less travelling time but paid him a larger salary: £160 a year, with a free dinner and tea included. It was a preparatory school, which meant that his classes were considerably younger than they had been at High Wycombe. It was also a school strongly imbued with Church tradition. Here Eliot taught the upper forms of the school for the three terms of 1916.[23] Among his pupils one was later to rule the Great Western Railway from Paddington Station, but the celebrity (who was a small boy of nine or ten at the time) was John Betjeman, destined to become a lifelong friend.[24] Even though so young, Betjeman was already conscious of his poetic vocation. He had soon presented Eliot with a colourfully bound volume: the collected poems of John Betjeman. To some extent, no doubt, Eliot helped to stimulate his pupil's impulse towards poetry. But however salutary his effect, and however stimulating his lessons, Tom rapidly came to feel that schoolmastering was not for him. In fact, he even confessed that he disliked teaching. When he began work at High Wycombe, he had imagined that the long summer vacation would give him ample time for his own writing, but—as he told W. T. Levy[25]—he had not bargained with the fact that the task of projecting his own personality to a class of schoolboys would drain away so much of his nervous energy. So strong was his reluctance to continue in this career that he gave in his notice for the end of December 1916 without having any other job to go to. For the first two months of 1917 he was out of work, but in March of that year he was finally successful in obtaining a post with Lloyds Bank in Queen Victoria Street.

6

Widening Horizons

THE decision to join the Colonial and Foreign Department of Lloyds Bank, where he began his duties on 19 March 1917,[1] was by no means as startling a move as might at first appear. It shows what was to determine his life over and over again, that business was in his blood. He was, after all, the son of a brick manufacturer from whom he had imbibed a sense of the value of money, a sense which he never lost. Besides, the regular hours in a bank relieved him from the strain of personal relationships of which he had quite enough when he returned home in the evenings. Not that he did always return to Vivienne when the day's work was done, for at least once he was sent away by the bank on a fairly protracted tour of the provinces.[2]

The post he was offered involved him in settling pre-War enemy debts,[3] after an initial assignment of dealing with documentary credits, bills of exchange and foreign currency. Thus, he soon had a chance to use his French and German, and to assess the fundamental relations of Britain to the Continent—a subject which never failed to fascinate him. It also showed him how ruinous the War had been: within three weeks of his joining the bank (6 April 1917) America had entered the war against Germany, and Tom had been patriotic enough to volunteer his services to the American Navy. On account of his hernia these services were refused; he was not even admitted into the United States Intelligence Service,[4] and so it was that at Lloyds Bank he dealt with the aftermath of war without ever having been involved in its operations.

When the question of pre-War enemy debts had been eventually settled, Tom was transferred to the bank's Foreign Information Bureau, where he began as joint head of the office and later assumed sole charge. Each day he had to study over twenty foreign newspapers and distil from them an *Extract From the Foreign Press* which was then circulated through the bank. He also produced a monthly analysis of foreign-exchange movements. This work in the key service department of Lloyds foreign branch gave him a much greater sense of fulfilment than at either of the schools; it also gave him a much larger income than he would have obtained in schoolteaching, unless he had been lucky enough to become a headmaster: for though the move to Lloyds meant an initial drop in salary (from £160 to £120 a year), he was earning £600 a year after tax by the time he left the bank's employment in November of 1925.

Once or twice during the nine years he was at the bank men with literary interests sought him out. One of these was Bonamy Dobrée, who had first heard of Eliot from E. M. Forster when the latter pressed a copy of *Prufrock in Alexandria* into his hands. The other visitor was to play a bigger part in his life for many a year to come. This was Ivor Richards, who from 1922 lectured at Magdalene College, Cambridge on English literature. Later, when Richards married, he used to ask Eliot to come and stay with him in King's Parade, looking out on to the splendours of the great chapel which Wordsworth called an "immense and glorious work of fine intelligence."

These two men found Eliot at work in a little room in the basement of the Colonial and Foreign Department, a room filled almost entirely by a huge table and extending under the pavement. In fact, it was lit almost entirely by a skylight on which the hard heels of those days were constantly tapping as Tom pored over his account books and worked out the matters of individual accounts such as that of Houston Stewart Chamberlain, whose property had been impounded because of his pro-German sympathies.

These nine years at the bank saw an immense widening of Tom's literary horizons. To begin with, there was still Ezra Pound. Throughout his year and a half at High Wycombe and Highgate Tom kept in touch with the man from Idaho, for whom things were no longer going as well as in the balmy days of his friend's first visit.[5] Yet it was hardly surprising that his aggressive flamboyancy was failing to vanquish England. As his keen admirer, Eliot argued that strangers would need time to become accustomed to him. Another discerning American, John Gould Fletcher, was disconcerted by his only too apparent desire to gain notoriety by infuriating people.[6] So much so that, despite the occasional admirer, Ezra gradually found himself surrounded by an ever spreading antagonism. He had deliberately chosen the path of hostility. Edmund Gosse found him unspeakable: he had been disrespectful to their housemaid. Of one of the leading academic poets of the time, Lascelles Abercrombie, Pound wrote that "stupidity carried beyond a certain point becomes a public menace"; after which he actually challenged Abercrombie to a duel. The challenge was answered by the apposite suggestion that they should fire at one another not bullets but unsold copies of their books.[7] Sometimes Pound adopted a loftier tone. He would dismiss new aspirants in one crushing phrase: "Il n'est pas dong le mouvemong." For Edmund Gosse, on the other hand, he was "that outrageous American filibuster." Literary circles in London were finding it impossible "to accept this vulgar clown as *a poet*."[8] How different Wyndham Lewis found Eliot: that sleek, tall, engaging apparition on whose features flittered a Gioconda smile! Prufrock was very attractive indeed and shrewd into the bargain. While Pound made brutal attacks, Eliot was shyly ironic: as he assumed the role of mocker or teaser he faintly blushed, but he was not slow in thrusts of satire, which he delivered with an alert and dancing eye.[9]

The shyer Eliot seemed, the more devoted Pound became. Not long afterwards Arthur Waugh, now remembered only as the father of two brilliant sons, referred in the course of a review of *Prufrock* to this "drunken helot." At once Ezra sprang to his friend's defence. Was Waugh punning on Eliot's name by any chance? "Since when," he asked in an article published in June 1917,[10] "have helots taken to reading Dante and Marlowe? Since when have helots made a new music, a new refinement, a new method of turning old phrases into new by their aptness?" In illustration of this, he then proceeded to quote delicately woven lines from two of Eliot's poems in the *Prufrock* volume, *Conversation Galante* and *La Figlia Che Piange*.

"Let us leave the silly old Waugh," Pound continued. "Mr. Eliot has made an advance on Browning. He had also made his dramatis personae contemporary and convincing. He has been an individual in his poems. I have read the contents of this book over and over, and with continued joy in the freshness, the humanity, the deep quiet culture. *I have tried to write of a few things that really have moved me* is, so far as I know, the sum of Mr. Eliot's "poetic theory." His practice has been a distinctive cadence, a personal modus of arrangement, remote origins in Elizabethan English and in the modern French masters, neither origin being sufficiently apparent to affect the personal quality. It is writing without pretence. Mr. Eliot at once takes rank with the five of six living poets whose English one can read with enjoyment.

"*The Egoist* has published the best prose writers of my generation. It follows its publication of Joyce by the publication of a 'new' poet who is at least unsurpassed by any of his contemporaries, either of his own age or his elders. . . ."

"Let us leave these bickerings, this stench of the printing-press, weekly and quarterly, let us return to the gardens of the Muses. . . . Mr. Eliot's melody rushes out like the thought of Fragilion 'among the birch-trees.' Mr. Waugh is my bitten macaroon at this festival."

Such was the contrast between the established academic criticism of the time and the enlightened attitude of *The Egoist,* of which, admittedly, Eliot was assistant editor from 1917 to 1919; he had replaced its regular assistant editor, Richard Aldington, when the latter had gone to fight in the War,[11] and its salary of £1 a week was a very welcome supplement to his fairly meagre income from the bank. Despite his connection with *The Egoist,* it was still gratifying, however, for Eliot to find such comprehension among "the happy few." Already he was becoming a man of mark with the publication of *Prufrock and Other Observations* (1917).

Eliot's friendship with Pound and his work at *The Egoist* brought him into contact with other writers of the new generation. One of the men in Pound's circle was an Englishman two years older than Pound himself, and from whom both he and Eliot were to derive many ideas. Born in 1883, T. E. Hulme had gone to St. John's College, Cambridge. He had been sent down from there, however, in 1904 for some infringement of college discipline, and in the years that followed led a life of his own pleasing in Canada, Belgium and Italy. But by 1912 he was back in Cambridge again with the support of no less a celebrity than the philosopher Bergson. He was still of too independent a temperament, however, to apply himself to the university curriculum, and went on from Cambridge to Berlin before returning to London. There his forceful personality and witty conversation were beginning to form a group and influence a generation. Eliot fell directly under his spell.[12]

Hulme held that ethical values are absolutely objective: behind them is the eternal reality. Man, for his part, is weakened by original sin. To escape from this weakness he must discipline himself and look to the eternal order. Only in this manner will he obtain the strength to lead a creative and constructive life. This outlook was, of course, the very opposite of what had been taught both by the humanists of the Renaissance and Jean-Jacques Rousseau. These had insisted that man is born free and that his natural impulses are good. Hulme, on the other hand, had close affinities with Irving Babbitt. Romanticism, he maintained, confused human and divine things instead of strictly separating them. It presupposed perfection. But where is perfection? In all of us is sin, which should be admitted and confessed. Otherwise political thought is confused; worse still, the whole realm of passion is idealized.

Speaking even more plainly, Hulme argued that Romanticism was wrong in its literary treatment of sexual love. Philosophy had changed from being a scientific discipline to the differentiation and investigation of certain abstract categories; allied to a form of sentimental idealism, it became a substitute for religion. This alliance sought to supply canons of satisfaction which beguiled men from the tragic significance of human life. Of this Hulme saw the worst contemporary example in Bertrand Russell, whose pamphlet *A Free Man's Worship* he condemned as "a piece of false and sickly rhetoric." Man being essentially bad, he can accomplish things of value only by ethical and political discipline. For this reason, order is not negative. Order is freedom, and freedom is found in institutions.

These ideas of Hulme were to combine with those of Maurras to make Eliot into a monarchist, a classicist and eventually a Churchman; they were to compel Pound—or rather, the bison element in him—to rush in the direction of the organized state, which developed into Fascism in 1922. As an antidote to the philosophy of President Charles William Eliot, on the one hand, and George Meredith, on the other, it gave Tom something that he found congenial not only to his Puritan origins but also to those unconscious influences seeping in from the old Catholicism of St. Louis and to his taste for European tradition. Ten years later he was citing Hulme along with Sorel, Maurras, Benda and Maritain as one who advocated the severe control of the emotions by reason; but behind all their thoughts was Irving Babbitt's book *Democracy and Leadership*.[13]

Hulme, who served as an artillery officer in the War, was killed in action in September 1917. His influence on Eliot remained deep, leading the younger man to consider more highly the qualities of reason, order and authority.

Richard Aldington, the former assistant editor of *The Egoist* whom Eliot temporarily replaced, was another man with whom he came into contact in Pound's circle. There was much of tragedy in Aldington's life. As a boy he came to realize that his mother detested him. He changed the Christian name she had given him to Richard. As Richard Aldington, he made a name for himself at the University of London and was a close friend of one to whom this book owes much, Sir Alec Randall, who wrote criticisms of German books for *The Criterion* year after year, and who ended his career as British ambassador in Copenhagen. Just as Alec Randall is a specialist in German, so Aldington had a marvelous understanding of French. With a high complexion and a robust physique, he had a mind which radiated vitality. Not only was he indebted to Pound for his post as assistant editor of *The Egoist*, he even owed his wife to Pound, who himself had proposed in Philadelphia to a girl six foot two inches tall, with blue eyes and masses of blond hair. Her family name of Doolittle was so false to her phenomenal energy that she always signed herself "H.D." Although H.D. had refused Pound, she followed him to London, and before long had accepted the advances of Richard Aldington. They were a fine pair and for a long time succeeded in satisfying each other's passion. Then came exhaustion, and off she went with another admirer. Yet at the very end, after Aldington had retired to the shores of Provence near the coastal village of La Lavendue, she came back to tend him in the weeks before he died.

Although, inevitably, Aldington did not play any great part in Tom's life at this particular time, being on military service when Tom was most closely associated with *The Egoist*, he was to have a deep effect on the poet's life a few years afterwards: first introducing Eliot to Bruce Richmond, and later writing the most savage lampoon imaginable about Tom and Vivienne.

Life was hard for Tom Eliot in the first few years of his service with the bank. His editorial work for *The Egoist* was not the only expedient he resorted to in an endeavour to increase his income. He gave Workers' Educational Lectures two evening a week,[14] and reviewed books for several journals, including *The Egoist* itself. Frequently, he found himself working fourteen or fifteen hours a day. But at least this helped to dull the pain of his domestic troubles. Indeed, even when teaching at Highgate, he had indulged in a certain amount of reviewing: from time to time, under the signature of T. Stearns Eliot, profound philosophical articles would appear. In 1916 he wrote four critiques for *The International Journal of Ethics:* the first a review of *Theism and Humanism*, by A. J. Balfour;[15] the second on *The Philosophy of Nietzsche*, by Abraham Wolf;[16] the third on *Conscience and Christ*, by the Oxford theologian Hastings Rashdall, afterwards Dean of Carlisle;[17] the fourth on *Group Theories of Religion and the Religion of the Individual*, by another Oxford don, Clement Webb.[18] All these show how far Eliot's metaphysical bent was turning towards religion. Also in 1916 he published two articles in *The Monist*,[19] comparing Bradley's philosophy with that of Leibniz, who for many years had been a speciality of Bertrand Russell. Even in 1917 he found time for further philosophical work, but as with the *International Journal of Ethics* reviews, once again the trend was definitely towards religion. In July 1917 *The International Journal of Ethics* published his review of William Temple's *Mens Creatrix*, in which he examines Temple's theme with an open mind, weighing how far the faith of a Christian depended on belief in the Jesus of history:[20] later, one of Eliot's detractors complained that in this review he had rejected Christianity as a myth, but this was an unjustified allegation, for Eliot approaches the problem with complete impartiality, setting forth both aspects of the question.

From this masterpiece of Temple he turned to a study of religion and philosophy by my friend R. G. Collingwood.[21] Eliot noted that Collingwood seemed to postulate (and this he certainly did) that orthodox Christianity was founded on the unique fact of the Virgin Birth. Eliot found his philosophical interpretation of the Incarnation, Miracles and Atonement to be extremely well handled. Temple had already shown him that particular types of metaphysics, aesthetics and ethics may be made to form a whole with Christianity. In the next issue of *The International Journal of Ethics*[22] Eliot was praising *A Manual of Modern Scholastic Philosophy*, by Cardinal D.-J. Mercier, then one of the intellectual heroes of Europe. What he especially admired was the skilful way in which this great Belgian theologian refuted Kant. When we also take into account the fact that ever since his early Harvard days he had been constantly studying Dante,[23] we realize that the Christian faith was already securing its place at the back of his mind, ten years before his conversion.

But by the time he was launched into *The Egoist*, it was literature rather than philosophy which occupied his energy, and his reviews. In a short article on Henry James, Eliot hailed him as the most intelligent man of his generation,[24] saying of him what was to be true of himself, that it is the final consummation for an American to become not an Englishman but a European, in a way that no one really attached to one European nation could quite be. To this he added that James had a mind so fine that no *idea* could violate it. In England, Eliot said, ideas run wild and pasture on the emotions: instead of thinking without feelings, we corrupt our feelings with ideas. In September 1918, just as he was approaching the age of thirty, he published in *The Egoist* a review of the sensational book, *Tarr*, which Pound's friend Wyndham Lewis had just brought out.[25] Lewis, said Tom, was more primitive and yet more civilized than any of his contemporaries: his experience was deeper than civilization; subtler, yet in certain respects much cruder. The careful and sophisticated Eliot was also capable of being crude, but only in his jokes and especially his practical jokes. That was why he delighted in others' brutally frank statements of the place and importance of sex.

Even in *The Egoist* Tom's penchant for jokes found a means of expression. Towards the end of 1917 it was decided to print readers' views on the articles and poems offered them by *The Egoist*. In order to get the correspondence off to a good start, Eliot invested himself with no less than five pseudonyms. It was typical of the ingenious playfulness with which he treated many things, and not least himself. He was Charles Augustus Conybeare of the Carlton Club, Liverpool, asking where the writers of philosophical articles in *The Egoist* obtained their ideas.[26] He was the Rev. Charles James Grimble of the Vicarage, Leays, who thought it a sensible policy to let people know about foreign ways and to keep their minds open. He was J. A. D. Spence, a master at Thridlingston Grammar School, deploring the way in which Ezra Pound had rehabilitated Ovid, and praising Ezra's enemy Gosse. He was Muriel

A. Schwarz of 60 Alexandra Gardens, Hampstead, N.W. who thought that an article written by Wyndham Lewis had cast a slur on "the cheery philosophy of our brave boys in the trenches" (this was a touch of satire to please Bertrand Russell); finally, he was Helen B. Trundlett of Batton, Kent,[26] who saw the War as a "Great Ordeal which is proving the well-spring of a Renaissance of English poetry"—a satirical reference to Rupert Brooke.

So it was that he combined playfulness, invention and satire while laying the foundations of a literary revolution. In 1921 he was to add to these disguises that of Gus Krutzsch, the pedant who refused to go to China because it had no native cheese. He could assume disguises and throw himself into fictitious characters as though from the beginning a playwright.

So much for *The Egoist*, Pound, Hulme and Aldington. But in the early years of his employment with the bank, horizons were also opening in a very different direction. Bertrand Russell continued his guardianship of Tom by introducing him to Lady Ottoline Morrell and also to Bloomsbury.[27] Russell himself belonged to the circle which was to make Bloomsbury famous. This circle had begun with Thoby Stephen and his two sisters, Vanessa (married to Clive Bell) and Virginia, who reigns in literature as Virginia Woolf—two young ladies as graceful, precious and fanciful as vases of Venetian glass. Here Lytton Strachey belonged; here Lady Ottoline kept a great house in Bedford Square which she was later to sell to Herbert Asquith; here was Roger Fry with his deranged wife, and Desmond MacCarthy, married to a Warre-Cornish whose father had been Vice-Provost of Eton, a woman whom we used to find very remarkable for her manner and her sayings.

I have not discovered whether it was Lady Ottoline Morrell

or Clive Bell who introduced Tom to Virginia. At any rate, she seems to have been immediately captivated, or at least amused, by his prim precision of speaking and the polish of his manner. Like theirs, his dress was what London required—perhaps even more than that. Yet in some ways Londoners were aware that he was not quite one of themselves. The English are too pleased with themselves not to find a foreigner, especially one from the New World, someone at whom they can poke fun. Tom was, however, as congenial as any of Leonard and Virginia Woolf's friends, and before long she was inviting him to stay at their little house at Rodmell, near Lewes—the simplicity of which was in sharp contrast to Garsington's satins and sumptuousness.

At the time when Tom first met Virginia Woolf, she was not actually living in Bloomsbury itself, but dividing her time between Richmond and Rodmell. She and her husband had gone to live at Richmond in 1914 and not until 13 March 1924 did they move back to Tavistock Square. It was in Surrey and Sussex, therefore, that Tom passed from a formal acquaintance with Virginia Woolf to close friendship. She noticed that, though his eyes were lively and youthful, the shape of his sentences, like the cast of his face, was often heavy. To her he looked more like marble than flesh. His sentences were far too formal and rigid. He knew he could be too pedantic and admitted that at Garsington he had talked like a priggish, pompous young ass. Whereas an Englishman would have written: "Forgive me if I have been a bit slow in answering your invitation," his phrase was: "Please pardon me for not having responded to your note immediately."[28] Leonard Woolf noticed how embarrassed he was to find his host dropping behind to relieve himself. That was something which Tom would never have done; he even told me that he never shaved in front of his (first) wife. Yet through this pose the Woolfs were able to penetrate to the essential warmth of his nature. Not that Tom was always able to realize this. "The critics say I am learned and cold," he once remarked.[29] "The truth is I am neither."

The reason for this was that American manners are always a little more precise than English manners when the Americans concerned come from anywhere near Boston. Bostonians, in fact, are more acutely conscious of class than anyone in London society. Yet the name of Eliot's family, so honoured in Massachusetts and so closely connected with Harvard, was not in itself a guarantee of being welcomed into the "upper ten" of Europe. Tom's claim to the attention of any inner circle was confined to a tiny record of work, known to very few, and sufficiently novel in style to evoke query rather than gain acceptance. As soon as he married, he was very short of money. From March 1917 he was earning his living as a bank clerk, and Virginia laughingly said that he might look forward to becoming a branch manager[30]—which, curiously enough, a senior in the bank promised him would be the reward of his financial efficiency. Despite her mockery, Tom gradually grew very fond of this "Queen of Bloomsbury" as Arnold Bennett called her, and by 1922 felt free enough to answer her invitation to lunch in an amusingly-worded rhymed letter.[31]

If Mrs. Woolf had qualities to make her the centre of a literary circle, if Lady Ottoline Morrell gathered together those who were the rising stars in the sky of literature and made her houses into a galaxy, there was another hostess resolutely attracting into her orbit every kind of celebrity. This was Sybil, wife of Dr. Arthur Colefax, who was soon afterwards to be knighted.[32] Somehow by 1917 Mrs. Colefax had heard of Tom and asked him to come to a poetry reading which she had arranged to collect money for a war charity. The occasion was presided over by Edmund Gosse, and although it was wartime, Mrs. Colefax had gathered together enough food for a little dinner party to which she invited those who were due to read; and these included both Eliot and Osbert Sitwell.

Osbert thought Tom "a most striking being."[33] He noticed a peculiar something in the colour and glint of his eyes. Sitwell greatly exaggerates the effect of Tom's face, however. When I met the poet ten years later, what struck me was the lack of light and colour in it: all seemed to be pervaded by a dovelike grey, agreeable but unremarkable. But perhaps Osbert Sitwell could see what others could not see: eyes "peculiarly luminous," eyes, he said, which might have belonged to a tiger, a puma, a leopard, or a lynx, but were less domesticated and placid than those of a lion. I myself would say that Tom's eyes looked placid even though one sometimes felt that they revealed strain. But I cannot pretend to the close intimacy with lions claimed by Osbert Sitwell, who said furthermore that Tom's face also "possessed the width of bony structure of a tigrine face, albeit the nose was prominent, similar, I used to think, to that of a figure on an Aztec carving or bas-relief." I do gather what Sir Osbert meant when, echoing so many others, he went on to say that "though he was reserved, and had armoured himself behind the fine manners, and the fastidiously courteous manner, that are so particularly his own, . . . his air . . . was always lively, gay, even jaunty." That is the salient thing which his friends always noticed, the gaiety, the sense of humour, the readiness for a joke.

The Eliot family's summer home at Gloucester, Massachusetts.

The Dry Salvages.

MILTON ACADEMY, MASSACHUSETTS

T. S. Eliot at 17.

T. S. Eliot with the housemasters, matron, and other students of Forbes House, Milton Academy. Eliot is standing in the back row, second from the right.

MILTON ACADEMY, MASSACHUSETTS

ABOVE: *T. S. Eliot in a group of Merton freshmen, Oxford University, October 1914. Eliot is in the third row, third from the left.*

ABOVE RIGHT: *T. S. Eliot and Lady Ottoline Morrell at Garsington Manor in 1920.*

RIGHT: *Vivienne Eliot in the garden of Garsington Manor, photographed by Lady Ottoline Morrell, about 1920.*

MRS. IGOR VINOGRADOFF

MRS. IGOR VINOGRADOFF

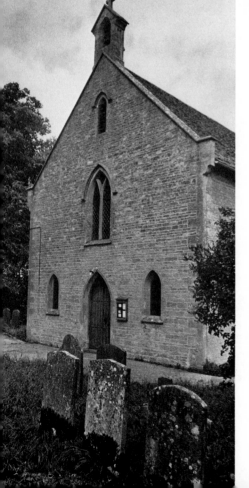

ABOVE: *T. S. Eliot, about 1927.*

LEFT: *Finstock Church, Oxfordshire: the place of Eliot's baptism in 1927.*

OPPOSITE: *T. S. Eliot, Virginia Woolf, and Vivienne Eliot. This photograph was taken by Leonard Woolf in 1932, just before the Eliots' separation.*

MRS. IAN PARSONS

T. S. Eliot's study at the Bungalow, Crowhurst.

Burnt Norton House and the rose garden.

T. S. Eliot on the film set of Murder in the Cathedral.

The drained pools at Burnt Norton.

BELOW: *East Coker Church.*

John Hayward in 1935.

The drawing room at 22 Bina Gardens where Hayward and Eliot gave brilliant parties.

T. S. Eliot receiving the Nobel Prize for Literature at Stockholm on 10 December 1948.

OPPOSITE: *T. S. Eliot lecturing at the Institute for Advanced Study, Princeton University, in 1948.*

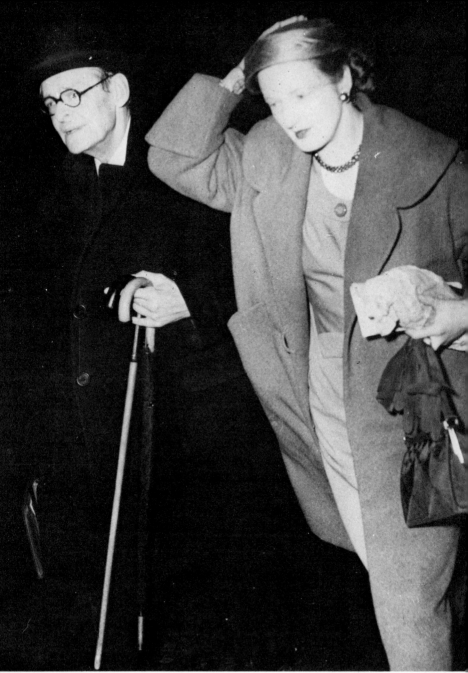

T. S. Eliot and Valerie Eliot returning to London after their Riviera honeymoon, in February 1957.

T. S. Eliot in 1958.

Mrs. Valerie Eliot at the unveiling of a stone in her husband's memory, Westminster Abbey, 4 January 1967.

Sitwell suggests that Tom must have been exhausted by his "long hours of uncongenial work," but at that time Tom had hardly left Highgate for the bank and the work at Lloyds was anything but uncongenial. The other impression that Osbert Sitwell recorded of Tom strikes me as pure fancy: that "the range and tragic depths of his great poetry were to be read in the very lines of his face." In 1917 Tom was far from writing tragic poetry. When he *had* written it, we who saw much of him were struck rather by the mildness of his gaze, his recurring chuckling whenever he showed up the seriousness of what he was discussing. I would have said that, if one is to compare him with any animal but the opossum, better the cunning combination of the sleek and caressing cat with the unobtrusiveness and quietness of a mouse.

But neither cat, nor mouse, nor lion can furnish a simile for the check trousers and black coat—the garb of a bank official in the earlier part of this century—which, always correct, were also even elegant, and Sitwell rightly noted that Tom walked with a cheerful, easy movement. This is all he has recorded of his meeting with Tom at Mrs. Colefax's. The fact is, however, that in the ensuing years the three Sitwells (Osbert, Sacheverell and Edith) were to provide him with constant and generous hospitality.

And well they might, for they too (in spite of a friendship with Edmund Gosse) belonged to the avant-garde in literature: they spoke warmly of Pound and were full of praise for another young poet who wrote for *The Egoist* and was closely associated with art and letters. This was Herbert Read, who was to be one of Eliot's particular friends for many a long year. Each of the Sitwells was a unique individual, yet they were, if not a movement, an entity presenting their own front.

Osbert was the most official: he moved with ease among the established literary men of the time and was on excellent terms with Edmund Gosse, the librarian to the House of Lords and author of *Father and Son*. In the attitude Osbert took to himself there was something faintly reminiscent of the ducal connection of Lady Ottoline. As yet he had no title but his place in *Burke* was assured.[34] His father was a baronet and his mother the daughter of an earl. Besides that, the Sitwells had a large ugly country house in Derbyshire, Renishaw, which, although it looked onto factory chimneys, they took very seriously indeed. Unlike Lady Ottoline, all three were actually writers, and Osbert and Edith were already established in a commanding intellectual and social position at the time of Mrs. Colefax's poetry reading. Eliot and Osbert Sitwell felt great mutual respect, and with Edith Tom shared the two interests of poetry and religion. Edith Sitwell also wrote flamboyant prose depicting, in rainbow colours of the Impressionists, a few portraits embracing such widely different subjects as Queen Elizabeth I and Queen Victoria—and also the poet Alexander Pope, who was then outside all the current fashions. Tom told me that when his firm published her book, many would be keen to see what such a poet as she would have to say about *The Rape of the Lock* and *The Dunciad*. But in the year Tom first met her, her phase was still the impish, modish verse of *Façade*, later set to music by Sir William Walton. She did not yet seem too important a writer, but as a strong and original personality she made her due impression on the young American. Edith Sitwell was a year older than Tom.

It was Sacheverell, her brother ten years younger than herself, who became Tom's special friend. Sacheverell Sitwell was, in fact, just twenty when they met. Being just a little

younger than Karl Culpin, he was the youngest of the friends
to whom at that time Tom felt especially drawn. Their common bond was less books than boats: they both loved to sail
and for the next eight years saw a great deal of each other. In
the 1920s, when their financial position had improved, the
Eliots rented a cottage and a little yacht at Bosham on the
Sussex shore, and there they would be joined by Sacheverell
Sitwell and Vivienne's brother, Maurice. In fact, there came a
moment when Tom and Sacheverell were both in real danger
of being drowned. As the years went by, Tom also forged a
deeper link with Edith. He became an Anglican, she gradually
became a Catholic, and so they shared the Christian faith until
she died[35] less than a month before him.

The final widening of Tom's literary horizon in these early
years of marriage came from his meeting, at Garsington, with
Katherine Mansfield. Here was a woman who snapped her
fingers at convention and tradition, who had mixed with
"certain lewd fellows of the baser sort" and who, settling in a
dubious German *pension*, had discarded chastity before she
somehow got taken up by Lady Ottoline. Her talk was
piquant, her jokes were in dubious taste, she reeked of cheap
scent. For some years she had been the mistress of Middleton
Murry, who gradually changed her from ineffective pensive-
ness and ribaldry to a woman who could write beautiful short
stories and vivid letters. Love and disillusionment, Murry remarked, were to mark her life until the end. She could enjoy
the beauty of a flower, and yet be aware of the snail crawling
up its stem; her impressions of love comprehended both joy
and sadness. She could feel as much of the joy and thrill of
passion as Russell himself.

It was through Katherine Mansfield that Tom met Murry,

who not long before had resuscitated a literary weekly known as *The Athenaeum*. Like Bonamy Dobrée, Murry had been much captivated by *Prufrock*—so much so that he invited Tom to join his staff even before being sent copies of *The Egoist*. Here was a dilemma: Tom could immediately embark on a literary career with adequate pay and a wider influence; he would be working under the direction of a man who admired his poetry; nevertheless, after talking the matter over with Vivienne, he said that he thought he would do better to stay on at the bank, earning his living as a business man and adjusting the war debts of German subjects. What he could do, however, was to write frequently for *The Athenaeum*, as incidentally he also did for *Art and Letters*[36] and *The Chapbook*.[37]

In the years that followed, Murry gained for *The Athenaeum* an enviable reputation. Vivienne told me that she found the Murry pair more scintillating than anybody she knew, that the evenings when they all dined together were incomparably brilliant. It was Murry who, in his review of *La Jeune Parque*, brought Paul Valéry to an English public. Valéry appreciated his praise, but remained slightly sceptical as to the admirer. When I mentioned Murry's name to Valéry during a visit the poet paid to Madame des Burgues, at Giens near Hyères, the answer was: "Murry! The man who kills off all his wives—the Bluebeard of today." Yet this was the man who gave a new direction to Tom's thoughts, inspiring him to write about contemporary subjects while each, despite their scepticism, already felt an attraction towards the faith in Christ which they would later develop in such different ways. Both could agree that civilization must not be confused with material comfort: it was less an affair of gas or electricity or the internal combustion engine than of eliminating the traces of original sin, as far as was possible within the limitations of perverse human nature.

For no one was to become more clearly aware than Tom of mankind's severely limited powers to change human character. Both during and after the war, married life stretched taut the highly-strung structure of brain and nerves. He should have been able to relax, but every evening there was Vivienne, whom neither poppy nor mandragora could sedate. To the restlessness of her nights she added the exhaustion, disarray and illusion which ruthlessly pursued her ineffective sedatives. How often her days darkened into misgiving and despondency, which might however be suddenly lit up by the lightnings of her surprises of her elaborations of the daring jokes of Katherine Mansfield. Elaborations much chastened, however, for Vivienne's talk, though it often insinuated scandal, no more bordered on indecency than Tom's own. They both liked to be risqué, and Tom delighted in quoting the first lines of current ditties without pursuing them to the point at which they ended in ribaldry.

The clearest and most vivid portrait of Vivienne at this time comes from a woman who died in 1965; she had begun life as a Morrison-Scott, married a grandson of Coventry Patmore, but aften ten years of married life with this successful business man abandoned him and their two sons to replace H.D. in the affections of Richard Aldington. She was, in fact, one of his four wives and much relished the literary atmosphere in which Aldington lived. She has given us a remarkable portrait of both Tom and the wife whom he then adored. Eliot himself was in no way striking, she observed;[38] and here, as against Osbert Sitwell, I feel that Mrs. Patmore was undoubtedly telling the truth. One had to hunt for an explanation of his undoubted force. She felt that inhibitions and a critical attitude prevented him from indulging in really genial humour. His appearance was distinguished, but she longed for a grace and a carelessness which would have made him really attractive.

Then comes the vivid description of Vivienne, whose personality (Mrs. Patmore thought) suited Tom's "quiet elegance." Slim and rather small with light brown hair and shining grey eyes, she had an incisive manner and shimmered with intelligence. She was only a little simpler in character than Tom, and in her frailty resembled a tangara figure.[39] One day she asked Mrs. Patmore: "Are you ever free on Sunday afternoons?" What she wanted to do was to take Tom to a little *thé dansant* in Queensway, Bayswater, where he could dance and relax. Tom held his partner lightly and gracefully and danced adequately. Vivienne was much more of an expert; though she had never been a professional dancer, she had studied ballet technique. One afternoon in a chemist's shop she actually attempted an imitation of the Russian dancer Karsavina, Tom supporting her with spontaneous tenderness.

There was social life, too. One of the women the Eliots most admired was Mrs. St. John Hutchinson,[40] who remained their friend for many years. Mrs. Hutchinson was also a friend of Herbert Asquith, and Tom was never prouder of Vivienne than after they had spent a weekend at Sutton Courtenay as the guests of Lord and Lady Oxford and the former Prime Minister had been subjugated by Vivienne's charm and beauty.[41] Bertrand Russell, helpful as always, lent Tom and Vivienne his house at Marlow,[42] where Tom gardened and, with the help of Mary Culpin as cook, entertained friends of whom perhaps Lucy Thayer, Mary Culpin's brother Karl and

Mrs. St. John Hutchinson were the closest. As a hostess, says Mrs. Patmore,[43] Vivienne was "endearing, quiet, attentive to her guests without fuss and a very intelligent listener."

Nevertheless, the heaviness and strain of Tom's life in his younger days were all too frequently exhausting. He often looked tired and run down. One of his friends has told me that somewhere about 1918, when he heard the word "insane" mentioned in conversation, he caught it up with pathetic intensity. The tragedy of Vivienne's lunacy loomed like a spectre before him.

Those who find insanity in the ones they love add to life's burdens the tormenting question whether they themselves are alleviating or worsening the malady. The time was to come when, after tender care and long, despairing reflection, he must face the fact that the doctors had pronounced their verdict.

CHAPTER

7

James Joyce and Richard Aldington

ONE day in April 1918, as the British and American armies in France were reeling under the last convulsive furies of the German attack, Leonard and Virginia Woolf received a visitor at their home in Richmond.[1]

This was Miss Harriet Weaver; she came at Tom Eliot's instigation; and she brought with her a brown paper parcel containing the uncompleted manuscript of *Ulysses*.

Miss Weaver, the champion of Pound, Eliot and Joyce, the original impulse of the whole *Egoist* revolution, and the admirer of Herbert Read and Richard Aldginton, was not only a Quakeress but the very model of the conventional Victorian spinster. Leonard Woolf describes her as mild in nature. His wife Virginia found her unalterably modest, judicious and decorous. Her neat mauve dress seemed to fit her soul no less than her body. Her grey gloves, like her simple blue eyes, were yet another sign of domestic rectitude. Yet it was she and Tom who wished to sponsor the publication of *Ulysses*.

She had come to ask Virginia Woolf, who with her husband ran her own publishing company, the Hogarth Press, whether they would be interested in publishing Joyce's outstanding novel.

But, however outstanding, *Ulysses* is also sensational and verging on the obscene. What was it that induced Tom, with all his correctness, to champion such a book? We have already noted his interest in *Bubu de Montparnasse* and his liking for risqué jokes. Moreover, from the time when he first began to write for *The Egoist*, he believed that D. H. Lawrence was the most interesting of the rising novelists. Why? Because, convinced that the really absorbing regions of life and mind are those which border the unconscious, Tom welcomed an exploration of them which brought the reader into immediate touch with human passion. He admired Lawrence's freshness, directness and frankness in dealing with sexual relations.

In his *Portrait of the Artist as a Young Man* Joyce had succeeded in giving a naive account of his own youth, first as a pupil of the Jesuits, then as one who sought emancipation from them. Without inhibitions, he set down the sensations of his early years. He was, as it were, the Van Gogh of writers, living what Keats desired, a life of sensations rather than thoughts. His whole talent was concentrated on the memory of his upbringing in an Ireland at once Catholic and unsophisticated. He recognized religion there but lived independent of it. This we see in each of the sketches in *The Dubliners*, the last of which Eliot thought the best short story he knew.

Just as the appearance of Virginia's visitor offered a complete disguise to her literary daring, so her brown paper parcel contrasted strongly with the lurid phantasmagoria of the most revolutionary novel then published in the twentieth century. What Eliot's own *Prufrock* had already hinted, this book displayed in the completely unrestrained flow of its descriptions and sensations. To *A Portrait of the Artist as a Young Man*, and its stream of consciousness, *Ulysses* added a frankness in its treatment of eroticism which until then had been taboo in serious literature. This part of life was the more interesting to the correct Quaker lady because she knew nothing of it in her own experience. Her instinct was to do things hitherto unattempted in the realm of print. Joyce, after all, had written with artistry, imagination, picturesqueness and beauty—despite the vulgarity of much of the subject-matter in *Ulysses*. (Likewise, Eliot was to portray banal life in mean streets and a vulgar Irish-American in his bath.) Joyce had exploited the device of contrast. Then why not approve him for going the whole gamut of Dublin life, even to the extent of describing a girl in a brothel? As soon as the manuscript of *Ulysses* came into Miss Weaver's hands, she and Eliot decided to publish it in *The Egoist*—but they were also determined, if possible, to have it brought out as a book.

Miss Weaver, Eliot and Joyce were soon apprised of the facts of the situation: no British printer would dare to touch the book. Yet Eliot still remained convinced that Joyce was a supreme master. Twenty-two years later, when Joyce died in 1941, *The Times* brought out a balanced, if somewhat muted, appraisal of his achievement. Still passionately convinced of Joyce's merit as a novelist, Eliot thought the obituary too lukewarm in tone and wrote a vehement protest about it to *The Times*—so vehement, indeed, that the newspaper refused to publish it. Eliot persisted in making his views known to the world, and found a chance to bring them out in a literary magazine, *Horizon*.[2]

It was not until 1920 that he had a chance of meeting the man he so deeply admired.[3] After spending some time in

Zurich, Joyce came over to Paris where Eliot and Wyndham Lewis visited him.[4] Lewis, in fact, was accompanying Eliot on a summer-holiday excursion to Quiberon, in Brittany: Tom, as so often, was run down and overworked, and Vivienne felt that the change would do her husband good.[5] Before leaving London, Tom had mentioned to Ezra Pound that he was going to France for a holiday, and Pound had entrusted him with a parcel to be delivered to Joyce.

As Joyce's address was in the Quartier Latin, Eliot and Lewis took rooms in a small, dingy hotel in the Rue des Saints-Pères, the sort of hotel meublé with which that part of Paris is still crowded. The rooms were high, the parquet dirty, the furniture faded, the curtains frowzy. But there was many a little place nearby where one could eat well and at that time cheaply, as cheaply as at the Petit Savoyard in Soho.

Eliot sent off an express letter to Joyce, telling him of the parcel that had arrived for him from Ezra Pound and inviting him to dinner. At about six o'clock Joyce turned up in the Rue des Saints-Pères, bringing with him his son Giorgio. "Ah! Wyndham Lewis," he said under his breath as he sat down, dangling his straw hat while Eliot offered him the parcel.

"Is this the parcel you mentioned in your note?" he asked. Then he attempted to untie the crafty knot with which the cunning old Ezra (as Lewis calls him) had tied the parcel; failing in this, he asked for a knife, and was given a pair of nail-scissors. Gingerly he opened the parcel, only to find inside it an assortment of nondescript garments and two old brown shoes.

"Oh!" Joyce exclaimed. Then followed a pause during which Irish social poise, on the one hand, adjusted itself to Bostonian reticence, on the other.

"Oh!" he repeated with a laugh—while no one dared to touch the brown shoes. With a slow smile, Eliot pressed Joyce to stay to dinner. Turning to his son Giorgio, Joyce said to him in Italian to tell his mother that his father would not be home to dinner. With a deep bow to the hosts, Giorgio picked up the parcel and rushed out of the room.

Unexpectedly, Joyce then insisted on inviting Eliot and Lewis to dine with *him* at a restaurant, paying for everything himself. He even dashed out of the taxis to forestall them in their attempts to pay. But what was rather irritating about his hospitality was that, throughout a whole evening's conversation with Wyndham Lewis, Joyce always spoke of Tom as "your friend Mr. Eliot," as if he were referring to some obscure friend whom Lewis allowed to accompany him to Paris only out of politeness. Joyce uttered not one word about Eliot's writings; he was merely the messenger who had come with the old brown shoes, not the author of *Prufrock, Gerontion* and the essays, articles and reviews published in *The Egoist* and *The Athenaeum*, some of which were reprinted about that time in an anthology entitled *The Sacred Wood.* Eliot was naturally nettled. Joyce, he said, "is exceedingly arrogant. Underneath. That is why he is so polite."[6] But this mood of annoyance did not long cool Eliot's admiration for all that Joyce had written.[7]

After *Ulysses* had eventually been published abroad, he wrote in *The Dial*[8] that here was the most important literary expression of the age. He felt that it had given shape and significance to the immense panorama of contemporary history, which so often seemed to be merely futility and anarchy. Only those, like Joyce, who had some inner system of belief could make sense of the disorder that surrounded them.

A creative mind is always vitally concerned with more than it can encompass; Eliot was vigorously analysing and comparing things whose meaning still eluded him. His own mind was a chaos like the one depicted in narrative form in *Ulysses*. He himself, a year or two later, was to set down in a poem which is the sequel to *Ulysses* the vivid picture of a mind struggling to keep a hold on order while culture is met with chaos.

Meanwhile, however, he was still largely a critic and reviewer—apart from his regular work at Lloyds. He had by now given up his post as assistant editor of *The Egoist*, but still contributed both to Miss Weaver's journal and to *The Athenaeum*.[9] Richard Aldington had come back from the War, and it was not long before he had formulated the idea of introducing Tom to the editor of *The Times Literary Supplement*, Bruce Richmond. Here, he felt, would be another outlet for Tom's critical genius. But it was by no means easy to persuade Richmond to meet Eliot. Aldington, in fact, describes this episode as the most complicated piece of diplomacy he ever undertook. Richmond had more than enough distinguished contributors to *The Times Literary Supplement*, and perhaps he was somewhat put off from meeting Tom by the memory of *Prufrock and Other Observations*.

"After about six months of cautious work," Aldington has written,[10] "I finally talked Richmond into agreeing to have lunch with Eliot. I felt quite sure that he had only to meet Eliot and hear him talk for all the prejudice to melt away, and for him to realize that he was in the presence of an exceptionally gifted man."

It was 1919 or thereabouts, and Tom appeared in London in a complex guise. He had cultivated a beard in Switzerland in the Uncle Sam style and on top of this he set a Derby hat.

"I had always thought of him as handsome," Aldington continues, "certainly very distinguished in appearance; but with the combination of that hat and beard he looked perfectly awful. . . . Richmond shook his head and blinked; I shook my head and blinked; Tom smiled urbanely, and looked more awful than ever. . . . All's well that ends well. Over a steak and a pewter pot of bitter, Eliot began talking. In five minutes he had completely captivated Richmond, as he can captivate any intelligent person. Afterwards Richmond made a discreet Oxonian jest about the beard, but when we next met Tom, it had vanished; and all was forgotten and forgiven."[11]

Aldington places this meeting somewhere about 1922, which would be when Tom returned from Switzerland via Paris after writing *The Waste Land*. But his first contribution to *The Times Literary Supplement* was dated 13 November 1919,[12] and in any case Aldington followed Pound to Paris in 1921.

It is Richard Church who tells us how Aldington announced his intention to cross the Channel.[13] Church first explains his own place within that set. Like Herbert Read, he had originally worked in the Civil Service. One day a newcomer with a head of fine fiery hair burst into his Whitehall office. "Are you Dicky Church?" the stranger asked in a loud cheery voice. He was six feet tall, his green eyes were restless, his hair fluttered and flickered continually, he was a furnace of nervous passion. "I'm Flint. Frank Flint," he said, "as good a poet as you are. Ever heard of me? Of course you haven't! Who has? No! No! No silver spoon in my mouth. Gutter-born, gutter-bred! Oh God! Forget it, man, forget it." Courage and ability, Church explains, had raised from a dreary grey Victorian slum of east London this man who was now in charge of foreign statistics in the Ministry of Labour. He had written a book dedicated to Herbert Read, to whom before very long he introduced young Church.

At the Commercio, in Frith Street, Soho, Church would meet Read, Eliot, Pound and the whole coterie of the Imagists. He says—and I sympathize—that he could make nothing of the scorn the Imagists poured on their contemporaries, nor of their contention that D. H. Lawrence was superhuman.

It was at the Commercio, early in 1921, that Church met Eliot and at once felt his nervous intensity and noted the reserve which countered the naivete natural to the young man from St. Louis. Flint waved his long arms and fired his salvos, Herbert Read occasionally let fall a monosyllable from his granite lips, while Eliot sat there quiet and calm. His voice was soft—of course, there was no trace of an American accent— and every syllable was pronounced with precision; in many a phrase was the cutting edge of satire. But there was a Montparnasse side of him, in Church's eyes. As for Pound, he was dreadfully self-conscious. Like hypercivilized European decadents, these uprooted Americans always gave Church the sensation of being in the presence of withered flowers—withered flowers like those Eliot wrote about on his arrival at Harvard. No matter how aggressive Pound might be, Eliot never offered Church anything but his characteristic quiet courtesy.

Soon another man entered the Commercio. As though presenting a police warrant, he announced his name: Aldington. Read's eyes fixed him with a glassy stare, Eliot looked up quizzically at a figure in whom Church found a certain suggestion of rugged nobility: bold and authoritative in his manner, he was still a handsome animal who, even in his defiance, exerted a certain fresh magnetism. In a tone of voice then, as always, disgruntled and rasping, Aldington snapped out the words: "I am leaving" (he meant for Paris). He seemed to be expecting protests that never came; on the contrary, Eliot gently nodded his approval. At last Flint, mellowed with chianti, grasped him by the arm. "Dear fellow" he said, "dear fellow, you mustn't, mustn't go." But go he did. He remained in touch with Eliot, however, and in the following year (1922) was actually collaborating with him in the new review of which Eliot became editor, *The Criterion*. He gave the highest praise to Eliot's anthology of essays, *The Sacred Wood*, but within a few years had become intensely hostile both to him and to Pound, both of whom, some ten years after the party at the Commercio, he subjected to savage satire in the lampoon *Stepping Heavenward*.[14]

Although it was not written until rather later in Aldington's career, I feel that this is the appropriate moment to discuss *Stepping Heavenward*, for the impressions which it records of Tom, Vivienne and Ezra date largely, if not entirely, from the years 1919–1921. It shows us that even then Eliot's mind was moving towards the time when Pound would give the name of "Parson Possum" to his prize discovery of 1914.

The method Aldington chose was to represent Eliot as an historian, giving him the name Cibber which incurs such mockery in Pope's *Dunciad*. Pound became Lucas Cholmp, "who had won much praise in England by his vigorous exposures of Washington and John Paul Jones." Vivienne was renamed Adèle Paléologue, a creature of "exquisite melancholy." "Is it really, really true that you are American?" she asked Cibber. "I can scarcely believe it. You're not a bit like the others. . . ."

"America must really be a *wonderful* country," she continued. "Ye-es," replied Cibber thoughtfully, "ye-es, but it has many defects. It is essentially a country with too many moralities and too few manners. It can only be rescued by a disciplined aristocracy and a dogmatic Church."

Aldington naturally loved to satirize religion. In this regard, a typical quip was when he said of the legend that Cibber walked barefoot on a pilgrimage to Lourdes that it could be dismissed as a pious exaggeration of the fact that he once took a holiday with a countess in Biarritz. Much in Aldington's lampoon is cheap and nasty, but there are many touches in it which are truly revealing, among which is an echo of the gossip that surrounded Eliot's marriage. "This marriage is one of the major mysteries of Cibber's life."

"How explain this infatuation in so cool a fish?" Aldington continued. "All men and large numbers of women are human, but when we consider the profundity of Cibber's studies, the growing New England austerity of his appearance and morals, the almost arid bleakness of his life and the imposing nihilism of his philosophy at that time, this marriage can only be explained as a savage freak of Hazard or as the Head of Providence using strange means to bring a Great Soul to God."

With extreme ingenuity, Aldington adds further satire to this mixture of fact and imagination. It was wartime. "London was raided. . . . The responsibilities of matrimony weighed heavily upon him. (His father) did not increase his allowance, and prices were rising, rising; historical genius had no commercial value; a household had to be supported somehow. With superb energy, Cibber made a decision and—what a mad world it was!—accepted work as the guiding spirit of a haberdashery department, where his courteous manners and distinguished appearance found full scope." So much for the bank. Then, returning to the marriage, Aldington suggested in the crudest possible way that the cause of Vivienne's malady was finding her husband more like an angel than a man.

It is not surprising that after *Stepping Heavenward* was published, Eliot refused to allow any mention of his marriage even from the friends in whom he had most fully confided. The silence that came into everything that was printed about Eliot left the back door open to those suggestions of scandal which were made by his enemies both in Britain and in the United States.

Aldington may or may not be returning to fact when he says that Cholmp, who had been rather in favour of the marriage as a means of linking Cibber with Europe, watched his friend's marital disharmony with growing dismay. He is certainly right in saying that those hours in the bank were a relief to Eliot's jaded nerves and that that was why for nine years he gladly remained a banker. But was not refusing to leave Lloyds' Colonial and Foreign Department the supreme touch of *chic*? Aldington wittily asks. "It turned mere publicity into fame." Everybody was commenting on the fact that so great a genius so employed his day. "Intense and arduous as his studies were," and here again Aldington is drawing direct from life, "he found time to become an enthusiastic and ardent follower of Monsieur Charles Maurras, defender of Nationalism, Monarchy, and Catholic Discipline. . . . The lean melancholy figure of the young American became familiar to all the more serious student gatherings of the time. Cibber made few intimate friends and spoke very rarely, but listened carefully. Yet already he was able to make his influence felt, and time and again would ruin an argument or wreck an enthusiasm by a well-placed criticism."

Here Aldington skilfully reveals the essential complexity of Eliot. He portrayed the lower life of prosperous cities repeatedly in his poems (a fact at which *Stepping Heavenward* can only hit, since Cibber is an historian), yet he was equally interested in the higher reaches of intellectual debate. Sometimes he would speak or write words as cutting as the sharpest cynic's. With *The Waste Land*, he put Ezra Pound quite into the shade.

In every sphere, Eliot was beginning to enjoy the prestige of rising authority; or, as Aldington puts it, "wherever you went in evening dress you were bound to hear people discussing Cibber."

CHAPTER

8

The Waste Land

I F everybody in evening dress was discussing Cibber, it was
not so much because of *The Sacred Wood* (though this
had been hailed by Bonamy Dobrée as the most important
book of criticism since the *Preface to Lyrical Ballads* and
Biographia Literaria) as after the appearance of *The Waste
Land* (October 1922).

In the spring of 1921 Tom's brother Henry had come over
to see him from America and they went one evening to hear
Stravinsky's *Sacre du Printemps*. At the end of the perfor-
mance Tom stood up and cheered.[1] In the world of music
Stravinsky was providing what Joyce provided in prose. He
dealt boldly with the sordid, as Joyce had overridden every
convention in describing the intimacy and at times the beastli-
ness of life in Dublin. To Eliot this sort of music came as a
welcome experience. There was tumult in him and he felt
relief when music met him with its own tumult.

In the year of Eliot's death A. C. MacGill, a Professor of
Religion at Princeton, wrote about these innovations in a
book which he called *The Celebration of Flesh*.[2] Poetry, he

claimed, was a celebration of the actuality and richness of our fleshly engagement with the insistence of the life of towns and factories. It should aim at revealing to townsmen more reality in their daily occupations than they usually notice.

Pound and his followers were, I think, unjustified in saying that the older poets of their time sought refuge from reality in mushy, conventional verse. Edward Arlington Robinson in America, and Thomas Hardy, A. E. Housman and Alfred Noyes in England had each developed new and direct styles far from the poetic norm. It is, however, undeniable that Eliot was to take verse further than ever before into the sordidness of the streets, and attain his effects by contrasting this sordidness with the splendours of traditional poetry. In such poems as *Prufrock* there were plenty of musical and poetic expressions among the reminiscences of sordid things. But the object of *Prufrock* was to emphasize the contrast, introducing into verse the language of ordinary conversation—just as Eliot's favourite French poets did. To combine these effects with the surprises of the Elizabethan dramatists was the novelty at which Eliot aimed.

He was to say later that the poet sees through boredom and horror to a hidden glory.[3] So Dante had done in his *Inferno*. It was for Eliot to juxtapose banality, vulgarity and even sordidness (all of which he knew well from direct experience) with echoes of great literature and lines inspired with the spiritual secret of all religions. Thus he produced a chaotic sequence of verse relevant to the predicaments and confusions of the years following the First World War.

As the summer of 1921 followed on his brother Henry's visit, Tom became utterly exhausted. His daily routine was to get up at about five in the morning and work at his writing in the early hours of the day. Then off to the bank for a day's work adjusting the war debts of German nationals and sympathizers, and finally home to Vivienne and the strain of their life together. It was a routine too arduous for flesh and blood to endure. In the fall of 1921 he had to take prolonged leave from the bank.

He went first to the Albemarle Hotel, 47 Eastern Esplanade, Cliftonville, near Margate, where he stayed from 22 October to 12 November, after which he moved to La Turbie, above Monaco. But it was at a sanatorium in Lausanne that he found the best relaxation for his nerves, after the accumulated strain and tension of years: and it was there that he composed many of the thousand or so lines which make up the original *Waste Land*.[4] (The poem had been begun in earnest at Margate.[5]) These lines reflect his extensive reading, his attempts to find a belief, his ideals, his memories of the years just behind him, and the ragtime when he escaped from his culture and his anxieties.

One of the best ways to understand *The Waste Land* is to turn back to the volume of his collected poems published in 1920, *Ara Vos Prec*. These three words of Provençal come from the twenty-sixth canto of Dante's *Purgatorio*. The whole Provençal passage haunted the poet's mind for ten years. Here is a translation of the last five lines of the canto:

> "[I] view with joy the day I hope to know.
> I pray you by that Goodness which doth deign
> To guide you to the summit of this stair,
> Bethink you in due season of my pain."
> Then he shrank back in the refining fire.[6]

Such was the theme of poem after poem which Eliot was then writing, now satirizing the vulgarity of vice, now expounding the astringent process which gives his diagnosis of the age its cathartic disillusionment.

> *Sovenha vos a temps de ma dolor.*
> Bethink you in due season of my pain.

This is the theme of the poem *Gerontion*,[7] which Eliot intended as his introduction to *The Waste Land*.

In writing *Gerontion*, Eliot recalled the fateful decisions made in 1919 in the Hall of Mirrors at Versailles. Those alone were cause enough for cynicism, even if he had had no disillusionment in marriage. And as for Vivienne, how little there remained in him of a joy that had once been eager. Why should he even strive to keep the embers of his passion burning?[8] Eliot did not shirk this question even before his nerves gave way in 1921. But once his breakdown had occurred, he determined to break away for a while from the thousand small deliberations of his daily routine, abjure the pursuit of Romantic illusions, and gaze into reality from the essential life of suffering. *Sovenha vos a temps de ma dolor.*

So exhaustion kept propounding to him the enigma, as it beguiled him into a wilderness of mirrors from which he vainly sought an outlet: vainly, until he eventually discovered it in a famous Sanskrit classic.

In after years, vehemently rejecting the idea that *The Waste Land* expresses the disillusionment of an age,[9] he maintained that there was no such thing as the disillusionment of an age and that, in any case, the subtleties, enigmas and allusions of *The Waste Land* were written in obedience to a plain command given in the voice of thunder and coming from the ancient wisdom of India. The command of the *Bhagavad Gita* is "Give. Sympathize. Control." Its recurrent theme is "Shantih," which is the Sanskrit word for "Peace."

What in Sanskrit is "Shantih" is "Salaam," in Arabic, the universal greeting which runs from Malaya to Morocco, the greeting also which the risen Christ gave to His Apostles. "Peace I leave with you, my peace I give unto you: not as the world giveth, give I unto you." How well I remember Tom repeating those words to me and saying that the peace of Christ is indeed different from any the world can offer, that it is in fact more often given when the world refuses peace.

He wrote to his mother that much of his life was in the poem. *The Waste Land* contains many a picture of his travels, many a recollection of his London (whether in the crowds walking over London Bridge or in the white and gold of the church of St. Magnus the Martyr in the city), there is even the sailing at Gloucester and Bosham, when the boat responded gaily to the breeze and the controlling hand at the rudder. There is also the recollection of that rash moment when he had rushed to the Registry Office and pledged himself in a bond which neither prudence nor patience could unloose. There are the moments when Vivienne complained of her bad nerves at night and when he ordered a taxi for her in the afternoon. There is his talk with a Lithuanian girl by the Starnbergersee. There is his love of opera and music-hall. There are his relaxations and his torments.

But what does the poem mean? The very fact that there is no answer to this question is the secret of *The Waste Land*'s immense success. People could puzzle about it endlessly, and in so doing find something to commune with their own confusion. Pound would not accept *Gerontion* as a preface to *The Waste Land*, but if Tom had persisted in his intention it would have been clear that *The Waste Land* is the poem of a man working his way through a nervous breakdown and dealing

partly with his own memories and partly with a mass of material—both classic and contemporary—too vast for him to digest.
The new poetry Tom inaugurated with *The Waste Land* was
to be a cry from the heart, an echo from the crowd and an
echo from the great classics. Bill and Lou jostle against Madame
Sosostris, Mr. Eugenides and Tiresias, and the metre echoes
first Shakespeare, or the rollicking lilt of a popular song.

No wonder that even cultivated people wondered what
Eliot was driving at. "Were the notes to *Wastelands* (sic) a
lark or serious?" asked Arnold Bennett, who "couldn't see the
point of the poem."[10] If one of the highest literary authorities
of the age failed dismally to understand *The Waste Land*,
could greater perceptiveness be expected of undergraduates?
After reading the poem to a literary society at Worcester College, Oxford, a year or two after its publication, Eliot was
asked by a puzzled undergraduate: "Mr. Eliot, did you mean
it all seriously?" With courteous patience, Tom insisted that
it was the very fabric of his life. Yes, but a fabric in which
seriousness was interwoven with mockery, even buffoonery.
Tom's reply to Arnold Bennett was that the notes were "not
more of a skit than some things in the poem itself."[10]

Yet another undergraduate of Worcester College asked
him: "Mr. Eliot, did you write it all yourself? Didn't that
passage about *The barge she sat in, like a burnish'd throne*
come from somewhere else?" And so, of course, though
slightly modified,[11] it did.[12] Indeed, the poet even added thirty-
five words from F. M. Chapman's *Handbook of Birds of
Eastern North America* (1895). Its four hundred and thirty-
three lines introduced no less than thirty-five quotations ranging from Shakespeare and Goldsmith and the dramatists of
the seventeenth century to the *Pervigilium Veneris*, Dante,

Gerard de Nerval, Baudelaire and Wagner. He was later to confess that, partly by subtlety, partly by effrontery, partly by accident, he thus acquired a reputation for immense erudition. Sometimes he used quotations to convey a sense of glory, sometimes for the contrast of ruthless satire. *In The Vicar of Wakefield* Goldsmith had asked:

> When lovely woman stoops to folly,
> And finds too late that men betray,
> What charm can soothe her melancholy,
> What art can wash her guilt away?

But when in 1921 Eliot wished to write of a woman's folly,[13] she was not lovely, she was a typist in a cheap room with her combinations drying on a line, and her slippers, stockings, stays and camisoles scattered around her. Into this cheap room arrived a pimpled vulgar clerk, perhaps of a type Tom met at the bank. After his departure, the "folly" completed, she automatically smoothes her hair and puts a record on the gramophone. In this manner the typist (whom no doubt Tom knew, as he knew Lou, his charwoman) thinks she can dispose of folly, melancholy and guilt.

What could be more sordid than an affair of this kind or the abortion engineered by Lou in the section preceding it?[14] The way in which he depicted all this, which was a squalid, dreary and vulgar subject, made certain readers feel that this was the aspect of life he himself really liked, while it struck others as the work of a man almost driven mad by disgust and cynicism. One writer in New York, Burton Roscoe, wrote that the poem gave voice to the despairing resignation arising from the spiritual and economic consequences of the War, from the cross-purposes of modern civilization, from the cul-de-sac into which both science and philosophy seemed to have drifted, and from the breakdown of those directive purposes which give zest and joy to the business of living. In London, Eliot's friend Harold Monro wrote that the poem was at one and the same time a representation, a criticism and a disgusted outcry of a heart turned cynical. It was calm, fierce and horrifying.

But by now Eliot had finished writing his thousand lines— no longer in the sanatorium but at Chardonne above Vevey, where one looks towards Chillon and the Dents du Midi. Returning to England via Paris, he halted in the French capital to consult Pound. What was his opinion of the newly delivered poem? Far from giving the text his full approval, Pound condemned its thousand or so lines as sprawling and chaotic and at once set to work whittling them down to less than five hundred, cutting out among other things a long passage in imitation of Pope, and rearranging the lines that remained.[15] To all these changes Eliot agreed without much demur; indeed, he came round to the view that they had immensely strengthened the poem's impact;[16] but whether Pound's judgment was competent I would strongly question. The surviving lines were divided up into five sections between which it is difficult to find the narrow way of ordered sequence. And, as we have already noted, Pound objected to Eliot's using *Gerontion* as a preface to his new poem. Throw it out in hard chunks and see if people can get their teeth into it, seemed to be his attitude. In different moods, many could pick out and emphasize something that suited them.

When it came to printing the poem,[17] Eliot suspected that Pound's obstetric effort had been anything but successful. The printing was done in sets of sixteen-page signatures. After the four hundred and thirty-three lines had been set up in print, there were too many blank pages left in the final signature, which offended the propriety of Leonard Woolf, the publisher. So Tom was instructed to fill them in. Rather than re-insert some of the discarded passages, which in my opinion might have greatly enhanced the symmetry and meaning of the whole, another expedient was chosen: to append explanatory notes, but these notes themselves led to fierce controversy, pointing to some sources but not others, and generally making confusion worse confounded.

Always the most eager admirer of her husband's poetry, Vivienne at once saw the immense range of prospects opened up by *The Waste Land*. She also thought of the old friend who had partly inspired it, Bertrand Russell: he must see it at once, even before it was published. But for some reason the four hundred and thirty-three lines of typescript were not sent to Russell in the spring of 1922.[18] A coolness seemed to have descended on the friendship of Russell and the Eliots. Tom confessed to Russell, however, that it was he and Vivienne who feared that Russell might not wish to have anything more to do with them.[18] Thus, Russell did not read the poem until it had appeared in print—and even then (it seems) belatedly, for his letter congratulating Tom on this great achievement was presumably not written until October 1923, eighteen months after Vivienne had mooted the idea of showing him *The Waste Land*. She had been right, however, in thinking that the poem would appeal to him. Russell much appreciated the fifth section, in which the work begins to emerge from incoherence into principle. Tom was immensely gratified by Russell's compliment, for he was someone who knew where he had done best.

Meanwhile, in the eighteen months between the finishing of *The Waste Land* and the receipt of Russell's letter, Vivienne's health had deteriorated still further. It seems that in the spring of 1923 she suffered a bad relapse, indeed nearly died.[18] She left London to convalesce in the country, and remained there for at least six months, with Tom visiting her at weekends. She was not at home to enjoy the satisfaction of Russell's letter when it arrived.

Someone else who read *The Waste Land*, and with equal admiration, was his mother. Ever since Eliot's visit to America in 1915, Tom's mother had felt anxious about her younger son. In the early years of their estrangement, she knew that he was unhappy in England. It had been wartime, and news from him had been infrequent and inadequate. She believed that his gifts lay in the direction of philosophy, not "vers libres."[19] What he sent her of his published works seemed meagre and strange. Her strength was giving way. In 1919 her husband died, still believing that Tom was "the boy who had taken a wrong turning" (as Eliot once told a friend); at the age of seventy-six she gave up her home in St. Louis and settled in Massachusetts. It was here, in 1923, when she was in her eightieth year, that she read *The Waste Land*—to which, he had confessed to her, so much of his inner life had been imparted. She read it to make contact with his life, its thoughts, worry and strain; and, with a mother's instinct, she found her way through its maze. She felt its greatness, accepted and defended it. He had hoped for recognition from his parents, and now at last he had obtained it. From that time forward, mother and son looked at one another with ever deepening respect. He arranged for her one long poem, *Savonarola*, to be published and actually wrote a preface[20] for it. Though he had moved rapidly away from the family's Unitarian worship, she was to have the satisfaction, two years before her death,[21] of witnessing her brilliant son's reconciliation with Christianity.

Meredith said that those who live much by their heart in youth have sharp foretastes of the issues imaged for the soul. This is true also of those who live on the scale of genius or who suffer from psychic illness, and plainly Tom was both of these: after a bout of influenza in January 1922, he found himself in deep depression. Yet as the year went by, it was to prove by far the most auspicious he had ever known. In literate circles the impression made by *The Waste Land* was that it marked a watershed in the poetic life of the century. In Germany the great critic Ernst Robert Curtius accepted it as the voice of the German soul in the sufferings of defeat. He translated it into excellent German verse. In America it appeared in *The Dial* and won a prize for two thousand dollars. Two thousand dollars! It meant emancipation from his financial straits, a better house,[22] even a car. But these benefits were small compared to what Eliot gained in the combination of a wealthy patroness and an admiring friend among publishers. The patroness was Lady Rothermere, the admiring friend Richard Cobden-Sanderson.

Richard Cobden-Sanderson was the grandson of the great Liberal statesman, Richard Cobden; his father had been guardian of the young orphans Frank and Bertrand Russell. He was of sparkling wit and elegant taste, whose wife, Sally, was adored in the wide circle of friends whom they entertained in their house at Hammersmith. Here Tom often came[23] and enjoyed himself so much that he was known as "the gay American." His heart glowed in such companionship, not only at the Cobden-Sandersons' Hammersmith parties but at their country house, Lavender Cottage, at Long Crendon, near Thame. It was a delightful village where the poetess Ruth Pitter afterwards came to live. Richard Cobden-Sanderson spent his life as a self-employed publisher dealing only in work which he judged to be of the finest quality, and steadfastly maintaining the highest standards of production. It was to him that Tom turned when, in 1922, he decided that he would like to found a literary review, and Cobden-Sanderson in his turn obtained support for the new venture (which was to be known as *The Criterion*) from a friend of his who was interested in both painting and literature. This was Lady Rothermere, wife of the first Viscount Rothermere, who was owner of *The Daily Mail, The Sunday Dispatch,* and *The Evening News.* For some time, as Cobden-Sanderson was well aware, Lady Rothermere had had ambitions of founding and supporting a literary review. She gladly assented to this proposal, for which she put up all the necessary money, disclaiming virtually all control over editorial policy.

So it was that in October 1922 Tom was blessed with the opportunity to edit a magazine of his own, a magazine which was to become so valuable both in the development of his own ideas and in its intellectual influence generally. Beginning with his own poetry (*The Waste Land* was in the first quarterly issue) and a study of *Ulysses,* it soon broadened its scope to describe cultural movements both in western Europe and America. But it was another commitment for Tom—unpaid evening work, for a bank official was not permitted to hold any other regular employment.

For three years Lady Rothermere continued as sole owner of the equity of *The Criterion* and its generous subsidizer.

Cobden-Sanderson often used to receive letters from Tom jokingly informing him of the amounts she was prepared to "cough up." But in July 1925 her three-year contract with Richard Cobden-Sanderson expired and she decided that she no longer wished to support this financial burden alone (perhaps she did not completely agree with its policy), and Tom then had to face the question of whether the magazine should go out of existence or whether a dose of strychnine would enable its heart to continue beating. He spoke about this to Bruce Richmond, of *The Times Literary Supplement,* one of whose protégés, Frank Morley (they were both from New College, Oxford), worked in the publishing-house of Faber & Gwyer. It was in this way that two momentous steps were taken in Eliot's life: Faber & Gwyer were induced by Morley to take over some of the financial burden of *The Criterion;* and indirectly, Tom was to find the congenial employment of a lifetime. The arrangement was that the equity of *The New Criterion*[24] (as it was now to be called) would be divided between Faber & Gwyer and Lady Rothermere, with Tom remaining as editor.

Within a year or two of this Lady Rothermere decided to make France her permanent home and so retired from the board altogether;[25] her share in the enterprise was bought by the publishing-house; but to her and Richard Cobden-Sanderson belongs the immense credit of the journal's initiation, with all that it meant for Eliot's intellectual development and the cultural life of Britain. Not only did it publish such writers as Proust, Hofmannsthal and Valéry,[26] it also took up lesser known writers such as T. O. Beachcroft, Algar Thorold,[27] myself, and that most fascinating of the unsophisticated, Desmond Hawkins, whose friendship Tom cultivated in the same way that he cultivated mine. Desmond would be invited to lunch with Tom and then return with him to his office and talk on for hours and hours.

Moving ahead to the later years of *The Criterion*, I find that my first contribution to it was published in 1929.[28] It was a paper I had written in the Dolomites on the poetry of Michelangelo, and its central theme was that artistic creation results from the generative contact of an artist's mind with something outside it enabling it to conceive. This idea was a favourite with Michelangelo, and as the great sculptor had been mentioned in *Prufrock* and as his thought was the direct development of medieval philosophy, I foresaw Tom's interest in my article, which he immediately accepted. I then offered him a paper on Maupassant, which he at first refused but soon afterwards agreed to publish. He also took an article from me on St. John of the Cross. Several times I reviewed books in *The Criterion*, and I was invited to one of its evenings, at which I met Bonamy Dobrée, who was Professor of English in the Royal University of Egypt some years before I myself occupied that post. The other guest I remember from that evening was T. O. Beachcroft, who first met Tom at Balliol when Tom came to address an undergraduate society, to whom (incidentally) he enlarged on the resemblances between Bach and Moliére.

Besides his editorial and critical work for the newly founded *Criterion*, Eliot was also engaged on new poetry and even a poetic drama. As early as 10 September 1924, after discussing *The Waste Land* with Arnold Bennett, he had told Bennett that "he had definitely given up that form of writing":[29] his interest now lay in drama. What he had in mind was to write a prose drama of modern life, but the prose was to be rhythmic and the high moments of the play were to be enhanced by the roll of drum-beats. He was thinking of getting down to this project immediately, and even persuaded Bennett to read the draft scenario and a few specimen pages of dialogue. The attraction of drama was indeed always strong for Eliot, drama in all its forms—from Aristophanes to the music hall. Much of his poetry in fact is couched in semi-dramatic form. Likewise his dramas were to be poetry exteriorized. His interest in the theatre remained with him from boyhood until death.

Now, with Bennett to advise him, he was thinking of writing a little play in which satire would be pushed over the verge of farce. This work, which was never finished, is what we now have as the fragment of *Sweeney Agonistes*,[30] headed by quotations from Aeschylus and St. John of the Cross. Sweeney was to be taken out of the bath in which we had first seen him in *Ara Vos Prec*.[31] He was to fulfil his ideal of spiritual bliss on a desert island in the South Seas, the sort of island painted by Gauguin and which Eliot himself had constantly before his eyes in the painting he brought back to America from Paris in 1911. Such islands had also been an ideal of Eliot's boyhood.[32] Here Sweeney was to combine fornication with cannibalism,[33] practising a philosophy of life summed up in the line from the *Upanishads:* "Birth, and copulation, and death."[34] Often in time to come he was again to elaborate from these works of brahminic mysticism on the closeness of birth to death and of death to birth. Not only was Mary Queen of Scots right to say: "In my end is my beginning"; he saw an end in every beginning, and a beginning in every end. Such was the timelessness of life. So, through time, time was to be conquered. How easy to turn the subtlest idea into the crudest, and to exalt fornication into the main object of life. Yet the very moment that that is done, the fullness and sacredness of life are denied. In this sense, fornication hardly falls short of cannibalism. Such was to be the theme of Eliot's next effort of satire and comedy in the real style of the music hall, which around the years when he was working at *Sweeney Agonistes* (1925–1927)[35] was one of his favourite relaxations. It was a poem which he always insisted should appear in his collected works. Without it we cannot understand *The Waste Land:* for otherwise we should have lost sight of "the gay American" who so often attended the Cobden-Sandersons' parties, we should overlook the current photograph of Eliot at that time, showing a young man successful and serene—such as to Vivienne he still so often was.

His next poem, *The Hollow Men* (1925),[36] again shows how short-lived was that serenity; or rather, how in Eliot the moods of serenity and despair coexist. We have seen how, at Pound's insistence, *The Waste Land* had ended repeating the brahminic invocation of cosmic peace. But when people are suffering from nervous depression, their minds are more preoccupied with the hopelessness of things. Involved through banking, as Tom was, in the full realization of the evils of war and the resulting wreck of Europe, and experiencing at the same time the breakdown of his own nerves, he took his place among those whom he called "the hollow men." His heart was beating weakly, it had been chilled with disappointments more numbing than his apparent success allowed others to think. A later poem, the sixth canto of *Ash-Wednesday*, was to tell that he might still indulge the hopes he had abandoned, see yachts moving again with the fresh breeze arising;[37] meanwhile, how often the instincts of his heart would fail; as he wakes in the night trembling with tenderness,

Lips that would kiss
Form prayers to broken stone.[38]

Ever since his Harvard undergraduate days, when George Santayana was still Professor of Philosophy, Eliot had deeply admired the author of *The Sense of Beauty* and *The Life of Reason*, works that are imbued with a sense of cosmopolitan culture and a keen feeling for the inter-relationship of beauty and religion. Writing of the *Divina Commedia*, Santayana had stressed that it was the Catholic Church which provided Dante's inspiration, enabling him to build a sublimely orchestrated masterpiece. "As in some great symphony," he wrote,[39] "everything is cumulative: the movements conspire, the tension grows, the volume redoubles, the keen melody soars higher and higher; and it all ends, not with a bang, not with some casual incident, but in sustained reflection, in the sense that it had not ended, but remains by us in its totality, a revelation and a resource for ever."

This sentence hung in Tom's mind for many years, though (unlike Santayana) he still could not accept the range and glory of Dante as his own guide in a disconsolate time. To the Father in Heaven belonged "the Kingdom, the Power and the Glory," but life was also human life.

"What is life?" Shelley had asked at the end of his last great poem.[40] Here was another poet asking the same question a hundred years afterwards. "Life is," he wrote,[41] but could proceed no further. Then, going back in his mind to the children's games he played in St. Louis, he echoed a line about the end of the world, and (as the final line of *The Hollow Men*) adapted with terrific intensity Santayana's phrase about "all ending not with a bang . . . but in sustained reflection," changing it into something expressive of his own tired mood and the time's uncertainties, a plaintive cry of misery lost in a vacuity painful, yet too inconclusive for precise expression.

When his intimate friend of Harvard days, Conrad Aiken, turned to the last pages of *Poems 1909–1925*, and read *The Hollow Men*,[42] he was filled with admiration and amazement. These poems surpassed anything being written on either side of the Atlantic. Aiken wrote Tom a note saying that he would rather have written that book than anything there was. The poet answered this compliment not with a letter but a clipping from *The Midwives' Record* on which the words "blood, mucus, shreds of mucus, purulent offensive discharge" had been underlined.[43] Happily their friendship remained unclouded by this unexpected reaction. Aiken realized that he had been put in his place for the very fulsomeness of his tribute, and replied to Eliot in a message of similar eccentricity. Having thus cleared the air, he could resume a friendship unbroken by any other vicissitudes till death intervened.

CHAPTER

9

Into Publishing

TOM's cryptic reply to Conrad Aiken was the clearest possible symptom of tired nerves and distraught anxiety. For one thing, work at the bank was apparently becoming less congenial to him.[1] Only two or three years earlier he had welcomed his duties at Lloyds. In March 1922 there had been a move among his friends to collect contributions amounting to some £300 a year for a period of not less than five years[2] —an income which would enable him to leave the bank and devote himself entirely to literature. When Lytton Strachey heard of the scheme, he ridiculed in his typical vein of mockery the idea that from his financial successes he should contribute to the maintenance of a virtually unknown poet. If Tom had ever by any chance learned of Strachey's remarks he would have been infuriated, for he never had any liking for Strachey, whose brilliant prose made the sharpest contrast to his own, and who furthermore had no background of either metaphysical or spiritual interests. But as soon as the whole project of rescuing him from the bank came to his knowledge, he very decidedly refused it.[3] At the time of *The Waste Land*, he preferred to be the business man who could make his own way.

This attitude of robust independence did not persist for more than a couple of years, however. We find Tom admitting to Arnold Bennett that though the digesting of financial information was interesting enough, "he would prefer to be doing something else."[4] The soothing effect of statistics was beginning to wane, in the face of overwork at *The Criterion* in the evenings, and the disquieting presence of Vivienne.

Letters from Tom to Bertrand Russell, dated 21 April and 7 May 1955,[5] paint the picture of her ill health in the starkest colours. What Russell had predicted to Tom[6] when the Eliots first stayed with him in 1915 had proved uncannily true.[7] Vivienne's health was now many times worse than it had been then. Her husband simply did not know how to cope with her:[8] there was something so mystifying in her behaviour. She seemed to have the brilliance of a precocious six-year-old; so great was her creative talent that her stories impressed him as much as Katherine Mansfield's; if ever they argued, her logic was incontrovertible. Eliot felt close to despair. He was even ready to take the blame for this domestic tragedy upon himself. For some undisclosed reason, he still felt—as he had in 1923[9]—that Russell might wish to have nothing more to do with them; or perhaps it was only against himself that Russell might bear a grudge?[10] Vivienne's moods were variable (meeting her in Gower Street about this time, Lord David Cecil found her both vivid and appealing), but even in the space of three weeks (21 April–7 May 1925) it was clear that she was deteriorating.

We have seen how it was through *The Criterion* and Bruce

Richmond that Eliot came into touch with Frank Morley and
Faber & Gwyer. At the end of this same year (1925) an
opportunity occurred which would combine literature and
business in his daily employment.

A Fellow of All Souls College at Oxford, Geoffrey Faber,
had become a director of Strong's Romsey Ales after a rather
unlucrative spell as an executive with the Clarendon Press. But
in 1925 he decided that he could do equally well in publishing
and resumed his connections with C. W. Stewart, whom he
had known in his earlier publishing days. By then Stewart had
also moved from the Clarendon Press, to become manager of
The Scientific Press Limited, a Gwyer interest. Faber bought
a substantial shareholding in the Gwyer firm, changing the
name of the Scientific Press to Faber & Gwyer Limited, general publishers. He had soon gathered around him a gifted
number of directors: Richard de la Mare, son of the poet
Walter; Frank Morley, the American from New College,
Oxford, who had worked with Richmond on *The Times
Literary Supplement;* and C. W. Stewart himself. It was not
long before Eliot, with his unique blend of literary genius and
precise business knowledge, had also been suggested to Faber
as a possible collaborator, for Morley was full of his praises
and so it seems was Hugh Walpole;[11] but always at the root
of Eliot's transfer to publishing was Bruce Richmond.[12] Faber
took up Morley's and Walpole's idea with enthusiasm. He met
Eliot, and was filled with admiration for someone who seemed
to him the most brilliant man he had ever met, even at All
Souls. Here was the shrewdest judge of value it had been his
good fortune to meet; not only was his knowledge astonish-
ingly wide, but his power of assessment was little short of
genius.

And so, in November 1925, Eliot left the Colonial and Foreign Department of Lloyds Bank to become a director of Faber & Gwyer at a much better salary than the £600 a year (after tax) which he was then earning in Queen Victoria Street. With him came *The Criterion*,[13] now jointly owned by Lady Rothermere and his new employer: under its new ownership it was incorporated as a limited company, of which Eliot was a director, as well as editor of the magazine. His directorship of Faber & Gwyer (reconstituted on 28 March 1929 as Faber & Faber Limited) was to remain his breadwinning job until the day of his death, though his subsidiary appointment with *The Criterion* ceased on the winding-up of that journal in January 1939. It was to prove an absorbing and congenial interest, and a profitable one into the bargain: for, as his financial position steadily improved, he and Vivienne found they were able to take a little house in Chester Terrace, on the edge of Belgravia. Both Geoffrey and Enid Faber became his firm friends: every year he went to stay with them at their holiday home, Ty-Glenn, near Aberystwyth; every year he confided more of his cares to them, taking them into his confidence with regard to Vivienne. In his working day he was less occupied with the business side of the firm (though, of course, he carried out some of a director's administrative duties) than with editorial functions: reading manuscripts, both commissioned and uncommissioned, and deciding whether to publish them or not, with or without revisions, and talking to authors.

So pleased was Geoffrey Faber with his board's acquisition that he was soon suggesting that Eliot should be elected a Research Fellow of All Souls. This was the unique Oxford college without any undergraduate or graduate students, where a group of distinguished men apply themselves in almost monastic dignity to the various branches of the humanities: history, philosophy, law, classics, English and foreign literature, theology. Faber himself had been elected to one of the Prize Fellowships awarded each November after a College examination taken by the most brilliant young men to have graduated in the University degree examinations. A Prize Fellowship like Faber's is of seven years' duration, during which the beneficiary can remain in or outside Oxford, pursuing academic or non-academic work; but no Prize Fellow need sever his connection altogether with All Souls. For the very reason perhaps that Faber's work took him into the diverse fields of brewing and publishing, he particularly chose to remain in contact with his adoptive College. And he was eager that Tom Eliot should become a colleague. But as soon as the Fellows of All Souls had taken a careful look at Eliot's verse, that question was irrevocably settled.[14] He was by no means the sort of man for a Research Fellowship of All Souls! Only one young man, a radical socialist, stood out against their decision: the historian A. L. Rowse, who later was to become so noted a contributor to *The Criterion*.

Another Fellow of All Souls, Dermot Morrah, told me however that rather later than this there was also some question of Tom's being offered a Research Fellowship (of which there are many in the College). His proposed line of research was to investigate the theory that the writings of seventeenth-century Anglicanism did not lead to any theological outcome. But this project also failed to command support.

This interest in the writings of Anglican divines in the seventeenth century was very much at the forefront of Tom's mind in the early years of his association with Faber & Gwyer, which was the time I first met him. When Bruce Richmond first asked Eliot to write for *The Times Literary Supplement*, it was to discuss seventeenth-century English drama. But in 1926 the poet's fancy had been taken by Lancelot Andrewes,[15] about whom it was agreed that he should write a "leader."

Preces Privatae, the devotional prayers of Andrewes published after his death, reveals a devoutness remarkable in its sincerity and elevation, in the beautiful and ordered variety of its spiritual cares, and the expressiveness with which it links mind and style. But until Eliot wrote of Lancelot Andrewes, few had thought of him as a writer or preacher of special eminence: he lacked the roll, the rhythm, the elated eloquence of Jeremy Taylor or Cardinal Newman, yet it was for this very reason that Eliot's enterprising soberness found him congenial. Here was a man not wrapped up in his own personality or wrought by his passions; his intellect controlled his sensibility; every line added something to his thought; his subject carried him on and fused his sentences with it. He depended not on passion or imagination, but on observation, wit, analysis, precision. He carried on the reasonableness of Hooker, sticking to the essentials of doctrine but careful to answer the needs of his own age.

Eliot believed that the genius of Hooker was one with the triumphs of Elizabeth I. In his view, it was Elizabeth who formed the Church of England. He found in Hooker, as in the later bishops Andrewes and Bramhall,[16] a breadth of culture and a balance which put them at ease both with the Middle Ages and the Renaissance, making them not Englishmen but Europeans. Latimer's sermons, although acute and colloquial, had been those of a mere Protestant; Andrewes spoke as a man of culture and authority.

Eliot pursued these reflections in the following year (1927), when a book was published on Bramhall, the prelate who contended against Hobbes that the state should not be a Leviathan, and whose *Just Vindication of the English Church* Eliot aptly compared with Hooker's *Laws of Ecclesiastical Polity*.

Literary work and personal circumstances interacted as ever. During the year, while he was writing on Bramhall and preparing for a reprint of his essay on Andrewes,[17] Vivienne suffered another extreme attack of insomnia, resulting inevitably in deep depression, which in its turn affected him. His anxiety turned back to Jim Clements who, in the crisis of 1921–1922, had brought him to Geneva and to the completion of his famous poem. Clements had told him that twelve miles from Geneva at the foot of the Jura mountains was a well-known centre for dealing with nervous disorders, Divonne-les-Bains; there the Eliots went in June 1927. They had not been there a week before their specialist was bringing them into touch with another patient in the hope that common interests would help in his treatment. This patient was myself.

What were my own first impressions of Eliot? Here was someone extremely approachable and friendly, even confiding, someone to whom one took immediately. One felt that he was sincerity incarnate, the most natural and the most modest of men. Like myself, he was a contributor to *The Times Literary Supplement*. He was now cherishing the interests which had dominated my own work at Oxford. He showed me his article on Andrewes[18] (and also the manuscript of *Gerontion*, published seven years earlier in *Ara Vos Prec*), he spoke of his enthusiasm for *The Burning Babe* of Robert Southwell, on whom he had also written an article for *The Times Literary*

Supplement,[19] and finally discussed with me what he was about to write on John Bramhall.

He and I had been at Oxford together in the autumn of 1914 (though without actually meeting), when I was already completing my dissertation on Donne, Browne and Vaughan, which I had published in 1922 under the title *Outflying Philosophy*. In 1924 I had offered Bruce Richmond an article on the poetry of Michelangelo, later accepted by Tom. My first contribution printed in *The Times Literary Supplement* was an article on St. Peter's, Rome for the New Year's Day issue of 1925, the Holy Year which brought so many pilgrims to the Papal city.[20] Not only was I devoted to the idea of Catholicism and its traditions in the Church of England but from the time I was a boy in New Zealand I had learned much about Indian religion from the theosophists and had read even then (in translations) the *Mahabharata* and the *Bhagavad Gita*; furthermore, I had spent three of the war years in India, and so personally witnessed Hinduism and Islam. I had had pupils among both Brahmins and Sikhs; in a regiment of Indian cavalry we had two squadrons of Hindus and two of Punjabi Moslems. For five years I had lived in Italy, either in Rome or at Fiesole, where I was steeped in the atmosphere and associations of the *Divina Commedia*.

Moreover, I was passionately interested in an *entente* between Rome and Canterbury. I knew all on both sides who under Cardinal Mercier had been present at the Malines Conversations, and for three years had been on terms of closest friendship with Lord Halifax, then the leading layman in the Church of England. As a specialist on Dante, a promoter of Anglo-Catholic ecumenism and one who had made extensive researches into three of the most attractive Anglicans of the seventeenth century, I knew in my soul the spiritual treasury at the threshold of which Eliot had just arrived. But what were these resemblances compared with the fact that I too suffered from insomnia and that my nerves, like Vivienne's, were often on a knife-edge? I understood both her predicament and Tom's. It was perhaps inevitable that we were drawn together in a deep friendship which lasted for the rest of our lives.

Tom told me that he had never been a practising Anglican and that there were one or two points he would have to settle before he could become one. What they were I did not inquire; but of one thing I felt convinced, that I must put him in immediate touch with two particular friends of mine; first with Lord Halifax, then with the head of Liddon House, Francis Underhill, afterwards Dean of Rochester and later still Bishop of Bath and Wells (in both of whose homes, Hickleton Hall and the moated Palace at Wells, Tom was afterwards to stay as an honoured guest).

How well I remember my first glimpse of Vivienne as she walked almost as though in a trance along a wooded path! Her black hair was dank, her white face blotched—owing, no doubt, to the excess of bromide she had been taking. Her dark dress hung loosely over her frail form; her expression was both vague and acutely sad. I saw at a glance how much she suffered, and was drawn towards her with the deepest sympathy.

The treatment at Divonne which the Eliots and I took and from which Tom profiited more than Vivienne, was a variant of the *douche écossaise*, in which strong gushes of hot, alternating with icy cold, water were played on the naked body. The doctors on the whole deprecated drugs and avoided psychoanalysis. Their idea was that once they had gained a patient's confidence, he would soon divulge the reasons for his strain. It was evident that the strain from which my new friends were suffering was that they no longer lived together in deepest unity.

A very little later Tom was driving from Doncaster Station in the Rolls-Royce which Lord Halifax had sent to convey him the further six miles to Hickleton Hall.

Although the old Churchman was then on the verge of ninety, he was still a captivating and lively companion. From his earliest youth he had radiated a charm enriched by his experience in central society. His father had been a Secretary of State to Queen Victoria, his son was then Viceroy of India and was to become both Foreign Secretary and Ambassador to Washington. In his young days he had been in the court of Edward VII, then Prince of Wales, but had left it not to embarrass the Prince with the accusation of being pro-Catholic. His sister, Mrs. Meynell Ingram, had the most princely home and the largest fortune of any woman in Yorkshire. He was a scholar who wrote delightful English and carried on a continual correspondence with the Archbishops of Canterbury and York, impelling them towards Catholic unity. But above all, he was a master of the art of conversation, with a spirit of boyish fun and a taste for the jokes Tom loved.

It was not long before Lord Halifax was writing to thank me for sending him a friend so admirable and delightful in every way: one to whom he was immediately drawn, in reciprocity of friendship. Tom had hardly been a day at Hickleton before he came to a full identity of religious outlook with his host, who not only specialized on Catholic claims and developments within the Church of England but was actually head of its special organism, the Church Union (then the English Church

Union). With the Church Union he shared a devotion to the Virgin Mother, recognizing her central place in the communion of saints. He sought absolution after confession to a spiritual director. Picturing the hopes he had nurtured during the Malines Conversations, he drew his new friend into this movement.

Tom, in his marriage, had made a swift surrender. He now made one equally swift and equally sweeping. He accompanied his host each day to Hickleton Church, the little church close by the Hall, where they worshipped in a form which only an expert could have detected was other than the Roman Catholic mass, and where the building was exactly arranged with lights, lamps, pictures, images and the redolence of incense so as to have what one could only call a Catholic atmosphere. Issuing from this worship, he bound himself to the causes of his host, even more completely and more suddenly than he had done twelve years before to his wife.

He too wrote to thank me for introducing him to a friend whose influence upon his life was destined to be so far-reaching. But he had not yet made the formal adherence to his new belief.

Working as a director of a rising firm of British publishers, and accepting (as he did) English ideas of social order, politics and government, where would he fit in better than if he accepted the English Church and became a subject of the English King? As he had chosen London rather than Paris as a place to live, so now he felt that an *ecclesia anglicana* that was one with the development of English history and literature was much to be preferred to a church worked out with relentless logic by Maritain. And just at this point, he found in the work and temper of an American friend the link he needed.

William Force Stead was of the same age as Pound. Tom had met him in 1923, on an introduction from Richard Cobden-Sanderson, whose friendship they both prized. (I met Stead in the following year, on an introduction from the then Archbishop of Canterbury, Randall Davidson.) Born in Washington, and a graduate of the University of Virginia, he had married a Washington girl of the best style and society and then come to England as an American consul. Hardly had he done so than he found that literature and religion were his real bent in life. He resigned from the consular service, was ordained in the Church of England (serving both as chaplain of Worcester College, Oxford, and as chaplain to the Anglo-Catholic church in Florence, where I met him), and did distinguished work both in prose and verse. His religious musings were called *The Shadow of Mount Carmel*;[21] Tom, writing to me, praised this book as one of the best examples of contemporary prose. Stead's verse, which was in the tradition of Coleridge, was also published by Cobden-Sanderson. In later years he concentrated on Christopher Smart, on whom he did brilliant research. He wrote a charming essay on Smart's affection for his cat Geoffrey; and that, being about a cat, and by William, Tom simply had to accept for *The Criterion*. (Tom Eliot was passionately addicted to cats.) Returning in 1939 to America, he became a professor at Trinity College, Washington, where his lectures were very much appreciated. This was the friend who, from their first meeting in 1923, steadily drew Tom towards the writings of seventeenth-century Anglicanism, and especially those of Lancelot Andrewes. He was also the friend who, after Tom's final decision to be received into the Church of England, actually baptized him.

10

A Convert to Anglicanism

THERE will be many who read this book who have no precise idea of what the religion of a Catholic or an Anglican really is. It is therefore essential to my memoir that I should make it clear what it was in this religion which drew Tom into such immediate accord with me between the Jura and Geneva, which was the basis of our thirty-eight years of intimate friendship and which from 1927 was a dominant idea of his life and thought.

It answered his scrutiny of time and eternity, appearance and reality, experience and metaphysics. It was a sharp contrast to what he had learned of the Church of the Messiah which his grandfather had founded on the banks of the Mississippi. So much so that he said that before 1927 he had never been a Christian. It is a religion which does much to explain what drove him from American to Europe and made him into a European. It was a sharp antidote to "the religion of the future."

At the College de France, in 1910–1911, Eliot had listened with eager ears to Bergson lecturing on Creative Evolution.

Now in 1927 he had to accept that at a certain point in this evolution—say, 2,000,000 years after the appearance of what Teilhard de Chardin has called "the Phenomenon of Man"—the Logos became more closely identified with man and man's environment. He entered time; He became incarnate; in other words, one Christ was both God and man, not by conversion of the Godhead into flesh but by the taking of manhood into God—one not by confusion of two separate categories of being but by the union of the two separate categories in His own person. As far as His divinity was concerned, He was equal to the Father; but in so far as He was created man, He was not co-equal with His Creator.

Such was the fascinating belief on which Eliot's eyes were now open, not merely as a reader of Lancelot Andrewes but as one sharing in the inner life of his friend and host. It was the Anglican forms of Lancelot Andrewes to which Eliot had first been attracted. But how much more they meant to him when he saw the Church of England mirrored in a man so winning and saintly as his distinguished host at Hickleton.

Lord Halifax was not only convinced (as indeed he said to me) that he believed everything a Catholic should believe; but also that his own belief should help to redeem the Church of England from its separation from Rome, and lead it back to Catholic unity. Where did this Anglo-Catholic point of view stop short of Roman Catholicism? As far as he was concerned, nowhere. He had no objection to the primacy of the Pope. He saw nothing to disturb him in a word so negative and, when closely examined, so void of exact meaning as "infallibility." In fact, he *protested* against nothing. Each day he used for his meditations the devotional prayers of the Roman Catholic bishop, Richard Challoner.

What then was the place of the Church of England? Did he really think that the vast majority of its members agreed with his outlook? Those who did not share his view were, he felt, untrue to the real Church of England which during his lifetime had been so completely transformed by the Oxford Movement, with its accent on sacramentalism. At the time of Lord Halifax's birth in 1839, it was still the Anglican custom to celebrate the Eucharist only four times a year. What gave Cardinal Newman most satisfaction as Vicar of St. Mary's, Oxford was the institution of a weekly Eucharist. But when Tom arrived at Hickleton in 1927, there was a daily Eucharist, either in the parish church of the village or else in the Hall's private chapel.

As for the controversial question of the validity of Anglican orders, Lord Halifax never doubted that the Rector of Hickleton was validly ordained to celebrate the sacrifice of the Mass. Certainly, he had been disappointed in 1896 when Leo XIII published a Bull stating that Anglican orders were null and void. But he knew perfectly well that this had not been the dominant idea among Roman Catholic scholars, and that *Apostolicae Curae* had been engineered by reactionary elements in the Curia working in association with Cardinal Merry del Val. But Halifax, who had seen Merry del Val's ecclesiastical policy pretty well discredited during the pontificate of Benedict XV (1914–1922), not unnaturally looked forward to the time when the Cardinal's views on the validity of Anglican orders would be equally discredited.

Though Lord Halifax read Challoner daily, he had never read Dante. He adored Cardinal Mercier but knew nothing of the book on scholastic philosophy which Tom had so favourably reviewed very nearly ten years before. He led Tom, however, to the ecumenism of Malines.

And so it was that Tom came a stage nearer to living that sacramental life which afterwards became the centre of his being. On returning to London from Hickleton he met William Force Stead and asked if he might depend on him for a special favour. What he actually wrote a day or two later was to ask if he could be "confirmed in the Church of England." He felt that through his new Trinitarian sacramentalism he would be incorporated into the supernatural life which was the goal of all the religions he had studied.

Tom's request placed William in a difficulty. For Unitarians are not baptized "in the Name of the Father, and of the Son, and of the Holy Ghost," and that being so, are they (from a Trinitarian point of view) baptized at all? Marianne Moore told me that when a similar question had been raised by her Presbyterian grandfather in regard to Tom's grandfather William Greenleaf Eliot, the minister had replied that he would give a blessing in the name of the Lord Jesus Christ, and that, said Miss Moore's grandfather, "was good enough for me." But William had to explain to Tom that it was a question of receiving the sacrament of Baptism. They talked it over, and finally Tom said: "William, I want to be baptized into the one true fold of Christ."

It was now past the middle of June. William was living some fifteen miles distant from Oxford in a fine, seventeenth-century gabled house at Finstock, on the borders of Wychwood Forest. He arranged that Tom should come and stay with him there, and meet two friends who were to be his godfathers. One was B. H. Streeter, a famous theologian who afterwards became Provost of Queen's College, Oxford, where Stead himself had been an undergraduate. The other was Vere Somerset, an historian of puckish wit and eclectic taste, a Fellow of Worcester College, who had a fine country house at

Ross-on-Wye in Herefordshire. On the afternoon of 29 June 1927, St. Peter's Day, William went with his three guests and locked the doors of the little church at Finstock before pouring the water of regeneration over the head of one who in future years was to be as much the leading layman in the Church of England as Lord Halifax was at that time.

The next morning William drove Tom through Oxford to the heavy Georgian palace at Cuddesdon, on the hill above Garsington. It was no longer Charles Gore, the friend of Lady Ottoline, who was Bishop of Oxford, but Thomas Banks Strong, who had been Dean of Christ Church when Tom was a research student at Merton. He led the two Americans into his chapel and laid his hands on the head of the newly baptized man with the words: "Defend, O Lord, this thy Servant with thy heavenly grace, that he may continue thine for ever; and daily increase in thy Holy Spirit more and more, until he come unto thy everlasting kingdom." From that day onwards my friend followed in the footsteps of Lord Halifax and daily strengthened soul and body in the mysteries of the altar.

He found this very different indeed from the sterile Unitarianism he had abandoned with its sectarian controversies and the element of worldliness he found in the well-dressed congregation. It was this he afterwards admitted which had driven him into agnosticism. Asked by Unitarians in Massachusetts why he had left their persuasion for the Anglo-Catholic Church, he replied that he had done nothing of the kind. From Unitarianism he lapsed into agnosticism, and out of agnosticism found his way (after inclining towards Buddhism around 1922) to the Catholic idea which he preferred in its Anglican form. He said at another time that he was driven to belief by seeing agnosticism pushed to its limits by

Bertrand Russell—who, though so good a friend, was never his guide as a metaphysician. Another who influenced him was Pascal, about whom he was to write in 1931,[1] and who had the mind to conceive and the sensibility to feel that life without God the Redeemer was disastrous, meaningless and futile. There is another point worth noting in a man who is too often discussed simply in relation to other books: going into a church one day (as he later told Maurice Reckitt) he had felt something extraordinarily moving in the sight of people kneeling in silent prayer. Thus, Tom's baptism and confirmation were no sudden conversions. For twenty years he had been in a spiritual "waste land," first cutting the deeply emotional links with his family's worship, then toying with Indian mysticism, then impelled by Dante towards the one Catholic and Apostolic Church, and finally drawn towards Anglicanism by his meeting with Lord Halifax and by his love of England, of which he became a naturalized citizen on 2 November 1927.

His deeply meditated commitment to Anglicanism was not made, however, without violent denunciations from many of his friends, both as to his moral character and mental calibre. As he said to me later, it was not the Christians but the pagans who thundered self-righteousness and claimed infallible wisdom. "I was not only a lost soul," he chuckled, "but a lost sheep." At times he would give vigorous rejoinders to such ill-founded criticism. Lord David Cecil has told me that once at a party of Lady Ottoline's, Tom turned sharply on Koteliansky when he suggested that Christian faith was merely escapism. Never had Cecil heard anyone speak with such intensity as came into Tom's voice while he explained that Christian faith, far from softening the edges of life, made each of them more cutting, because it gave a fuller and therefore more intense life; it also made life more poignant because it brought every issue of the soul into direct relation to Infinity; it made every obligation more pressing; at every turn, it demanded greater sacrifice and commitment.

Sacrifice and commitment were indeed essential to Tom's religious outlook. Deeply as he pondered the mysteries of the Christian faith, he realized that—as Pascal always insisted—there was something in it beyond the power of mind to grasp. This meant that, like myself, he was ecumenical, tolerant, and impatient of religious controversy. We both believed in stating our views but never argued to convert people to religion. Indeed, Tom once said at Magdalene College, Cambridge that if any one had ever tried to convert him, he would have failed.[2] Combined with this element of commitment was a residual agnosticism. For, as Dryden had asked: "how can finite grasp infinity?" If one really believes in the infinite, one has entered into a realm of mystery where intelligence soon becomes a trespasser; in any acceptance of infinite mystery, a certain agnosticism is inherent. Not that his acceptance of mystery meant an acceptance of mysticism. In fact, in his last years he categorically denied that he was a mystic. He could not understand the theology of St. John of the Cross that so absorbed me nor calm his whole being in that "oblivion blest." Holy Communion must surely at times have given him feelings of near-mysticism, but if so, his poetry (unlike Wordsworth's) leaves no record of the fact. His spiritual life was centred rather on the ideas of travail and stress in the complexities of a life in which he was strengthened and consoled by sacramental worship. As for Rome, though he read and paid tribute to Friedrich von Hugel, he was accustomed to think of it as something intolerably rigid and narrow and exclusive, a Church which denied salvation to those outside it.

This is a tone he might have heard often enough among the Americans of his youth. He looked, he said, with deep respect on the great cosmopolitan church, but could never regard the hopes of humanity as confined to one institution. When his friend Sally Cobden-Sanderson was thinking of becoming a Catholic, he warned her that she would have too much to swallow. The truth is, of course, that whatever our Church allegiance, we have to accommodate it to our needs. And this he recognized when he said that Christianity is always adapting itself into something which can be believed. He might have added that in doing so, it discovers more of its true self and of infinity.

After his baptism and confirmation, Tom paid his usual summer visit to the Fabers' holiday home near Aberystwyth. It was a roomy house four miles out of the town, built on hills overlooking the sea. Here he relaxed in the ease and peace of country life, as in earlier years he had relaxed in the sea and sunshine of Gloucester. Cool as the water is in Cardigan Bay, Tom often stayed in for a long swim, picnicked afterwards, and then came back to the house in the afternoon where he might join in a game of tennis. This was not a game which he played well, but at times he could surprise his opponents with a peculiarly savage cut.

Now that he was a baptized, committed Anglican he found a new engagement with the Fabers. During the summer of 1927 another son had been born to the Fabers who decided that the poet should be asked to become the boy's godfather. Tom accepted, and the baby was named after him. From that time on, Tom Faber was the object of his particular regard; it was marked by his receipt of presents from Eliot more valuable than the rest of the family ever received. He was never happier than in making enormous presents.

Year after year he would come back to Ty-Glen and watch the family grow up. The years followed the set pattern: swims, picnics, tennis, reading aloud in the evenings. Tom was just part of the household and fitted perfectly with both parents and children. In due course his godson became a scientist and, after studying at Cambridge, was elected a Fellow of Corpus Christi College. Whenever his godfather was in Cambridge, he never forgot to entertain the young don sumptuously.

Meanwhile, I was still holidaying in Switzerland and France, but as soon as I returned to London I renewed contact with Tom, who had of course already written to tell me about Lord Halifax. Not long afterwards he entertained me at the Royal Societies Club, introducing me to Tom Burns, who afterwards became managing director of Burns & Oates, and to Father Martin D'Arcy, whom he described as "one of the most brilliant young men in England." He also took me to lunch at a little restaurant in South Kensington so that I could meet Herbert Read, whose book on English stained glass I had just reviewed.[3] Dining at 57 Chester Terrace, I met Lady Ottoline Morrell. But it was not until 1930 that I was invited to stay with Tom and Vivienne in the flat to which they had quite recently moved, 68 Clarence Gate Gardens.

Close by this flat was the very church that cultivated the ideals of the English Church Union, and where the clergy venerated Lord Halifax. The Vicar was Father Mayhew, the church St. Cyprian's. It was here that Tom became a daily worshipper until, with a change of residence four or five years later, he transferred his worship to St. Stephen's, Gloucester Road. Vivienne seldom, if ever, accompanied her husband to St. Cyprian's. Indeed, she seems to have been positively hostile to his new-found church affiliations, deriding them as "monastic." Tom also continued to visit Francis Underhill, with whom I had first put him into touch, and who until 1932 was still Warden of Liddon House, London—an Anglican centre for the pastoral care of young university people. In fact, rather than Father Mayhew, it was Francis Underhill who became Tom's first spiritual counsellor,[4] and who was also responsible for introducing him to Kelham Theological College, near Newark in Nottinghamshire, where he frequently stayed in the 1930s. About this time Tom also met George Bell, who after being Dean of Canterbury from 1924 to 1929 was nominated to the see of Chichester, and in whose delightful palace he stayed in December 1930.

Here was a man who appreciated to the full the role which Tom was to play in the Church of England, and without whom there would be no such play as *Murder in the Cathedral*.[5] But this project would not mature for another four years. All that the Bishop could do for the moment was to appoint Martin Browne as a sort of dramatic director to the diocese; and it was Browne who ultimately directed *Murder in the Cathedral* in 1935. In exactly the same way, Bishop Bell appointed Quentin Nelson to be a diocesan psychiatrist, a man who could watch over the connection between mental illness and healing, which after all is one function of the Church. He used to say that the Church holds all the cards in her hand, but so often fails to play them. He looked on Tom as an ace of trumps.

Vivienne did not accompany her husband to the palace of Chichester. Writing a warm letter of thanks to Mrs. Bell on 18 December 1930,[6] Tom blamed her absence on the chilly weather, adding that he looked forward to another visit to Chichester, perhaps in the summer, when his wife might be able to come with him. But that summer never came, or at least not that particular opportunity. Yet with each succeeding year, Tom's bonds with the Church of England were becoming closer.

When in 1930 the Anglican Communion collected its bishops for a congress, his critical mind was soon at work on one of the most pungent of his essays. This essay, "Thoughts after Lambeth," published in 1931, dealt with the statement issued by the Anglican bishops after their Lambeth Conference. What pleased him in this statement was the bishops' realization that if youth wanted religion at all, it wanted a religion that demanded sacrifice. Thought, study, mortification, sacrifice: these were the notions that should be impressed upon Christian youth. They wanted a religion difficult both to the disorderly mind and to the unruly passions.

From this it was but a step to the question of birth control. Eliot wanted both Rome and Canterbury to face the fact that neither of them had given clear guidance. The Roman attitude left unanswered the crucial question: when is it right to limit the family—and when is it wrong to do so? But the Anglican point of view also left an essential question open: when is it right to limit the family only by continence, and when is it right to limit by contraception?

And when the Conference declared that, while the historic episcopate was necessary to any union in which Anglicans could take part, yet no particular theory of the episcopate was required as a condition of reunion; did the Anglican bishops mean that Nonconformists should accept the episcopate as a harmless formality for the sake of a phantom unity?

The Conference had strengthened the Church, however, in its witness to a world more sharply divided than ever between

Christians and non-Christians. People were trying on all sides to build up a non-Christian civilization, but sooner or later the attempt must fail. Christian faith must be kept alive through the Dark Ages to come, so that at last it can rebuild civilization and save the world from suicide.

Such were the fundamental views of Eliot at this time.[7] In "Thoughts after Lambeth" he set out all his genius as a critic and thinker. He defined, he satirized, he jested. He was himself in all that he said and did as a churchman. But, at the back of his mind, he was sure that enormous principles were at stake and that in his spiritual stand he must always be uncompromising.

CHAPTER

11

Ash-Wednesday and Other Poems

ELIOT'S desire for reality in religion, about the time of his actual reception into the Church, is well expressed in the poem *Journey of the Magi*, published in 1927 as the eighth in a series of "Ariel Poems," which were single poems by various authors appearing periodically as pamphlets. This eighth "Ariel Poem" takes its theme from an Epiphany sermon of Lancelot Andrewes: the coming of the three Wise Men to the stable at Bethlehem to worship the Infant Jesus. They have travelled from far-off countries and through treacherous weather, sometimes looking back nostalgically to the hospitable warmth of their own palaces. Yet their mysterious awareness of a divine goal impels them to the manger, where, having seen the longed-for vision, they accept and worship their Master. Back in their own kingdoms, they do not regret the hazardous journey, on which they would set out all over again if the same circumstances (impossibly) arose. Years afterwards, however, they are still assailed by a nagging doubt: the doubt which we have already encountered in *Sweeney Agonistes*, concerning the closeness of birth and death. Hurrying after the star, they had had a clear premonition of Birth, yet it is the taste of Death which has remained on their lips: the lesson of the *Upanishads*, and the paradox of Jesus' own teaching, "Except a man be born again, he cannot see the kingdom of God."

A Song for Simeon, published as the sixteenth "Ariel Poem" in the following year (1928), expresses the calmer, resigned attitude of a man who has not merely found the Infant Christ but the solution of his religious quest. Like the prophet Simeon, of whom we read in St. Luke's Gospel, Eliot had waited long years for the coming of Jesus. Whereas the Magi had responded immediately to the summons of a star, only to find that the goal of their pilgrimage was disquiet and uncertainty, Simeon knew no sudden revelation, only the quiet certainty that "a light to lighten the Gentiles" was eventually to be revealed. Holding in his arms the Salvation of all people, he can welcome death not as an escape from perplexed alienation, but as a release into "the fulness of him that filleth all in all." How far is this modern version of the *Nunc Dimittis* a picture of Eliot's own frame of mind? In the years after I first met him, he seemed to share with Simeon the confidence of a new-found certainty, but to what extent he was picturing himself in Simeon's prophetic foreknowledge of the revelation to come, it is beyond the power of any of us to say.

In *Marina*, the twenty-ninth of the "Ariel Poems," published in 1930, we find the only example in Eliot's work of a really joyful poem. Connecting the Marina of Shakespeare's *Pericles, Prince of Tyre* with his recollections and evocation of what he had enjoyed as a young man on the shore of Massachusetts, he suggests that on the bleakness of his life until the time of his conversion there had now dawned a new hope.

"If only," Lady Ottoline Morrell once said to me, "if only Tom could get away to open fields and hills and the everlasting things!" Far removed from the life of sordid and disillusioned cities, this poem, centred on islands and pine-trees, rocks and the song of woodthrushes, is the nearest Tom ever came to the "everlasting things" Lady Ottoline had in mind.

Not that his other great poem of 1930, *Ash-Wednesday*, turns a blind eye to the everlasting issues of death, judgment, heaven and hell. If *The Waste Land* is Eliot's *Inferno*, this poem (as indeed its name implies) is his *Purgatorio*. Though hearing the sound of psalms and holy voices, the poet is still occupied with purging an unquiet soul tormented by company and environment uncongenial to his spiritual life. Nevertheless, he has found faith in Christ and in His sacramental presence. He prays never to be separated from it, though torn between it and the solicitations of the world. The six sections of *Ash-Wednesday* are all grounded in the liturgy, in the Rose Garden of Paradise and in the needs tormented by love unsatisfied and still more tormented by "love's sad satiety." As the Rose of section II becomes a whole Garden, so the poet moves beyond alternations of hope and despair to what worship can offer faith. And so in section VI he can still sit among the rocks, as he had sat by the sea on summer days in Massachusetts, watching the white sails fly out to sea.

So, despite the poem's strong accent on the vanity of human wishes, its satire of that hell on earth with which most people around him were familiar, *Ash-Wednesday* seems to end, centrally, in Paradise. Much of its language, however, inevitably remains obscure. Indeed, this is one of the poem's fascinations. Eliot was once asked by an undergraduate what he meant by the line, *Lady, three white leopards sat under a juniper-tree*,[1] to which he replied decisively: "I mean, *Lady, three white leopards sat under a juniper-tree.*"[2] Hardly an illuminating answer, but the best one in the circumstances. Indeed, he might usefully have called Paul Valéry to his aid in this emergency, by pointing out that an author's interpretation of his own work has no more force or validity than that of any other person.[3] It seems especially necessary to invoke this autonomy of the work of art when one remembers that Eliot's three white leopards were perhaps meant to be sitting under a *jujuba* tree. For, as recent research has shown, Eliot first uses the word "juniper-tree" in the same year that *Ash-Wednesday* appeared, in a mistranslation of a line of St.-John Perse. Eliot, who deeply admired Perse's *Anabase*, so much so that he worked for several years on a translation of it, failed to appreciate that "l'arbre jujubier" is a quite different botanical specimen from "l'arbre genévrier." But what is the relevance of such hair-splitting? Eliot's *Anabasis* is, in any case, a transposition rather than a translation of *Anabase*, for far from espousing the sense of the original Eliot frequently creates a new meaning of his own. So here in *Ash-Wednesday*, in the confusion of jujubas and junipers, he has created a new meaning. It ill behoves us to ask what is that meaning—as the undergraduate found to his dismay. Eliot was the first to admit that in *The Family Reunion*[4] there is no meaning in his line "harefoot over the moon."[5] Another poet, Shelley, countered the charge of meaninglessness in *The Witch of Atlas* by asking why he was not permitted to amuse himself with imagery as a kitten does with its own play. It is the musical cadences of the lines and the private visual images they evoke which create nine-tenths of the magic of hermetic poetry. Let the leopards sit under whatever tree they will, let jeweled unicorns be harnessed to gilded hearses[6]—the poet will rightly disclaim the necessity of minute interpretation. It is only the total effect of *Ash-Wednesday* which is capable of systematic exposition: the ascent, through a spiritual purgatory, to the Rose Garden of celestial happiness.

12

The Separation from Vivienne

JUST after the publication of *Ash-Wednesday* in 1930 I was invited to stay with Tom and Vivienne at their flat in Clarence Gate Gardens. I had not long returned from a trip to the United States, but was in close touch with them as soon as I came back to England, the more so because two New Zealand friends of mine, Tim Nelson and his mother, lived not far from their flat. While I was staying there Mabel Nelson made friends with Vivienne—a friendship on which Vivienne came increasingly to depend. Mabel was also the mother of the Quentin Nelson whom Bishop Bell appointed to his diocese as a psychiatric consultant, and like Quentin, she had a sensitive understanding of psychological abnormality.

I suppose that, apart from Vivienne's brother Maurice, I am one of the few persons who can recall a stay in that household; and perhaps I alone was invited to stay because of all their friends I had shared most deeply in Vivienne's illness.

In the few days I was there, the Eliots overwhelmed me with hospitality. It was during this visit that I met the poetess Hope Mirrlees. Another evening Vivienne gathered a number

of literary friends to meet the poet Ralph Hodgson. His published work was slim because Hodgson felt that if he could
not maintain his highest standard, he should not publish anything further. In personality he was a sharp contrast to Eliot's
fineness: his accent was homely, his figure portly and his manners hearty; but he was a man of acute sensitiveness and wonderful freshness, with a heart of warmest loyalty. All this Tom
appreciated, though in poetry their styles were as sharply
differentiated as their personalities—as Tom's lines to him[1] have
suggested. Hodgson had just come over from Toyko with a
very young and unsophisticated blonde girl. "He calls her,"
said Vivienne in her caustic way, "his secretary." The rest of
the party were mostly youngish writers who each read an extract from his or her work, but at the centre of it all was Lady
Ottoline, to whom Vivienne deferred as if to royalty (of
whom, in fact, she was close kin).[2] Tom read *Difficulties of
a Statesman*,[3] with its emphatic ending: "RESIGN RESIGN RE-
SIGN."

At another time during my stay, I was reading to him from
his poem *A Song for Simeon*, with its reference to the Nativity
as the Word within the world unable to speak a word,[4] and I
felt moved to quote Edward Caswall's Nativity lines:

> Sacred Infant all divine,
> What a tender love was thine;
> Thus to come from highest bliss,
> Down to such a world as this![5]

Vivienne's response, then Tom's, was to be touched into
acquiescence.

Another time, when I was reading one of those passages
where Ruskin becomes most elaborately eloquent, and ex-

pected Tom to be as impressed by it as I was, his reaction came in one of those strange remarks by which he had so often killed a reputation with a snakebite: "How did Ruskin end?"[6] What I was admiring as the roll of fine frenzy struck him as the beginning of the years when eloquence was exchanged for insanity.

I remember three men calling at the flat. One was Vivienne's brother Maurice. Another was Montgomery Belgion, who has told us something of Tom's relations with the France of Charles Maurras.[7] The third was a Bolshevized aristocrat, Prince D. S. Mirsky. As soon as he had left, Vivienne said she had never felt more intense hostility than from the moment Mirsky and I exchanged glances. Her intuition was never clearer than in some apprehension of evil.

One morning while I was there I heard Tom speaking on the telephone. In his smooth, courteous voice he was saying: "Will you tell her Ladyship that I am unable to come to lunch with her because I don't accept invitations from ladies I have not met, nor from one who invites me without my wife, nor from one who is divorced." "Her Ladyship" was none other than Lady Astor, another American who had taken out British nationality, who was much better known than he was in 1930, and who was considered one of the most brilliant of hostesses both in her London home and in the country; her weekend parties at Clivedon were celebrated for their gatherings of men of power. On this occasion she had invited Eliot to meet Bernard Shaw and H. G. Wells, neither of whom he even wished to come into contact with.

Even at the time I stayed with Tom and Vivienne, nearly three years before their eventual separation, it was apparent that the sharing, trust and companionship essential to any marriage were sadly lacking in this one. Vivienne was becoming more and more wayward and unpredictable. At times, for no apparent reason, she would cancel invitations at the eleventh hour. In the agonized intensity of her own love, she found subtle ways of teasing and thwarting Tom. Sometimes her mood would verge on the very abyss of despair. I remember with what zest she quoted Hardy's lines during my stay:

> I'll tune me to the mood,
> And mumm with thee till eve:
> And maybe what as interlude
> I feign, I shall believe![8]

> Black is night's cope;
> But death will not appal
> One who, past doubtings all,
> Waits in unhope.[9]

How, I wondered, had she and Tom managed to live together for so long? I realized that it was only because, in addition to the anodyne of daily work at Faber & Faber, his own liking for kittenish jokes suited a mentality as elfish and stimulating as it was sad. Besides, his was never a passion like Aldington's. No wild horses had ever run away with him. He had no taste for the profuse richness of Shelley, or Turner's colours of fire and flame. I personally love to recall Shelley but when I once quoted to Tom the stanza:

> The keen stars were twinkling,
> And the fair moon was rising among them,
> Dear Jane!
> The guitar was tinkling,
> But the notes were not sweet till you sung them
> Again. . . .[10]

he burst into gentle but derisive laughter. Tom never cavilled at London's habitual pall. Much grey accorded with his undeviating correctness. His hair was never quite grey, but there was something in his complexion which toned in with the grey clothes of "the gay American."

The time was to come, however, and it was not long removed, when even the semblance of married life with Vivienne became impossible. Tom and she were leading lives apart. She was developing a tendency to find fault with everything, both in herself and in those around her. She did not join in his worship. She would not accompany him on his weekend visit to the Bells at Chichester. In fact, she never to my knowledge accompanied him on any weekend visit. At nights her tension and insomnia communicated their torment to his nerves. He had been the most devoted of husbands. He had tried every cure, even taking her to the French Riviera in 1930 in a last attempt to establish serenity between them; and more than once, above all in 1921, he himself had broken down under the strain.

At this point his spiritual counsellors became decisive: he had a duty to his career and his spiritual life. He must not wreck the work he was doing for the Church. Then, just as Tom was reaching to his painful decision, he received an invitation to return to Harvard in the fall of 1932 (extending into the spring of 1933), where the University was eager that he should deliver the annual Charles Eliot Norton poetry lectures. It was plain that he must accept this splendid opportunity to return to his old University, and lecture on the foundation of the man who, perhaps more than anyone, had confirmed him in his devotion to Dante.

Whether or not an instinct told Vivienne of some threat to

her own interests, Tom's decision to go to America without her certainly pushed her further over the confines of sanity. One friend saw her take off the stones of a necklace, throw them on to the floor and pretend they were animals which Tom must drive back into their stall. Often, whether alone with him or not, she would abruptly leave the table without a word.

His departure from her was dramatic. Vivienne, her brother Maurice, and his wife accompanied him as far as Southampton, from which his liner was to sail to Montreal. Tom got his wife into a cab outside their flat in Clarence Gate Gardens, and the others followed in another cab containing his ample luggage. On the way to Waterloo Station, however, Eliot discovered that some of his important papers had been locked up by Vivienne in the bathroom. He stopped his taxi on Constitution Hill to speak to the devoted friend who was following, begging her to return to the flat and try to recover the papers with the porter's help. Her taxi drove back to Clarence Gate Gardens at top speed, a page boy was thrust through the bathroom window, and the friend managed to get the precious documents to Waterloo a few minutes before the boat train was due to start.

On their arrival at Southampton, Tom and Vivienne went aboard the liner and walked together for a few minutes on deck, while Maurice and his wife sat and waited. Then all three waved Tom goodbye as his ship pulled away from the quay. Such was the last hectic day of this ill-starred couple. Eliot enjoyed a few days of peace during the Atlantic crossing.[10]

And what of Vivienne? Just before Tom left for America, she had invited a little girl to stay, but this girl became frightened and felt she must return home. To avoid being alone,

Vivienne then asked my friend Mabel Nelson to keep her company for a while, but soon Mabel too was feeling that she simply could not endure this situation any longer. Few of us are prepared to cope with mental illness. Vivienne's old friend Lucy Thayer, who had been one of the witnesses at her wedding, also stayed with her for a while, until the time came for her to return home to America.

But there was always the consoling thought of Tom's return after his six months' lecture tour. Vivienne fully expected that he would return to her, and indeed Tom had not given any impression to the contrary. In readiness for his homecoming she arranged for their flat to be redecorated, and her brother Maurice has told me how, during the long waiting period, she invited their friends to a little party at which all drank to Tom's health.

Meanwhile, however, the long separation led Tom to a fuller realization of the hopelessness of their marriage. At one point during his stay at Harvard a letter was delivered from Vivienne asking if she might not come over to America and join him. As he read her entreaty, his arm recoiled from it as from an electric shock. His nerves could no longer face the prodigious effort he had made over seventeen years.

It was in February 1933, just as he was occupied with his fifth Charles Eliot Norton lecture, that Tom wrote to his solicitor instructing him to prepare a Deed of Separation and enclosing a letter which the solicitor was to take personally to Vivienne, breaking the news. He told me later that as he dropped the letter and its enclosure into the post he quoted from *Julius Caesar* the following lines:

> Between the acting of a dreadful thing
> And the first motion, all the interim is
> Like a phantasma, or a hideous dream.

The settlement was generous. Vivienne stayed on at the flat, where she remained until her final breakdown just before the outbreak of World War II. She even took up an advanced course of study at the Royal College of Music. Tom never saw her again except on the other side of a solicitor's table.

Eliot was received in New York as though he were a reigning prince. He might have given up his American nationality but the United States had no intention of giving him up. They were already recognizing him as one of the greatest poets they had produced. It was a difficult matter to assess American poetry in 1932. But the acclaim for the author of *The Waste Land*, *Ash-Wednesday* and the "Ariel Poems" seemed to indicate that no American poet of the twentieth century had surpassed him.

He enjoyed the return to Harvard. Eleanor Hinkley, his cousin, was still living in her old home in Berkeley Street. There were his relatives the Lambs in Boston. His old friends Richard Hall and Leon Little were at hand, both with wives who were also dear to him. Best of all, there was his sister-in-law Theresa, widow of his brother, still living where she and Henry had lived in Prescott Street, Cambridge; and she, to tell the truth, meant more to him than his own sisters. And then there was the ambiance of Harvard itself: the pleasant life of Eliot House (which I myself enjoyed in the year of Tom's death), the constant hospitality of the Merrimans at the head of it; there were his eight lectures comfortably spaced out between 4 November 1932 and 31 March 1933; there were his weekly meetings with his students; there was his friendship with John Livingstone Lowes and still more with Theodore Spencer, both of whom he was constantly dropping in to see; and above all, there were the memories of twenty to twenty-five years before, when Harvard—though so much less impressive then in its buildings—had been the scene of his emergence into the world of letters, Harvard which he still distinctly preferred to Oxford and which was still to him the "fair Harvard" whose appeal his own undergraduate lines had voiced.[11]

The Charles Eliot Norton Professor of Poetry's lectures were entitled "Studies in the Relation of Criticism to Poetry in England." They were to be published in 1933 as *The Use of Poetry and the Use of Criticism*, and ranged in time from the Elizabethan period to the twentieth century. It is usual in such cases to give a foremost place to Shakespeare and Milton. Eliot's method, however, was very different from this sort of academic treatment. He was not, and never wished to be, an academic critic. At the end of his course of lectures, his friend Theodore Spencer said to him that a professorship at Harvard was assuredly his, if that was his ambition. Eliot's immediate reply was that he did not know enough. And, in a sense, this was true.[12] He had never undergone the discipline of learning English as a subject on the degree syllabus. How then could he teach English to degree students?

And so, just as the articles he had been writing in England were the thoughts of a poet with a mind of his own, so now he gave these lectures at Harvard not as tuition in a school of English literature but as the animadversion of independent genius on familiar authors, throwing a new and astonishing light by the vigour of an attention that was always fresh and individual. Attacking accepted opinions from a point of view so novel that it took his listeners by surprise, these lectures established him as the leading critic of the time.

Throughout his course wit, taste, philosophical judgment, metaphysical analysis and a habit of reading outside the usual run of prescribed texts startled professors and undergraduates alike. His whole career, even his career as a professor of poetry, was marked by the urge for exploration—the desire to create by a combination of the unexpected.

With superb skill he began his introductory lecture (delivered on 4 November 1932) and his sixth lecture (devoted to Matthew Arnold on 3 March 1933) with quotations from Charles Eliot Norton himself. "The rise of the democracy to power in America and in Europe," Norton had lamented to Sir Leslie Stephen,[13] "is not, as had been hoped, to be a safeguard of peace and civilization. It is the rise of the uncivilized, whom no school education can suffice to provide with intelligence and reason. It looks as if the world were entering on a new stage of experience, unlike anything heretofore, in which there must be a new discipline of suffering to fit men for the new conditions." And it was true that economic enterprise, unlimited competition and unrestrained individualism had not led to the vast moral and intellectual revolution for which C. E. Norton had hoped. The same thought preoccupied Eliot. He was the earnest thinker wishing to preserve in Europe the "sweetness and light" of which Arnold had written in *Culture and Anarchy*, and so renew its spiritual life. Five years before his return to Harvard, he had become an orthodox and devout believer, and now in the travail of personal anguish he looked at literature for something which mattered to morals, religion and, in its way, theology.

When it came to historical development, he began with the Elizabethan period,[14] stressing the fact that the literary criticism of Sir Philip Sidney and Thomas Campion was not basically at variance with the achievements of Marlowe, Shakespeare and Spenser; he then proceeded to the Augustans.[15] Dryden's criticism is praised for its discernment, openness to new impressions, and just awareness of the workings of the poetic imagination; Addison, as a critic, is trivial by comparison. In his final lecture of the autumn term,[16] Eliot then turned his attention to the literary criticism of the early Romantics. Wordsworth's *Preface to Lyrical Ballads* and Coleridge's *Biographia Literaria* have, he said, a range and fulness denied to all earlier critics. For the first time, poetry and the criticism of poetry reflect an integrated outlook on a wide variety of intellectual interests.

After this conspectus of early Romanticism, the Charles Eliot Norton lectures were interrupted by examinations and holidays lasting for nearly two months.

The fifth lecture, on Shelley and Keats, was not delivered until 17 February 1933, when the students had come back from their recess. Eliot's attack on Shelley is now notorious: here was the poetry of adolescence, of one who had written far too magniloquently about the function of poets. Eliot recalls that at the age of fifteen, at Smith Academy, St. Louis, he had been intoxicated by Shelley—before his acute critical faculty had been awakened by philosophy. There were, in fact, two reasons why in 1933 he now abhorred the poet who had once intoxicated him: first, that he had by now searched into Shelley's beliefs, and found him too much under William Godwin's radical and anti-Christian influence; secondly, that knowing what he now did about the scandal of Shelley's moral life, he considered him more or less a scoundrel as well as being pedantic and self-centred. And indeed, it was certainly unconscionable of Shelley to expect his young wife Harriet, then expecting her second baby, to pay for his elopement with a girl of sixteen whom he had seduced on her mother's grave. Against that kind of moral laxity Eliot's every instinct revolted. The recoil was all the stronger at that moment because of the effort of loyalty he was still making to a marriage which he felt bound to terminate in a separation. The example Shelley offered was hardly less than Satanic. He must put it behind him with all the force of his unconscious mind.

There was, of course, more to Shelley than this—as Eliot later came to realize. No English poet is closer to Goethe in the purity of his lyricism; none has surpassed him in the description of natural beauty; *Epipsychidion* must surely rank as one of the finest poems in the English language. But the objects he pursued, both in life and literature, were almost diametrically opposed to those of Eliot, who shrank from ethereal descriptions of the beauty of nature but who cultivated a beauty in his personal life totally foreign to Shelley. Keats, however, Eliot did admire, in that he was a poet of intuition whose ideas did not force themselves upon the visual and auditory imagination.

A fortnight later, on 3 March 1933, came the lecture on Matthew Arnold.[17] Eliot agreed with Charles Eliot Norton that, if culture were to be preserved from anarchy, "a new discipline of suffering" would be needed. What Matthew Arnold advocated, on the other hand, was a discipline of intellectual sobriety—or of "plain living and high thinking," to use Wordsworth's phrase. For, whatever may be our opinion of him as a poet, Eliot considered that Arnold had a jejune and puerile understanding of philosophy and was frankly indifferent to religion. This meant that he attached undue importance to the efficacy of moral precept, believing (in common with Pelagius, Condorcet and, his own father Thomas Arnold) that mankind was ultimately perfectible through the exercise of human reason.

As a poet, Arnold can "see beneath both beauty and ugliness";[18] his outlook on the world encompasses "the boredom, and the horror, and the glory"[18] of human existence. Yet, full of discernment as he is, he lacked the faith to see beyond the fleeting impermanence of the things around us. Nor did he have an auditory imagination. By this Eliot meant the feeling for syllable and rhythm which penetrates far deeper than the conscious levels of thought and feeling, invigorating every word, sinking to the most primitive and forgotten, returning to the very origins of language. It fuses the old, the obliterated and the trite with the current, the new and the surprising. It brings into fruitful proximity the most ancient and the most civilized mentalities.

In this criticism of Matthew Arnold we have something as far-reaching as Shelley ever claimed for poetry. Eliot's words tell us much of the secret recesses of his own genius. Another thirteen years were to elapse before he could be sure that here was the secret of his own contribution to the treasury of poetry. But already in *Prufrock* and the two *Sweeney* poems of 1920 he had given expression to the boredom and the horror. In *The Waste Land* and *Ash-Wednesday* were the horror and now and again glimpses of the glory.

On 17 and 31 March 1933 Eliot delivered his last two Charles Eliot Norton lectures at Harvard. He chose as his subject the contemporary situation of criticism. Maritain, Brémond, Rivière and his own friends Herbert Read and Ivor

Richards were the critics he had most closely in mind. But the substance and value of his course had been in his revelation of himself, and that revelation at its deepest is at one with the story of his personal and religious life.

CHAPTER

13

33 Courtfield Road

WHEN Eliot returned from Harvard in June 1933, the plan was that Mrs. Faber would do what she could for Vivienne, making joint arrangements with Maurice and his relations. Tom, meanwhile, remained out of London, finding company and friendship with a co-director of Faber & Faber, Frank Morley, and his family, whose home was an old farmhouse near Crowhurst in Surrey, called Pikes Farm. This was a battered seventeenth-century brick building with a wavy red-tiled roof and a circular pond between it and the road. Tom preferred not to stay at the farmhouse, however, fearing that Frank Morley's children would disturb his quiet. Instead, he took two rooms at the next-door cottage about thirty yards from Pikes Farm; his landlady was Mrs. Eames, wife of the deputy manager of the adjacent brickworks, and the house came to be known by the Morley children as "Uncle Tom's Cabin."[1] He arranged to have breakfast, lunch and tea at the "cabin," but dined at Pikes Farm, often remaining there until ten or eleven. The Morley household was entirely unconventional. Their food was homemade, their clothes homespun, they lived in the style of America's colonial days (Morley being himself an American). Tom learned to bake bread, and occasionally travelled up to London on the firm's business. When at the "cabin," his writing, reading and meditation were incessant; each Sunday he walked nearly a mile down the country lanes to attend the early morning communion service at the twelfth-century church of St. George's, Crowhurst, where a yewtree 1500 years old stands in the graveyard.

He also found time that year to write an introduction to the poems of Harold Monro,[2] to address the Anglo-Catholic Summer School of Sociology at Oxford and, in the fall of 1933, to pay yet another visit to America—this time to Charlottesville, where he gave the Page-Barbour lectures before the University of Virginia. These lectures were published in the following year (1934) as *After Strange Gods*, and in their intolerant asperity, their attempt to apply the labels of orthodoxy and heresy to contemporary literature, reflect the tragedy of Eliot's separation from Vivienne.

As winter approached, he left the rustic surroundings of Pikes Farm and the genial company of the Morleys to take up his abode once more in London. Having myself lived for some time in a large house, I chose for him the place to which he went: 33 Courtfield Road, in south Kensington.

There a lodging-house had been established by a personage who, although impressive, was almost sensationally dubious and odd. He had a great booming voice and the manner of a man who was determined to brazen out the fact that he had been a failure either as brigadier-general or archdeacon. This was William Edward Scott-Hall, who had begun life as a Roman Catholic and, as such, went to Oriel College, Oxford, which in those days had what Worcester College kept for a longer time, a number of gentlemen commoners. He was Oriel's last attempt in this kind. There he drifted towards ecclesiasticism, joined the "Old Catholics" and before long was actually ordained a bishop by Archbishop Matthew, himself sensational enough as an Old Catholic without a diocese, yet with an ordination unarguably valid in the eyes of Rome. In certain quarters this gave Scott-Hall a prestige greater than that of the legal bishops of the Church of England, because whereas many Roman Catholics denied the validity of Anglican orders and their place in the apostolic succession, here was a man who could undoubtedly pass the test.

Indubitably ordained a bishop, Scott-Hall set himself up in an establishment at Oxford called Folly Bridge House, and reigned over a little chapel. Money was always short, however; indeed, there came a moment when he began to wonder how he could live at all. Just at this point a supreme crisis in European history came to his rescue. World War I provided him with a career as an officer, but only at the expense of renouncing his activities as a bishop.

It was at the end of the War that he decided to keep a guesthouse. For this he chose one of those gaunt Victorian mansions which overlooked the spacious lawns of Harrington Gardens. It was a select neighbourhood. Next door lived a prominent Anglo-Catholic, Miss Muriel Forwood; among those who lived in houses opening onto the inner lawn were Axel Munthe, author of *The Story of San Michele*, and the leading Anglo-Catholic layman, Athelstan Riley.

Everyone who came to the house realized that its ruling spirit was not the fussy old man who was always making difficulties and seeking an occasion to bully people, but his friend, Miss Freda Bevan, who spent most of her time in the kitchen and seldom appeared. She was not (as he claimed) his niece, but only a woman who had befriended him when he got into difficulties at the Ministry of Munitions after being invalided out of the War, and who treated him with both pity and respect.

One of the most important considerations for Eliot was that 33 Courtfield Road was only a few minutes' walk from the church of St. Stephen's, Gloucester Road, which was well-known for its Anglo-Catholic services. Here he made friends with the incumbent, Father Eric Cheetham, with whom he was afterwards to share a home.

From the solemnities of its worship he would walk back to the space, quiet and companionship of the house at the back of Courtfield Road, and the pleasant conversation of Miss Bevan. She could offer a further attraction, too, for her cat Bubbles soon took a foremost place in his affections. If at times he felt the bereavement thrust upon him by his wife's illness and separation, if his heart craved for expressed affection (as it did always), then the tabby Bubbles came to his rescue, and to Bubbles he dedicated the same sort of playful verses he would at times indite to Virginia Woolf—with the added satisfaction that Bubbles' brain would never be unbalanced. A right-minded cat was to him the almost perfect companion. Its playfulness always responded to his own, and so did its affection. It always welcomed a caress. So in his gratitude he set Bubbles among the immortals, an elegant counterpart to Sweeney Agonistes, and equal in its consoling power to the burning candles and the waves of incense at St. Stephen's.

Besides Bubbles and a majestic Persian cat Xerxes, there was the friendliness of his next-door neighbour Miss Forwood, who would drive him about in her car. Once she was taking him to a poetry reading. "I hate reading my poetry aloud like this," he told her, "it's like undressing in public."

"You needn't worry," she reassured him. "You never take off too much."

What struck Miss Bevan most about Tom at this time was his sadness. He would come in and sit in the garden listlessly. He seemed dazed by the poignancy of life. "I wonder," he would keep repeating, "I wonder." He was in the state of weariness when every decision seems to be wrong. He knew that Vivienne's malady meant endless suffering. He sympathized with her, and he too suffered from loneliness. His mind was obsessed with this gloom.

Yet it was while he was at Courtfield Road in 1934 that he worked at *The Rock*, a pageant play staged at Sadler's Wells Theatre, London, between 28 May and 9 June that year. This was at the instigation of Martin Browne,[3] whom Eliot had first met while staying with Bishop George Bell at Chichester in December 1930. The Bishop had appointed Martin Browne as his "Director of Religious Drama in the Diocese of Chichester," but Browne's activities were not confined to this diocese (large as it is); they also extended to London. Here a pageant was to be staged in aid of the "Forty-Five Churches Fund of the Diocese of London"—the proceeds to be devoted to building new Anglican churches for the rapidly growing suburbs. Martin Browne seems to have invited Eliot's assistance in this project long before the removal to Courtfield Road; they were certainly discussing the pageant, rather inconclusively, at the time when Eliot was living near Oxted. Then it suddenly occurred to them that the pageant should consist of distinct scenes linked by an episodic plot, and recited to the accompaniment of music. These scenes were to become the Choruses from *The Rock*, and they were written at Courtfield Road.

In the earlier work of Eliot there is nothing so revealing as the "Book of Words" of this delightful and successful pageant to which Dr. Martin Shaw wrote the music. The Choruses from *The Rock* proved that he was born to be the playwright whose theatrical work furthered the spread of religious ideas. The time had come when people no longer looked to the pulpit for the message of redemption. Very few people have any chance to see *The Rock* as Eliot conceived it, but the ten Choruses are always printed in his collected works. Yet they have been too much neglected: these pages on the relation of the Church of England to contemporary London are the believer's answer to the searchings and confusions of the agnostic, twelve years earlier in *The Waste Land*.

The Church was not flourishing in London. Everywhere the twentieth century had emptied Christianity's places of worship, and had brought men further from God and nearer to the dust. What did the poet find in London, and in the foreign trade floating up the Thames? The complaint that there were too few chop-houses and too many churches. Why should there be any churches at all when men came there only to work? It would surely be better if they had their churches in the suburbs to which they commuted. But if one got out into the suburbs, what did one hear? Six days have we laboured, on the seventh let us motor to Hindhead and have a picnic. Families tear about in their cars; a young man dashes off on his motor cycle with a girl behind him on the pillion. Is this what C. W. Eliot meant by "the religion of the future"? What is the monument our young men of today will leave around the town? A thousand lost golf balls.

Meanwhile, politicians neglect the problem of over two million unemployed. No one has hired us, these two million men complain; no one is interested in what we say. But how can one have right relations between men unless one first has a right relation to God? Why, on the other hand, should men love the Church, when she tells them of evil, sin and other unpalatable facts? People go about their business well dressed, self-contented, enjoying themselves. Not so in a Church. There a man must repent and cleanse himself so as to be worthy of the Communion of Saints. Outside the Church, people's way of escaping both from the world and themselves was to devise some system so perfect that nobody need practise virtue. But this is to overlook the soul, which out of the music and liturgy of the Church can draw new forms of life. Let men build a Temple where they can learn of religion and the Redeemer.

The vividness of Eliot's lines seems like a restatement of Samuel Johnson's *Vanity of Human Wishes*, with its vigorous satire of London and its insistence on the value of prayer and belief. It was not in Eliot's nature (any more than in Johnson's) to lose himself in a sense of glory. In one of his sonnets on the *Divina Commedia*, Longfellow had written:

> Sing the old Latin hymns of peace and love
> And benedictions of the Holy Ghost;
> And the melodious bells among the spires
> O'er all the house-tops and through heaven above
> Proclaim the elevation of the Host![4]

Wordsworth, again, had pictured the glory of High Mass in a mountain church in Switzerland, where clouds of incense veiled the rood and each pale brow bent low as "dread hosannas" followed the Elevation.[5] Pope had a similar picture in his *Eloisa to Abelard*,[6] and (contemporary with Eliot) Alfred

Noyes, having attained to belief, was writing moving verses to echo the songs of adoration at the Mass. But in *The Rock* there is no hosanna and no glory.

These Choruses should not be dismissed as unworthy of the volume in which they are generally found. They combine satire and sagacity, colloquial vigour and classical dignity, and are a clear exposition of their writer's mind at that time. Speaking at the Concord Academy in 1944, Eliot said that poetry should not persuade us to believe but show us, as Dante and the *Bhagavad Gita* do, what it feels like to believe.

So closely did Eliot associate himself with the religious life of St. Stephen's that it was not long before he transferred himself from 33 Courtfield Road to live with his Vicar, Eric Cheetham, with whom he remained for the next five or six years. This was to be his home while he was writing *Murder in the Cathedral* and *The Family Reunion*. He had first attended a Mass at St. Stephen's in 1933, during the centenary year of the Oxford Movement, but it was not until his arrival in Courtfield Road that he became Vicar's Warden at the church, a post which he held from 1934 to 1959. This meant that he was an ex-officio member of St. Stephen's Parochial Church Council, the joint body of clergy and laymen who ran the parish's affairs. The post which Eric Cheetham invited Eliot to occupy was indeed the highest lay position in the parish, and even after Eliot relinquished its duties, feeling that they had become too onerous, he still remained a sidesman and a member of the Parochial Church Council. Altogether, therefore, his active connection with St. Stephen's, Gloucester Road, spanned a period of more than thirty years.

Eliot did not live with the clergy as one of them. Eric Cheetham and his curates ate their meals together; he had his alone, and frequently ate out. Sometimes, of course, he would chat with them after meals or at other times during the day, but the clergy house enabled him, on the whole, to lead a life of contemplation and withdrawal.

It was in the church that Father Cheetham and his assistants felt Eliot's presence. "It was a spiritual experience," said Father Nicholson, "to administer the Bread and the Wine to so devout a worshipper. At such a sacred moment the officiating priest could not but be aware that he was in the presence of a sublime spiritual reality." It is, of course, usual to observe with what recollection—and not least in Anglican churches—those who have received the sacrament leave the altar rail and return in stillness to their seats. With Eliot, this sacred moment was a more absorbing and radiant reality than with any other parishioner over the course of the years. The consummation of his surrender to the urgent immanence of the God-made-man was an act by which those who witnessed it were touched as by an event in the life of grace. Similar was his absorption in a night vigil.

He had not long settled down with Eric Cheetham before he found himself drawn to join a retreat at St. Simon's, Kentish Town. Here he met the two priests whom for the rest of his life he chose as his spiritual counsellors. These were Philip George Bacon and Frank Lucas Hillier. Father Hillier was of his own age, Father Bacon was some years older and already an invalid.

Suffering can add to a soul a power all its own, and with that power a penetrating sweetness. This was what Tom immediately felt in Father Bacon's presence. Here was a priest who understood because he was withdrawn by his disabilities into that closer communion with Christ which is the privilege of those called to share in His sufferings.

One cannot discuss the intimate trials of the soul with those with whom one lives. Someone more remote is needed, someone who deals with the soul not in the traffic of daily life but in its sacred inwardness. Once every two months or so, Tom would escape from all his accustomed haunts and drive out to Kentish Town, where no one would recognize him if he walked among them. He was as free there from the constraint of his gathering celebrity as he was from the routine of his life with the Vicar or from the business of the publishing house. So he would make his appointment, arrive in the morning for a long talk on the development and difficulties of his inner life, receive the salve and toning of absolution, and then, with the freedom of the soul strengthened and refreshed through penance, join the two fathers in complete and happy confidence at lunch.

As long as Father Bacon lived, he was Tom's "ghostly Father"; when the invalid's life failed, then Father Hillier was there to take his place in those changed years when Tom lived in the infinite solace and refreshment of his second marriage. By that time, as Father Hillier constantly noted, strain had been exchanged for complete serenity. In fact, the problems of his spiritual life had by then practically disappeared.

But this is to anticipate a later chapter in Tom's story, a chapter, however, which has its origins in the fulness of the sacramental life of St. Stephen's. At first living with his priests, and always turning to them for spiritual advice, he found in religion the sustaining power to bridge the twenty-three years or so between his first and his second marriage. And what did the priests think of the man whom they knew so well? The quality they always noticed in him was his humility. They saw that, far from asserting his taste or his individuality, he sought to pass unremarked and to regard himself as an instrument fashioned by God to do a certain work.

In fact, it was during the time he lived in the clergy house of St. Stephen's that he indulged in one of his gayest and most sustained jokes. Along with Geoffrey Faber and Frank Morley, he would frequently spend an evening with the noted bibliophile, anthologist and littérateur John Hayward, whom he had first met through his contributions to *The Criterion*.[7] The parties which Hayward gave at his home, 22 Bina Gardens, did not merely consist merely of Faber, Eliot and Morley: there were barristers, judges, diplomats, actors and other poets (such as John Betjeman), but of all these the three directors of Faber & Faber were perhaps the most regular attenders. Hayward greatly relied on these evenings, having suffered since the age of eleven from muscular dystrophy and consequently being more or less unable to leave the house. But this had not impaired his sense of fun, which not only appealed to all his guests but stimulated their jokes and wit. There was always great hilarity at the parties in Bina Gardens.

One little record of their intellectual skittishness remains. Called *Noctes Binanianae*, it commemorates the happy evenings in Bina Gardens, showing how the powers of Faber & Faber relaxed. These twenty-five pages of playfulness and parody were never issued to the world, but preserved for the delectation of the most elect in twenty-five privately printed copies. Hayward, Faber, Eliot and Morley, the masters of the night revels, were largely (if not entirely) responsible for this book, in which they chaffed each other under assumed names. Faber was Coot, Morley was Whale, Eliot either Elephant or

Possum, while Spider, or alternatively Tarantula, was the name given to their host who gathered them like flies into his parlour.

Not content with verbal jokes, Eliot and his friends often turned their ingenuity to jokes of a more practical variety; and Eliot was the most assiduous joker of them all. Sometimes, indeed, his taste for practical jokes would almost exceed the permitted bounds. It reached its acme one morning when the Fabers found themselves presented with a pair of human ears. Not even the original stage direction in *The Cocktail Party*, where Celia was not only to be crucified near an anthill but her face was to be smeared with a special grease attractive to ants, could ever surpass the opening of a receptacle of human ears! Confronted with such a gift, even the Fabers were shocked. Yet not only is there an echo of Van Gogh's celebrated quarrel with Gauguin, the lover of Yeats also recognizes a parallel in *The Tower*:[8]

> Beyond that ridge lived Mrs. French, and once
> When every silver candlestick or sconce
> Lit up the dark mahogany and the wine,
> A serving-man, that could divine
> That most respected lady's every wish,
> Ran and with the garden shears
> Clipped an insolent farmer's ears
> And brought them in a little covered dish.

So much for the pleasantries of 22 Bina Gardens and elsewhere, which were at one with a deep vein in Eliot's character, with much of his poetry, his endless banter—and even his attractiveness to Vivienne.

Equally essential to his nature, however, and the serious preoccupation of which banter was the relief mechanism, was

Eliot's new-found commitment to religious poetry, and especially the religious poetic drama. *The Rock* had been his first attempt in the field of religious drama; *Murder in the Cathedral* was to be the second. He was invited to undertake this second assignment by Bishop George Bell, his host of 1930 who had come to Sadler's Wells to see *The Rock*. It was intended for the Canterbury Festival of 1935, and was to be the first commissioned play staged in the Chapter House. (Earlier Festivals had performed existing plays.) The invitation came in the summer of 1934, and Eliot had about twelve months in which to write his new drama. Combining once again with Martin Browne,[9] he hesitated for some months about the form the play should take; not until the winter of 1934–1935 did he seriously set to work on it, visiting Canterbury about the same time to refresh his memory on the cathedral and its precincts. More than fifty years before, Tennyson had written his *Becket*, and just fifty years earlier Henry Irving had died on the stage at the very moment he was declaiming Becket's final lines:

> At the right hand of Power—
> Power and great glory—for thy Church, O Lord—
> Into Thy hands, O Lord—into Thy hands!

chapter 14

The First Plays

Time was to show that *Murder in the Cathedral* had a more continuous appeal to the mind of his age than any other play. The reason for this was its combination of splendid and original poetry, full of the grimness of winter and December wind, with a great and historic theme presented in forceful originality; also there was the excellence of Eliot's dramatic arrangement, the subtle studies in human psychology, and the play's profoundly spiritual and mystical qualities. All this was enhanced by the brilliant device whereby, at certain moments in the play, the actors thrust home their points by speaking directly to the audience. Everyone present at the play is thus involved in the drama of the competing claims of Church and State at all periods of history, as also in the conflict between what is temporal and what is eternal.

Writing on dramatic poetry in 1928, Eliot said that if drama was to be occupied with the deep, lasting things of life, then it should turn as its medium of expression. For in intense emotions, and in its approach to the permanent and universal, the human soul tends to express itself in verse. If, therefore, one wanted to write a religious drama of the kind that had been popular throughout the Middle Ages, one was bound to consider using verse in drama. When Eliot was invited by the Bishop of Chichester to write his Canterbury drama, he was still living in a time of intense personal distress. His religion, though leading to frequent and sincere worship and though completed by his living with clerical friends, had not brought his life to a thoroughly peaceful integration. He was often lonely, and always at the back of his mind was his preoccupation with his lonely wife.

If he could have forgotten Vivienne, she could not forget him. She would return to his office in Russell Square and try to waylay him on the stairs, but when it was suggested that he might see her he answered, and rightly, that it would be madness to do so. There are stories of her coming to his lectures wearing on her back a placard bearing the words "I am the wife he abandoned," and she was to be a regular attender of his plays.

So it came about that when the theme of martyrdom was set before him, he thought out the whole subject with a peculiar intensity of sympathy. This personal feeling was deepened by the growing intensity of the international situation. In the year in which he was completing *Murder in the Cathedral*, Mussolini had come out with the prophecy that if the nations of Europe persisted in their current mentalities, there would be general war by 1939.

Tom's second religious drama was an immense success at Canterbury, more so than *The Rock*. Soon it was being staged in London, where it was seen by a growing circle of admirers, which in 1937 included King George VI and his Queen. The approval of the King greatly delighted Tom, who told me how, each wearing a dinner jacket, the King and he had sat together in the stalls.

It was the beginning of an official recognition which was to lead not only to the Presidency of the Classical Association, the Virgil Society and the London Library, not only to honorary Fellowships at Magdalene College, Cambridge[1] and Merton College, Oxford,[2] but also to the Order of .Merit, the Nobel Prize, the Hanseatic Goethe Prize, the Dante Gold Medal and the American Medal of Freedom. The next ten years (1935–1945) were to see him pass from being a slightly dubious revolutionary to becoming the accepted master whose dignity was unimpeachable and whose word of authority final.

Meanwhile, undeterred by the somewhat unfavourable reaction of the Bishop of Chichester,[3] Eliot continued as a dramatist—quite determined, as he told Martin Browne, to move away from ecclesiastical and historical subjects, and deal instead with modern themes.[4] In the years preceding the Second World War he was planning, and then writing, *The Family Reunion*—a theme poignant in its acute relevance to his own youth.

Like *The Rock, Murder in the Cathedral* had been commissioned. It did not enable Eliot to express the need of his own soul. He now wished to find a subject that would provide him with a release from the pent-up strain and tension of his adolescence and marriage. It was to be a catharsis, a purging of the soul, an attempt to present in objective terms the intensely subjective drama of his return home to East Gloucester in the summer of 1915.

So, with a second World War upon him and in endless loneliness, he pictured a family reunion still sadder than his own, in the bleak home of a nobleman in the north of England, a country house which, in spite of its ample scale and comfortable dignity, had much of the dreary chill of Wuthering Heights.

Though interspersed with passages of real poetry, *The Family Reunion* remains a curious play. The question which every critic asked himself was to what extent it related the story of Eliot's own marriage—and even of his own adolescence. How far was Eliot responsible for the breakdown of his wife's health? (To Bertrand Russell he had admitted the damage which living with him had been causing Vivienne.[5]) The play itself leaves unresolved the question of Monchensey's responsibility for his wife's death: had he or had he not pushed her overboard? Perhaps he only thought that he had done so. "Je voudrais bien le disculper," the author once told a friend. Similarly, the problem of Eliot's own involvement in the wreck of Vivienne's happiness must remain an eternally insoluble enigma. Perhaps, as he confessed to Russell, he was in some degree responsible for that disaster, but could he (or should he) take the whole responsibility for it onto himself?

And what of the parallel between Eliot's childhood and Harry Monchensey's? Many have remarked that Mrs. Charlotte Eliot was the dominant personality in the East Gloucester household. But had her influence on Tom been as detrimental as Amy Monchensey's was on Harry? It would be rash to assume so close a relationship between the two cases. *The Family Reunion* is an imaginative treatment of potentialities, not the picture of an actuality. It certainly contains fragments of actuality, however, and it is intriguing to speculate whether the mysterious refusal to return to a settled career in America in 1915 might not have had much in common with Monchensey's refusal to remain at Wishwood. But the fact remains that *The Family Reunion* is much less interesting as a piece of dramatic craftsmanship than as an exploration of its author's state of mind.

CHAPTER

15

The War Years

WHEN the Second World War came, Tom was forced to retreat from the pleasant clergy house of St. Stephen's to Shamley Green, near Richmond in Surrey, where he lived as the guest of Mrs. Mirrlees. I often used to hear of her daughter Hope from my friend Charles Du Bos, who, in fact, published a little essay on her verse in *Approximations*.[1] I also met Hope Mirrlees when staying with the Eliots in Clarence Gate Gardens, and she entertained me on my return to England from the United States. She was undoubtedly one of Tom's greatest friends, as were her sister Margot Coker and, of course, their mother. "Mrs. Mirrlees is a remarkable woman," he said to me with great emphasis, and she certainly looked it.

The house which became Tom's retreat from the bombing stood high above the village and was run on the large scale. Among Mrs. Mirrlee's interesting neighbours were Sir Philip Gibbs and the Chapmans, who were in charge of G. F. Watts's collection near the Hog's Back. At that time Ronald Chapman had just left Eton, and Tom took a particular interest in seeing that he kept up his studies. In due course, he took a first at Oxford and became one of the staff at the Bodleian Library, where he often spoke to me of the help Eliot had given him in guiding him towards an academic career.

Except when he was firewatching on the premises of Faber & Faber on Tuesdays of each week, and working in his office for the whole of Tuesday and Wednesday,[2] Tom's practice was to spend most working days and weekends in Surrey, though he also worked many Thursdays in London travelling there and back in the day. Even in wartime conditions, however, he still managed to attend congresses, meetings and retreats, in all of which his participation became increasingly appreciated.

I was the guest of Mrs. Mirrlees during this period for an hour or two one afternoon. It was a time, however, when Tom was at Shamley Green. I was staying not many miles away at Albury Park as the guest of the Duchess of Northumberland, and when one day the Duchess was travelling in the direction of Mrs. Mirrlees's house I asked if I might accompany her and spend the afternoon with Tom and his hostess. After we had had tea, Mrs. Mirrlees sent me back to Albury in her car, and I took Tom with me. It seemed to me a great pity that he should see nothing of the splendours of Albury when so often living in its vicinity, and especially as it contained among other treasures two magnificent Turners. It was while we were looking at these paintings that the Duchess came in, and I explained to her that I had brought my friend over with me to give her an opportunity of meeting him. I detected, however, that she knew nothing of Tom's work and it was therefore with some diffidence that I introduced them. Tom noticed this at once and said with his usual good humour: "Are you getting to be ashamed of me, Robert?"

Tom always kept up with the Mirrlees, and not least with the elder daughter Margot, whose great house in Oxfordshire he loved above every other house he visited. This was Bicester House. When in Boston, I was much puzzled to see a letter from Tom to Sam Morison saying that his only friends in Bicester belonged to the hunting set.[3] The enigma was resolved when I discovered that the wife of the hunting man was Margot Coker. As a hostess she was absolutely irresistible, and not the less so because she thought Tom's prose dull. But if his prose was dull, his personality was scarcely less irresistible than hers. In her company he let himself go completely. At any rate, he fitted in perfectly with Aubrey Coker, as also with Margot's brother, General W. H. B. Mirrlees, and indeed with the whole set of hunting people who gathered around. One who joined the house parties was Ernest Simpson, whose personality I should have said was also extremely attractive. The ex-husband of the Duchess of Windsor and Tom struck up an immediate friendship.

As a matter of fact, Tom Eliot and Ernest Simpson had a common friend in Francis Underhill. Ernest Simpson had wanted Mary, the wife who succeeded Wallis, to be buried in the shadow of Wells Cathedral, when Francis was living in the moated palace beside it. But Anglican bishops have no control over their cathedral precincts; and the decision rested with the Dean and Chapter of Wells, who refused their permission, Ernest Simpson having been twice divorced. At the Bishop's suggestion, Mary Simpson was eventually buried in the churchyard nearest to the Cathedral.

Such was his busy life at Shamley Green, and his friendships with the Mirrlees, Cokers and others. But though no one had a keener appreciation of social nuances than Tom, it would be inaccurate to suppose that he moved only among county people, or even that his closest friendships were among such men and women. He was constantly renewing his friendship with John Hayward. He had his colleagues in the publishing house, especially the Morleys and Fabers. He remained in touch with Kelham Theological College, Nottinghamshire, where he had spent many happy days between 1933 and 1939, and with one of whose lay brothers, George Every, he kept up a steady stream of correspondence. In Kentish Town there were Father Bacon and Father Hillier; not to mention the life of his own parish and his friendship with its Vicar. Moreover, it was in the early years of the war that one of the closest friendships of Eliot's old age was formed, his friendship with the Corsican Jo Chiari.

It was the French authority on Milton, Denis Saurat, who brought young Chiari to Eliot's office in Russell Square. Here was just the sort of personality which Eliot most appreciated: a brother foreigner among the conventions of England; a man with the vigour and simplicity of his native island, and not much older than Jean Verdenal had been when Eliot first came to Paris. He was also a special admirer of the plays and poetry, while his own poetry was redolent of the coast of Corsica where he had so often bathed as a boy. The atmosphere of this Mediterranean coastline, with its resinous scents and wild vegetation, its hinterland of gorges so savage that one is said to have inspired Dante with imagery for the *Inferno*, was stranger and richer in odours and contrasts than anything Tom had known in Massachusetts. Chiari's thought was European, not English: he had spent much time in Paris and knew and loved its culture. Tom immediately formed with him the frank, easy friendship he had enjoyed at Oxford with Karl Culpin; and as with Culpin, he could share with Jo

Chiari the same simple jokes, renewing his old pleasure in the music hall and a regular enjoyment of cowboy films.

But what did Eliot think of that other pageant of slaughter, the Second World War? How did he react to the tremendous catastrophe in the midst of which he worked and even sometimes lived? In 1940 he accepted for publication my *Winston Churchill*, which showed the then Prime Minister as a man of moderation who had deprecated the too harsh treatment of Germany after the First World War and had exposed with the rush and drama of his own unique style the follies of the Allies both in strategy and tactics. My object in writing this book was one with which Eliot wholly agreed: to protect Churchill from the excesses of war propaganda and to urge that a reasonable settlement should be sought at the earliest possible moment. We agreed, too, about Churchill's majestic command of words, his range as an historian, his fascination as the author of *Thoughts and Adventures*. But we did not agree with his later policy of carrying the War to its ultimate oppression, a policy which too closely reminded us of the "follies of the victors" in 1919.

I recall a saying of Tom's during the War, that if one tries to fight evil with material means one will soon find oneself infected with the evil one is fighting; and when later he discovered that his warning had proved all too true, he became more and more concerned about the means and methods of rebuilding Christian order after the devil's joyride. Like everyone else he paid lip service to the total war effort in a few jingoistic lines, lines which he wisely allowed to slip into utter oblivion when the war was over; for they expressed only a passing mood of conformity to the aggressive narrowness and self-assertiveness of a country at war, or else perhaps were a satire of the country's attitude. Yet it is interesting to note that even for the shortest time he was able to adapt his fine mind to bellicosity; like Bertrand Russell's, his antipathy to Hitler was long, deep and well-founded.

This question of the rebuilding of Christian order was indeed one of his keenest preoccupations during the war years. Nobody, however, realized more clearly than he that it was not simply a question of rebuilding the *status quo ante*, but of reformulating the forms, attitudes and outlook of the Christian church for its mission in the latter half of the twentieth century. His ideas on these subjects were expounded in March 1939 in a series of lectures at Corpus Christi College, Cambridge, where he spoke by invitation of the Master, Sir Will Spens; later the same year, they became available to a far wider public in *The Idea of a Christian Society*. Delivered six months before the actual outbreak of war, they were planned at a time of mounting international tension and fearful expectancy; they were, moreover, only the first of his series of pronouncements on the restatement of faith at a time of imminent and far-reaching change. As such, he was the lay counterpart to Archbishop William Temple, who at least once had been his host at Bishopthorpe (from 10 to 12 October 1933), and who was striving equally hard to equip Britain with a spiritual outlook adequate to her post-war needs: adequate also to the commands of Christ the Redeemer!

Eliot's key argument in *The Idea of a Christian Society* is that even in the England of 1939 people were gradually becoming dechristianized. In those years of Hitler's increasing supremacy on the Continent, British people liked to pride themselves on the belief that they lived on a higher moral plane than the Germans—or even the Russians, who until 1941 were Germany's allies. But, he said, to speak of ourselves as a Christian society, as opposed to the societies of Fascism and Bolshevism, means nothing more than that we are not penalized for professing the Christian religion. The plain fact is that we do not commit our lives and actions to our professed beliefs. But then tolerance is intolerable, or at very least difficult, for a Christian because it means that he need make no particular sacrifices, and so may drift into conformity with materialism. We cannot give society the controlling balance of Christianity unless we are prepared to encounter discipline, inconvenience and discomfort. The British were too apt to think that to be under Hitler—or perhaps even under Stalin—was hell, as contrasted with the complacency with which they pursued their material existence. Complacent materialism is not Christianity. The Christian alternative to hell on earth is to accept the pain and sacrifice which on earth are purgatory.

Early in 1941 Eliot joined with the late J. H. Oldham (editor of *The Christian News-Letter*, to which the poet frequently contributed from then onwards and which, until its extinction in 1949, deeply influenced his social thought) in a project very similar in its intentions to *The Idea of a Christian Society*. This was a symposium of broadcast talks, "The Church Looks Ahead," which asked how one could move towards a Christian Britain. In his contribution to the book[4] Eliot insisted that for Britain to be called Christian at all, it would need to be reconverted from its paganism and that the notion of sacrifice must be the "head stone of the corner" of any attempt at evangelism. The pitfall into which many assemblies of churchmen fell was that their aspirations were confined to words, their reforms were not of their whole lives but some political or social scheme. We must rely on God, not clothe a human scheme in the drapery of Christianity. The people who will convert a nation are not those who are conventionalists, but prophets who may be unrecognized or even stoned.

One of his particular interests during the war years was the St. Anne's Society, founded by an Anglo-Catholic, Patrick McLaughlin, and centred on the parish of St. Anne's, Soho, where McLaughlin was vicar. The purpose of this society was to bring together Anglican intellectuals in such a way as to strengthen the Church's influence and leadership. For this purpose St. Anne's, Soho, was ideally suited. Close by were the Inns of Court, the nucleus of the English legal profession, and not far away were the theatres. It was almost at the edge of Bloomsbury, and on the way to Bloomsbury was the British Museum, with its incomparable Reading Room. Hardly further were the central administrative buildings of the University of London; a little to the south was King's College, London. It served, therefore, for all the professions, and was exactly what Eliot would have wished for as a Christian counterpart to *The Criterion.* For many years it was one of his favourite rendezvous, and at any of its meetings he might well come across Dorothy Sayers, Rose Macaulay, John Betjeman, C. S. Lewis, Eric Abbott or David Cecil. But the value of the St. Anne's Society was not only that it threw him into closer contact with such people as Dorothy Sayers, with whom in any case he had the threefold link of Anglo-Catholicism, an interest in Dante, and a passion for detective stories; it also introduced him to men and women whom he would not otherwise have met and some of whom, like T. M. Heron, were in the world of business. Heron combined social ideals with a conviction of the need for sweeping financial reforms—a view which Eliot had held ever since his experience of enemy debt settlement and banking in general. Eliot formed a warm friendship with T. M. Heron and his wife, and he was always happy to stay with them at their ample home in Welwyn Garden City.

Various as were his involvement in church affairs, social thought, charitable work and publishing, Eliot still found time —as any poet will—for further contributions to literature. Sometimes, indeed, these various categories merged, as when his religious interests impinged on the reconstruction of the social order, or his publishing coalesced with his own writing, or as when in 1939 he contributed to *The Queen's Book of the Red Cross*, in aid of the Lord Mayor of London's Fund for the Red Cross and the Order of St. John of Jerusalem. Not that Tom's offering outshone that of his distinguished fellow contributors! Rather the reverse: his poems *The Marching Song of the Pollicle Dogs*[5] and *Billy M'Caw: the Remarkable Parrot*[6] are the very acme of mediocrity. Yet they are worth noting as examples of his playful and observant eye.

The second of these exercises is about a parrot who was the chief magnet of a local bar, but the first is unique in that, instead of concentrating on cats (like the vast majority of his animal poems), it is dedicated to dogs. W. T. Levy relates how, long after the War was over, Mrs. Reinhold Niebuhr made Tom thoroughly disgruntled by asking him to choose a name for her dog:[7] that was asking too much! I am glad, therefore, to possess verses which, no matter how mediocre, show that his affections—like those of Vivienne—did not confine themselves to cats but could at a certain moment extend even to dogs: a predilection which must have been the final bond of sympathy between himself and that first wife whom he so often said that he adored.

On an infinitely more serious level, Eliot completed during the war the work which he had begun in the poem *Burnt Norton*, first published in 1936 in his *Collected Poems 1909–1935*. The second of his series of "Four Quartets," *East Coker*, followed in 1940; in 1941 came *The Dry Salvages*, of which something has already been said in relation to Eliot's boyhood holidays in Massachusetts; *Little Gidding* closed the series in 1942. Finally, all appeared together in New York in 1943 under their destined title of *Four Quartets*. Combine these, and you have the last poetic account of the evolution of the poet's soul at the approach of old age. For at last the sense of fading vitality which had haunted him in youth was halted and overcome in the creative achievements of the years between forty-five and fifty-five.

Friends noted, however, that as in his thirties and forties he had looked mature, so now in his fifties he looked no older. No grey showed in his hair, his sallow face showed no wrinkles and had no colour to lose, his figure remained lithe and graceful, his expression kept its slightly strained serenity. His humour was delightful in its effervescence, his talk engrossing in its surprises, in his judgments of men, literature and things he dazzled in his alternations of mildness and severity.

CHAPTER

16

Four Quartets

BEFORE beginning his Canterbury play in 1934, Eliot had visited friends at Chipping Campden, one of the most picturesque of the small Cotswold towns. Two or three miles out of Campden he found a spacious mansion with fine lawns, the name of which, Burnt Norton, he had made famous.[1] Its paths led him to a dry concrete pool, and there were shrubberies and a rose garden. It seems that, although he thought he was alone, some children had hidden themselves in the shrubberies; finally, they burst out laughing, so he was in pleasant company. He returned to London and busied himself with thoughts of *Murder in the Cathedral*. But during the summer of 1935, after the play had been acted at Canterbury, his thoughts went back to the lonely garden.

What now preoccupied him in his poem *Burnt Norton*[2] was the idea that each moment of time gives us an opportunity to sense timeless being, just as one night Henry Vaughan saw Eternity "like a great ring of pure and endless light," he was familiar with the notion of timelessness from his boyhood, having met it in transcendental philosophy, among the mystics and in the *Paradiso*.

For a moment at the outset of this poem he communes with the Timeless, but the mystical experience never lasts long: its "weight of glory," to use St. Paul's expression, is too heavy for us to bear. Nevertheless, that moment left behind it a conviction of attained reality, inherent in things of former years and in those of years to come.

If the idea applies to time, it applies also to movement: at the centre of the whirling planets is the stillness of the sun. This is the thought which the poem elaborates in new and intricate imagery typical of Eliot's mind.

Could he regain in London the transfiguring moment in the garden of Burnt Norton? With his images playing backwards and forwards between sunflowers, clematis, yew and a Chinese jar, he does come back to that sense of immediacy, when all is always now, though in doing so he has to strain expression to the utmost. The laughter of the children hidden in the leaves returns with its delight; memory makes it his own again, offering him joy against the boredom and misgiving of so many London hours—the waste, sad time stretching before and after, among the winds that sweep its gloomy hills.

Such had been his thoughts several years before the outbreak of war. Now, with his editorship of *The Criterion* abolished, working for part of the week in bombshelled London, seeing savage hatred unleashed between nation and nation, and with his separated wife Vivienne still living in torments of mental distress, he writes three further meditations on the mystical life of the Christian. In *East Coker*, he looks back to his English ancestors, who had sailed from the village of that name to the New World as long ago as 1669. *The Dry Sal-*

vages recalls his youthful sensation of the flow and expanse of water beside the shore of Massachusetts. In *Little Gidding* we are taken to a house in the Huntingdonshire village of that name which, to an even greater extent than the Usk of Henry Vaughan or the Bermerton of George Herbert, is the shrine of Anglo-Catholic withdrawal into a life of liturgy and con-templation.

Vivienne, in earlier years, had been at hand to appreciate the melancholy seriousness of *Gerontion*, *The Waste Land* and *The Hollow Men*. Now it was John Hayward who appre-ciated *Four Quartets*, even (like Vivienne) criticizing and making improvements to them. Modelled on such admired composers as Mozart, Beethoven and Bartok, they contained his reflections on the spiritual life, set down in a variety of idioms and metres that constitute the summit of his poetic achievement. In a unique personal way, they express his ar-dours for mystical experience and for the expression of mysti-cism. They reveal also the fidelity with which he still turned from the Anglican liturgy to the *Divina Commedia* and the *Bhagavad Gita*, classics which were now even more familiar companions than they had been twenty years earlier: they interpenetrate his memories of boyhood, his explorations of the life and home of his English ancestors, and his deepening communion with the seventeenth-century church which had first made him a believing Christian.

One reason for the success of the *Four Quartets* was that they were also poems of wartime, poems which met the stress of bombed towns and irrational aggression. It is true that, find-ing their inspiration in the counties of Gloucester, Somerset and Huntingdon and in the rocks off the shore of New Eng-land, they barely hinted that there was a war on; but they wove memories such as these into an experience of London at war, they combined a Londoner's attempts at the contemplative life with many records of acute personal observation.

Yet the composition of these poems was so complex as to make Eliot's meaning still more elusive than before. Each requires that the reader shall peer into it for any meaning and for many meanings. The allusions are as wide and intriguing as ever. Eliot still plays hide-and-seek with quotations from unexpected sources; and the gist of it all was what the mystics were saying then and always, that to attain the final goal of life one must sacrifice oneself and one must endure.

From the East Coker of his English ancestors, he turned back to the river and the sea of his American boyhood and youth. The year of *The Dry Salvages* was a time when private griefs were swallowed up in the tragedy of nations. The latest agony abides in history like the savage rocks which will always menace sailors when rough winds blow at night. This was Krishna's message to Arjuna[3] and the meaning of Pascal's remark that "Jésus sera en agonie jusqu'à la fin du monde."[4] The time of death is in every moment, and the bell's clang may be death-knell or angelus. Pray the prayer of the angelus that the Virgin Mary, in whom the Eternal Word was made flesh and came into time, may pray for us sinners now and at the hour of our death. Who can tell if death is not so embedded in the present moment as to be almost identical with it?

So much for private mysticism, but what of the corporate religious life of the Anglo-Catholic? At the village of Little Gidding during the Civil War between Charles I and Cromwell, Nicholas Ferrar and his family lived a life not unlike that of a medieval abbey. Such involvement in a community dedicated to the worship of God and the search for perfection was the true vocation of every devout soul. It was the vocation not only of Eliot himself but the unrecognized vocation of a warring world.

The poet's religious quest had taken him far. In *Four Quartets* he used words that cut deep into the soul, words as incisive as any written by St. John of the Cross. He wrote not only for himself but for a period of history more destructive than any the world had known. With advancing age, he often experienced a sense of disillusionment. He saw how mixed his motives had been, and in the psychology of depression became aware of errors and sins in what he had once thought was the exercise of virtue. But above all, he felt how powerless he was against the avalanche of folly which was destroying the traditional Europe he had admired and made his own.

The only escape from this revising work of conscience was not to plunge into the refining fire but, as he tells us in *Little Gidding,* to move rhythmically in it like a dancer. This was not only a personal experience, it was part of the drama of history. He saw it in the Second World War, and also in the English Civil War which had dispersed the Ferrars' community at Little Gidding. After his supreme lyric achievement in *East Coker* and the other meditative poems, he turned his attention to drama again. The only other piece of pure poetry he was to write came some fifteen years afterwards as a lyric of rapture in nuptial bliss.[5] As deep as any of his mystical urges was his longing for tenderness.

CHAPTER

17

At the Zenith

IT was, as I have mentioned, through *The Criterion* that John Hayward first came into touch with Eliot. They became friends and Hayward used to call on Tom and Vivienne at Clarence Gate Gardens. Later, in Bina Gardens, he inaugurated the series of parties commemorated in *Noctes Binanianæ.*

When the war was over, Eliot thought of leaving his luxurious shelter with Mrs. Mirrlees at Shamley Green. John Hayward, meanwhile, had transferred himself from Bina Gardens to the more distinguished neighbourhood of Cheyne Walk. Here he occupied a large flat overlooking gardens beyond which was the stretch of the Thames between Chelsea and Battersea which Turner and Whistler had so often painted.

Hayward invited Eliot to join him in his new home, a suggestion which Eliot accepted, though—with his usual modesty and unselfishness—he refused the big room with the view onto Cheyne Walk. This was to be his home until January 1957, a period of some eleven or twelve years. It was a comfortable establishment, furnished in the very best taste (Hayward had a liking for French furniture), in which Tom was given his own bedroom and library while the dining room and drawing room were shared between the two friends. Not that they often ate together, however; Hayward would usually have a tray brought in to him in his bed-sitting room. It was in this room, surrounded by Hayward's beloved books, that Tom often came for a friendly chat. Eliot's own rooms were spartan, almost monastic, in comparison; a chair, writing-table, and bookcase in his study, a crucifix on the unadorned wall of his bedroom. When Hayward discovered by chance that Eliot's bedroom was lit only by an unshaded sixty-watt bulb, he managed to persuade the poet to indulge in the luxury of a better light and a suitable lampshade.

Tom's day was to get up early and take a bus to his church in Gloucester Road. After returning to breakfast at the flat, he would set out for the office in Russell Square, where sometimes he would remain the whole day and sometimes only for a morning, or even go just for the afternoon. He often went out to dinner parties, but most evenings when the weather was fine he still found time to watch the boys playing football in the gardens of the Royal Hospital, Chelsea. Now and again the French housekeeper prepared a meal for a guest or two, but it was recognized that in this she went a little beyond the duties expected of her, and most guests were simply invited to tea.

Tom's most frequent visitors were Henzie Raeburn and her husband, Martin Browne, the friend who had directed both *The Rock* and *Murder in the Cathedral* in the playwright's ecclesiastical days, and *The Family Reunion* in secular idiom. Now Eliot intended to remain a secular playwright, and become a writer of comedy, and so Martin Browne would arrive in Cheyne Walk evening after evening, and work with him first on *The Cocktail Party* (1950) and then on *The Confidential Clerk* (1954), though on the latter play he was only consulted after the draft script had been prepared.[1] These two plays, apart from various lectures and speeches, were his only creative work in the time he was with Hayward, and Martin Browne thought that, in view of Eliot's heavy work-load at Faber & Faber, he did well to get through those in eleven or twelve years.[2]

With his keen interest in poetry, it was a delightful thing for Hayward to have Eliot's friendship and companionship; Eliot, on the other hand, felt compassion for Hayward's physical infirmity and deep respect for him both as a scholar and a man. One thing in particular was most gratifying to Tom: the taste and skill with which Hayward criticized his work as it was being composed, and which enabled him from time to time to add some erudite improvement, such as the word "laceration" which was put into *Little Gidding*[3] to suggest a comparison with Swift.

It was always an enigma to me that once Tom had realized the strain of living with an invalid like Vivienne, he should decide some thirteen years later to settle down with another invalid. What Hayward said to me was: "I wanted to take him away from the sort of life he was living with all those parsons"; and of course, as long as Tom was in Eric Cheetham's household he had to go out for his meals, which was always rather exhausting, and always return to a little community of clergy. What could Hayward offer in exchange? Taste, wit, elegance, the continual stimulus of a different type of mind, intelligent appreciation of his works[4]—and a French housekeeper who was much impressed by the elevation on which

Tom lived. "Mr. Eliot était un homme très religieux," she said to me; "il ne lisait jamais les journaux du dimanche."

Hayward always referred to Tom as his "lodger," and indeed it is true that, thanks to Hayward's generosity, Tom's household expenditure was much lower than it would otherwise have been. Even the most generous lodger does not, or at least did not at that time, pay more than £3 a day, which meant that he kept his living expenses down to £1,000 a year. This enabled him to put by a good sum of money all of it shrewdly invested by his stockbroker brother-in-law, Maurice. For quite apart from his salary and dividends as a director of Faber & Faber, he had the steady sale of his own work which swelled the stream of incoming royalties, he had the £8,000 or so of the Nobel Prize for Literature, and above all, the huge box-office success of *The Cocktail Party*. He told me that this play brought him no less than £29,000 and that, of this £29,000, he found to his unspeakable disgust that £25,000 was seized by the rapacity of Income Tax collectors. "I thought," he remarked bitterly, "that I had at last provided something for my declining years; but I was disappointed."

And not only was there a sharp improvement in his financial position (notwithstanding the deduction of £25,000 from the profits of *The Cocktail Party*), it was also a time when national and international honours began to be showered upon him. The first of the international honours was, in fact, the Nobel Prize, conferred on him in the year of his sixtieth birthday (1948), when he also dined with the King and Queen of Sweden. But earlier that year came the honour which perhaps gave him the greatest satisfaction of all, when from the hands of King George VI he received the Order of Merit.[5] This is an order conferred not on the Prime Minister's advice but by the Sovereign himself, independent, therefore, of all political considerations. It is given to the twenty-four men and women whom the Sovereign judges to have done the most distinguished work in their various walks of life.

At about this time, he dined with the King and Queen of England and was received in private audience by yet another sovereign, Pope Pius XII. Tom told me all about his visit to the Vatican, adding with a twinkle in his eye that the Holy Father had seen fit to discourse to him on poetry's relation to religion. Also to mark his sixtieth birthday, a Festschrift was put together by distinguished contributors.[6]

Travel was another occupation which absorbed more and more of his time, and not only the journeys to receive these distinguished marks of recognition and meet heads of state. He went on lecture tours to America, and had actually taken up an invitation to work at Princeton on *The Cocktail Party* when he received news of the Nobel award for his literary work. It was not long before a New York reporter was asking him: "For which work?" To which came the reply, "the entire corpus"—which the journalist took to be the title of either a play or a poem. He also kept up his visits to English religious houses like Mirfield, near Huddersfield in Yorkshire, occasionally stayed with bishops, and sometimes accepted the hospitality of friends, one of whom, Edgar Behrens, lived sumptuously on the Riviera.

Almost as if it was the penalty he had to pay for this tremendous reputation and worldwide recognition, ill health—an affliction of the lungs—was beginning to dog him as he passed his sixties. Almost every winter that he was in Cheyne Walk he sailed to Cape Town, generally with the Fabers, to strengthen his damaged lungs with the combination of sea and air. But in spite of everything, this painful illness (diagnosed as emphysema), sapped his energy, bodily strength and resistance. During the final year of his stay with Hayward (1956–1957) his strained heart led to a crisis, after which he seldom went so far in the mornings as St. Stephen's. He was fortunate to have just by his door the church where Sir Thomas More had worshipped in the time of King Henry VIII.

One chill morning (23 January 1947) it was Hayward's unenviable duty to tell his friend that Vivienne had died during the night at her nursing home in Stoke Newington, a London suburb. It was now almost thirty-two years since Tom and Vivienne had been married. For fourteen years he had felt that it would be madness for him to see her again and yet she had often sought to waylay him in the early years of their separation, and so renew the wonder of which her illness had deprived her. When he had decided to arrange for their separation, her brother Maurice had asked whether he could not find any less cruel way of telling her than by writing to her through solicitors. His answer was final: "What other way *can* I find?" He simply could not face the personal strain of saying cutting words to those he loved. When death comes, it throws a new and intense light on many relations of the heart; now once again he knew how deeply and constantly he had loved her, and how she had loved him as no other person had ever done. Hayward's message overcame him. He buried his face in his hands, crying: "Oh God! Oh God!"

The widower kept in close touch with his brother-in-law concerning the last arrangements. On an icy morning with snow still on the ground, they drove with the Fabers down to

Pinner in Middlesex where her body was laid to rest beneath the frozen earth.

Eliot, who had chosen to study at the Sorbonne before coming to Oxford, and who had visited Marburg before his arrival in London in 1914, always remained an admirer of Europe and an upholder of its cultural unity. Three years after the war ended, he was chosen with Arnold Toynbee to make a six-weeks lecture tour of Germany, with problems of European unity as his subject. He spoke first at Hamburg, and afterwards at Berlin, Hanover, Brunswick, Gottingen, Bonn, Frankfurt and Heidelberg, ending his tour at Munich. Everywhere he was received with enthusiasm, especially by the students.

He offered his listeners a recognition that they were cultured human beings in the unity of Europe. He spoke of the unity of the European cultural tradition as essential to Europe's progress. He wished to return to the rooted instincts of his ancestors at East Coker, instincts they shared with the whole of Christian Europe. Culture, he said, is made up of the elements of invention, intelligence, and a unified society not alien from the freedom of its individual families. Indeed, families, villages and neighbourhoods are the cells from which people spring. Progress is not the enforcement of uniformity: through the transformation of the ages, individual peoples can maintain their identity by cherishing their traditions, which means, of course, abandoning their resentments.

Then he developed his main ideas with regard to education. He certainly believed that the classics—Greek, Latin and Hebrew—should continue to be taught, but people should also remember that what had unified and civilized Europe was the brotherhood of the baptized. Christian tradition gives Europe a unity and a common heritage which is independent of geographical frontiers, which too often had no other justification than self-defense. No nation can attain self-preservation unless it looks beyond that to the good of the continent of which it is a part. Rather than have a triumphant nationalism alone, it was better to collapse.

Eliot's prestige, the deep moral earnestness of his talks, and the radiant force of his mind and personality emphasized the weight of what he was saying. Poetically, he had always been an innovator; politically, his object had been to conserve.

In his Hamburg lecture he spoke plainly of the manifold relations between Christianity and European culture. How important are the Christian writers of today, he asked. Only time could reveal the answer to that question. Art and literature cannot hand on to the future what they have not inherited from the past, and it was not easy to say how deep the Christian tradition was within them.

Turning to British and American culture, he stressed that the art forms of America, however European in origin, were taking on to a greater and greater extent an identity of their own. Local changes were constantly affecting them, producing differences of style and expression. Creative artists unconsciously search for new forms in their renewal of the traditional modes of personal confession. What was true of Anglo-American culture was equally true of German: that at no time can one tell whether a particular genius is at the beginning or end of a movement. His own sympathies he admitted were with the pioneers—to some extent, at least. For speech is a living organism: we cannot use the means of speech of our grandfathers if we are to explain what has happened in the interval between them and us. For this reason, and here he was giving the justification of his own verse, written poetic speech must be brought into the closest relationship with language as currently spoken by the generality of men.

Eliot had come over for these lectures as a diplomat of culture to bring Germany back to her rightful place in the unity of Europe, only to speak to his audiences in a region bordering on the unintelligible. What was perfectly clear to them, however, was his insistence that if cultural relations were to be resumed between Germany and the rest of Europe, then Germans must enjoy the utmost possible freedom: freedom to know other countries, to read their books, and to form friendships in countries sharing their interests.

Besides giving his German lectures in 1949, Eliot found time to visit the University of Munster, where a close friend of his, Josef Pieper, was a professor of philosophy. Pieper had been introduced to the poet a year or so after the war, when Alexander Dru called with him at the Faber & Faber offices in Russell Square. In this much younger German from Westphalia Tom had instantly felt an affinity such as he felt in 1911 for the now dead Laforgue. Their minds reached very similar conclusions from very similar points by very similar ways. "We understood one another immediately," was how the Professor put it to me. For his arrival in Munster, his new friend had prepared a festal afternoon, arranging that he should have a rest beforehand. So Tom was first of all taken after lunch to a small hotel where he managed to fit in a nap. At the Professor's home, his three children—then aged thirteen, eleven and seven—were introduced as the Pieper trio, and gave him a little concert with their recorders. This trio was mentioned several times in the ensuing correspondence between Josef

Pieper and Tom. From the point of view of philosophy, Eliot considered that this Munster professor was the closest exponent of his own views. He found in this thinker of the twentieth century what he had found in Aquinas's writings of the thirteenth: a form of the *philosophus perennis* which, rooted in Aristotle, had nevertheless developed in perfect harmony with Christian theology. He was constantly wanting to bring out translations of Josef Pieper, beginning with a little book for which he himself chose the English title, *Leisure: the Basis of Culture*.[7]

Within five years of the lecture tour, the country which so deeply admired *The Waste Land* in the 1920s and which had responded so eagerly to his message concerning the integration of European culture, was conferring upon him one of its most coveted honours: the Hanseatic Goethe Prize, awarded to him in 1954. It was not until 5 May 1955 that he actually went to Hamburg Town Hall to receive his award. Carl Burckhardt had been the first to receive this prize, and Martin Buber the second. It was expected of all recipients that they should deliver an address during the conferment ceremony, choosing some theme of special intellectual interest. "Goethe as the Sage" was the topic selected by Eliot.[8]

In his introductory speech, Dr. Albert Kolb (Rector of Hamburg University) traced the poet's place in the crisis of the history of culture. He stated his belief that the age of revolution was drawing to an end in Europe because on all sides social injustice was being so effectively stamped out. But even if the prerequisites for a Communist victory had gone, state interference in all walks of life endangered both the freedom of the individual and the life of the spirit. Eliot, he said, had recognized this fact as early as 1931, when he remarked that the world was then building up a life which, though civilized, was not Christian. Yet there was still hope, if Europe—realizing her traditional unity—could develop an awareness of her common past and her possession of the highest spiritual values.

Replying to these remarks, Eliot treated his audience to a discourse in praise of wisdom. He had been much less flattering to Goethe in 1933, when he had said that the sage of Weimar dabbled in both poetry and philosophy without making too great a success of either. Now when he reread these words in the mid 1950s, he was pained to find so many errors packed into so few words. Even in 1933, however, he had said that, like Vauvenargues and La Rochefoucauld, Goethe found his true place as a sage in the world of letters. Goethe, he now claimed, portrayed human beings in all the variety of their character, temper and circumstances; his wisdom flowed from the wellspring of the spirit; ranking among the greatest of Europeans, he was a citizen of the whole Continent. His wisdom was voiced in poetry, and was therefore a deeper and a more moving experience than it would otherwise have been. Indeed, Goethe's wisdom and his poetry are quite inseparable. He lived on many different levels and yet manifested at them all his serenity of wisdom: this placed him with Shakespeare and Dante in the very forefront of men, who while representing an age, were leading representatives of the unity of Europe.

Such was Eliot's final word to Germany, his final word too on what mattered so much to himself—his own position as a European figure. For while he still belonged (with ever increasing loyalty) to the Church of England, *The Waste Land*

and subsequent poems had also given him a place among the spiritual leaders of Europe.

He was almost equally, but not quite, as admired in France as he undoubtedly was in Germany and also Italy (where the Dante Gold Medal was conferred on him in Florence in 1959). Not only was he the translator of *Anabase*, he had himself written many skillful and witty poems in the French language. One instance of his immense prestige both as a Francophile and a European was that in 1951 he was invited to Paris to open the exhibition "Le Livre Anglais" organized by the Bibliothéque Nationale. This was a splendid occasion attended by the President of France, Vincent Auriol, by the British Ambassador and by numerous civic and national dignitaries. Here was the poet who, more than any other writer in the contemporary world (not even excluding Thomas Mann and Claudel), could be said to speak with the voice of cultural authority and spiritual leadership. Yet it was almost by a fluke that Eliot eventually arrived there on 18 November 1951. The purpose of the exhibition was to illustrate the history of British book-production through many centuries; it was inevitable, and fortunate, that John Hayward—with his immense knowledge of bibliography—should be asked to take a large hand in the planning of the exhibition, though only in a consultative capacity, and equally inevitable that he should accept. It so happens, however, that Charles Morgan is a novelist who has always been much more appreciated in France than in England, and the organizers of the "Livre Anglais" exhibition wished it to include the manuscript of an *Ode to France* which he had presented to the Bibliothéque Nationale. Hayward, on the other hand, detested the writings of Charles Morgan. Unless this (to him) obnoxious manuscript were removed from its showcase, he threatened to use all possible means to dissuade his "lodger," Eliot, from inaugurating such a display. And his efforts were successful, for the Morgan manuscript was rather ignominiously withdrawn, and few of the distinguished guests at the opening ceremony could have suspected how touch-and-go Eliot's participation had been![9]

In his opening remarks, the poet stressed his own inadequacy, as a mere man of letters, to do full justice to the immense array of manuscripts and books that had been gathered together for the exhibition. They were the true province of the bibliophile, and on that territory the man of letters would tread warily. Writers, he thought, should work in the silence of their studios, uniquely concerned with whatever contribution, great or small, they can make both to the reading public of their own generation and to posterity.

Relying no doubt heavily on Hayward's inspiration, he confessed that there were certain fields of bibliography in which France far outshone England. There had been no Jean Fouquet in English history, with his remarkable illustrations to Etienne Chevalier's *Book of Hours*, and Josephus's *History of the Jewish War*. Nor had there been any equivalent to the *Trés Riches Heures du Duc de Berri*. Nor could England rival the incomparable bookbindings of the eighteenth and nineteenth centuries, still less the sixteenth-century bookbindings commissioned by Grolier. Yet the exhibition did contain the *Benedictional of St. Aethelwold*, and Eliot was proud to be opening the choicest and most comprehensive display of British books and manuscripts ever organized.

Turning to the wider question of the relationship between creative writing and bibliography, Eliot stressed the writer's indebtedness to the patient scholars whose task it is to produce the best texts of the writings of his predecessors. For if the creative artist was concerned with the soul of literature, bibliographers were concerned to preserve its body. It was important to the impact of any poem that it should be suitably printed, in the right typeface and with the right layout and on the right paper. This again was the province of the bibliographer. And it was important that the contemporary poet should have available the precise texts, without any variation, of such earlier works as he might wish to study. The final purpose of bibliography, and perhaps the most important of all, was to help to ensure a continuing reverence for the works of genius handed down to us from the past. For if people at any time failed to appreciate those, then the outlook was grim for the writings of contemporary authors, and even grimmer was the prospect of transmitting cultural standards to the future.

Such was Eliot's tribute to John Hayward: a disguised tribute, for at no point in Eliot's address was he actually mentioned, though at every point the influence of his friendship was visible. Nor was Eliot fulsome in what he said on this occasion. He knew only too well the importance of a poem's layout, having seen Ezra Pound's obstetric efforts with *The Waste Land*. And remembering again the many constructive suggestions which Hayward had put to him, not only with regard to *Little Gidding* but to the other *Quartets* and *The Cocktail Party*, he realized, and publicly admitted, how great was the creative influence of textual scholarship. If further proof were required of the nature of Eliot's friendship with Hayward, it is surely here: far from their companionship being a mere arrangement of convenience, or the gregarious impulse of two lonely and aging men, it was a deep communion of interests in which each side contributed fruitfully to the other.

The Cocktail Party was by far the most successful of Eliot's plays. He had pondered it for many years before finally bringing it out in 1950. In fact, as early as 1939–1940 he spoke of it to a friend as "my comedy." It was half written by the time he heard from Hayward of his wife's death. But though Eliot spoke of it as "my comedy," it is a play with strong tragic undertones. Its subtle humour and the lightness of its conversation are what anyone would expect of a comedy, but its recurring themes of a troubled marriage and an expiation indicate a background of personal tragedy. Two ideas underlie *The Cocktail Party:* face the fact that you are as you are, and consequently have no right to expect the impossible of others (an idea both tragic and comic, and from which the play's comedy arises); and know that if evil is to be put right, there must be expiation. This second pivotal idea is an essentially tragic one. It will mean that in the last act the young woman with whom the husband of the play has committed adultery atones for her sin by dying crucified near an anthill.

There is so much of enduring value in this play that it must surely rank as one of the most outstanding plays written in the English language during this century. The subtlety with which Eliot expounds his ideas in act 2 must command the highest praise, and in the third act we have an unforgettable picture of the life of sacrifice, the dramatic horror of a beautiful girl going off as a nurse and being crucified before her corpse was eaten by ants. In the original production of the play at the Edinburgh Festival in August 1949, Eliot had put in a remark about Celia's face being smeared with a grease that would attract ants to her body; but this, as Martin Browne told me, was more than the theatregoers could stand and was therefore dropped for subsequent performances.

But apart from this repugnant detail, the crowds were delighted. At Edinburgh, Alec Guinness played the part of the psychiatrist. When the play moved to New York, it met an equally receptive audience, for, as Tom explained to me, it arrived on Broadway at a time when people were in the habit of going to psychiatrists to ease the strains of marriage. One of the secrets of its success, of course, was that Tom was well acquainted with the strains of marriage and the advice of psychiatrists. As I look back to my first meeting with Tom and Vivienne in June 1927, I realize how much of that holiday has gone into *The Cocktail Party*.

The style in which the comedy was written is, as one would expect, light, delicately amusing, and more to be acted than to be read. It depends upon its actors to bring out both its jokes and its wisdom. *The Cocktail Party* was, in other words, very different in style from *Murder in the Cathedral*, where there had been long passages of unequivocal prose mingling with verse that was not only metrical but frequently rhymed. Here, however, apart from a few sententious phrases put into the mouth of Harcourt-Reilly, and the libations at the end of act 2, there is nothing that departs from the ordinary level of sprightly conversation. And this is equally true of the style of Eliot's next play, *The Confidential Clerk*.

Indeed, it is only by considering *The Confidential Clerk* in relation to the earlier comedy that we can understand either. *The Cocktail Party* shows us that husband and wife must learn to put up with one another and not regard marriage as a veil for the indulgence of egoism. To this is added, with unmistakable clearness and force, the idea of sacrifice which is Eliot's most insistent theme. The concepts of self-denial and obligation to the good of the community had been derived in earliest boyhood both from his grandfather W. G. Eliot and from the novels of George Eliot, which his family so often read. From the days of his own personal tragedy came the further imperatives of penance and expiation: ideas that were essential to the Christian scheme to which he dedicated his whole life.

It is from such preoccupations as these that we are freed in *The Confidential Clerk*. The particular value of this charming comedy is that it fully conveys the wit, the adroitness, the charm and the gaiety of Eliot's habitual talk. Its lightness is what his friends expected of their daily life with him. Its adroitness and subtlety were also something constantly appreciated in real life by his many acquaintances. Compared with *The Cocktail Party*, it had "much more in layers to be meditated on and thought of as meanings of life."[10] Again, Eliot's phenomenal energy was shown in the untiring playfulness with which *The Confidential Clerk* treats both people and situations. It had been a somewhat satirical playfulness in earlier years. It was that quiet cut which Richard Aldington noticed as the way in which he could dispose of a reputation or clinch a discussion. But it grew kindlier as he advanced in the path of Christianity and is very well shown in the character of Eggerson. It is not too much to say that Eliot drew on his own character for that of the two personages (Eggerson and Colby Simpkins) who between them give rise to the play's title.

The Confidential Clerk owes much to a translation by Hilda Doolittle of the comedy *Ion* by Euripides,[11] but equally it belongs to an old Western European tradition of which *The Comedy of Errors, Twelfth Night* and Molière's *L'École des*

Femmes are outstanding examples; and of course, as with *The Cocktail Party*, it had had the benefit of John Hayward's and Martin Browne's advice. Helen Gardner considers it the best constructed of all Eliot's plays, and feels sure that it will survive. Martin Browne, on the other hand, doubts whether it is in harmony with modern taste.[12] Upper-class comedies based on mistaken identities, and with the love element muted in the present (as against all the illegitimacy of twenty or thirty years previously), belong rather to the world of Oscar Wilde and Somerset Maugham than to that of John Osborne and Arnold Wesker.

At the same time, it is a play worked out in a series of delicate, amusing and touching situations, not the least of which is when Lucasta tells Colby how she feels the stigma of illegitimacy, and he is unable to tell her that he shares it. Colby is a charming young man, perhaps the most attractive personality in the Eliot plays, and in Lady Elizabeth we have a satirical portrait of the woman taken up with modern religious quirks and fads. On seeing the play, Rose Macaulay said: "At last he has escaped from his preoccupations over his marriage." She was right. For the first time Eliot had written a play which did not deal with expiation.

CHAPTER

18

Eliot's Second Marriage

To return for a moment to the years immediately before the Second World War, when Eliot's review *The Criterion* was drawing towards its end, a young lady of exceptional charm and distinction was engaged by Faber & Faber as the review's production controller. This was Anne Bradby, who was to make her own name in the world of letters both for her poetry and plays and for her scholarly editions of James Thomson and Thomas Traherne. She belonged to a family well known at Rugby, where two housemasters bore the name of Bradby, one of them her father, and the other (G. F. Bradby) her uncle, who achieved a certain fame with a satire on public-school life, *The Lanchester Tradition*.[1]

She joined the firm of Faber & Faber early in 1936 and for the first three years of her employment was largely concerned with the innumerable matters, both large and small, in which any production department is involved. Almost all contributions to *The Criterion* had been directly commissioned by Eliot; it was also Miss Bradby's responsibility to sift through unsolicited articles and poems, and to recommend whether any of them should be published. In her editorial capacity, she soon understood Eliot's mind. She saw that although he always welcomed innovation, he was ruthless in his condemnation of anything pretentious or insincere. The simple query "Why?" would indicate his disapproval of any paper he felt that she had recommended too generously.

When the war broke out (by which time *The Criterion* had ceased to exist), Miss Bradby became Eliot's full-time secretary, and also did a certain amount of editing and reporting for the firm—work which she continued through the years. Sometimes Faber & Faber accepted badly written material from refugees, and this she would have to set in order. Then, in addition to her work for Eliot, she took over the secretarial work of Geoffrey Faber himself and assumed responsibility for the minutes and agendas of editorial committees. She attended meetings of the directors where she would notice Tom doodling or doing crossword puzzles. By this time she herself had a secretary under her. But in 1938 she had married Vivian Ridler, an employee in the printing department of the Oxford University Press, and now that he was liable to be called up for active service at any time, she eventually had to terminate her regular work for the firm.

During the five or so years of her work as Eliot's assistant, she attended one or two of the hilarious parties in Bina Gardens and one copy of the unpublished *Noctes Binanianae* was actually inscribed to her. She told me also of the immense amusement with which she had followed some of Tom's written arguments with a customs official. Playful and relentless was the development of his case until he had shown that the customs official's claims were utter nonsense.

It was after her marriage, and even more so after her retirement from Faber & Faber, that she won fame as a poetess, sensitive, fresh and original—a writer whose work was independent of schools and recognized for its distinction.

Some ten years passed, during which Eliot was served by a succession of secretaries. Then, about 1950, the post again fell vacant, and among some six or seven candidates Eliot's choice fell on an engaging girl from Yorkshire who had been private secretary to Charles Morgan. This in itself was no recommendation to Tom, who like Hayward, much distrusted Morgan's work. But this young lady, whose father, James Fletcher, was the manager of an insurance office, had gone to school with a cousin of mine, Hilary Quelch, who told me that she had always been noticed at school for her cheerful character and intellectual and physical competence. Even at Queen Anne's School, Caversham, Valerie Fletcher had one remarkable ambition, which was to become secretary to a celebrated writer. By securing her post with Charles Morgan, she had gratified her schoolgirl wish. But at Caversham she had been more deeply interested in T. S. Eliot than Charles Morgan, and great was her joy when she found that Eliot required a secretary: greater still when she herself was appointed to the job. It was the fulfilment of years of intent admiration for his works.

Whenever one called on Tom at 24 Russell Square, one would be aware of her pleasant personality, her air of unassuming competence. Tom's old friends from America found that she knew all about them. In the course of time she became the one person who knew every detail of his affairs.

Seven years did Miss Fletcher serve her principal in ever greater efficiency. None of us who saw her bringing the tea into his office ever thought of her as a particular friend, but how easy it is for any secretary to fall in love with her principal; and even in his sixties, Tom was not only the great celebrity of the age but a very attractive man with whom several women had fallen in love. Perhaps it was inevitable that before very long his devoted secretary should take her place among them; and then gradually the atmosphere was diffused, and he felt something quite particular for her. But in the meanwhile there were his bonds in Chelsea, and he could hardly think that a handsome and healthy young lady of thirty would wish to espouse an invalid of sixty-eight, so he said nothing.[2]

But it so happened that among his most intimate friends was a lady who recognized that in Cheyne Walk he was living under an increasing strain, that his twelve years' companionship with John Hayward was somehow wearing him out, and that the solution of his problem was to admit his secret love for his secretary. So she took the step of inviting Tom and Miss Fletcher to stay with her together, and in this way elicited his avowal.

Just how their love grew has been described metaphorically in Tom's last play, staged and published in 1958–1959, *The Elder Statesman*. When at last he began to return her affection the whole office gradually became aware of it. People who are in love radiate their bliss, and those who are closest to them become aware of their happiness and guess the reason why. Yet they kept a complete secret of their engagement: not a word of it was divulged except to her parents, one friend of hers, Tom's solicitor Gordon Higginson, and apparently Geoffrey Faber and the friend in whose house the proposal had been made.

He simply could not face a public disclosure, with all the sadness that it meant for Hayward, and this was why the marriage was prepared as secretly as if it had been a conspiracy. Yet the time must come for him to leave Hayward. On 9 January 1957, the day before his wedding, he came back to the flat for what was to be the very last time. He had firmly resolved not to breathe a word of his good news to Hayward.[3] But to the French housekeeper he explained that he was going away on a holiday and ended with the words: "Adieu, Madame," a greeting which naturally puzzled her. "Mais, Monsieur, pourquoi m'avez-vous dit 'adieu'?" she asked him in incredulous surprise; but Eliot turned on his heel and left the house.

It was not until the next day, when for the second time in his life he was indissolubly sealed in the bonds of matrimony, that he telephoned the news to the man who, only the previous day, had been his hospitable companion. "I am delighted. But why didn't you tell me before?" was Hayward's obvious reaction. And the reply was equally to be expected: "Well, John, I thought you would be so cross."

It so happened that on the afternoon of that day Hayward's nephews and nieces and their parents arrived for the Christmas tea-party to which he always invited them. Once inside the flat they found the French housekeeper unable to control her amazement and John Hayward greeting them with the words: "Can you believe what has happened? Mr. Eliot has eloped with his secretary!"

This, as Eliot had guessed, was a bitter blow to John Hayward. The full and exact circumstances of their twelve years' companionship and abrupt separation still await patient analysis,[4] and at times the evidence surrounding the incident may appear somewhat contradictory. Indeed, it is even possible that through the long months and years of Eliot's friendship with Miss Fletcher, the crippled invalid—his senses and intuitions heightened by incurable infirmity—suspected that a romance was gradually coming to fruition between Eliot and his secretary. If so, the news could hardly have come as a complete surprise. But it came with all the force of irreversible finality; it meant that their friendship of more than thirty years' standing was extinguished with scarcely a word of parting gratitude; it meant that, except for one chance meeting at an embassy, Eliot and Hayward were never to meet again.

And what of the wedding which had so suddenly parted the two friends? Some time before his disappearance from Cheyne Walk, Tom had consulted his solicitor, asking him to arrange a ceremony which should be taken to every extreme of secrecy. Gordon Higginson's great friend in undergraduate days at Balliol College, Oxford, had been C. P. Wright, now a clergyman of the Church of England and Vicar (until 1960) of St. Barnabas's Church, Addison Road, Kensington. Higginson naturally turned to him, and so it came about that though neither Eliot nor Miss Fletcher lived in the parish of St. Barnabas, they still chose its rather gloomy church as the place of their wedding. It is the normal practice in the Church of England for banns to be called on three consecutive Sundays, giving notice to the congregation that such-and-such a bachelor, spinster, widower or widow of the parish is intending to be married. It is also the custom of the Anglican Church that marriages should be celebrated within the hours of eight o'clock in the morning and six in the evening. But Tom would have nothing of this. Not only did he wish to be married in an unknown church, he wished no outsider to have foreknowledge of his intention, and he particularly hoped that it might be possible for him to be married in the dark—so as to ensure complete privacy. But in order for all this to be possible, a special licence was required of the Achbishop of Canterbury, enabling weddings to take place at any time and in any place. The time chosen for the wedding at St. Barnabas was 6:30 A.M.

So, not long after six in the morning, Tom was waiting at St. Barnabas's Church with his best man, Gordon Higginson, when at the appointed time Miss Fletcher's parents brought her in through the dark door to receive the Church's blessing on her union with T. S. Eliot.

Just before he was married, the bridegroom had made the most astonishing of discoveries: that the Parisian hero of his youth, Jules Laforgue, had been married in precisely the same church.[5] Nor was that the only odd coincidence about this wedding in the dark. Before the morning dawned over grey Kensington, the solicitor's clerical friend took the bridal party to breakfast with him at his home, 10 Kensington Church Walk, and this was exactly the house where over forty years before Eliot, on first arriving in England, had walked into the narrow, dingy parlour of Ezra Pound.

Although so many of the circumstances surrounding this marriage may seem unusual to the casual observer, it was characteristic of Tom Eliot. The psychological idiosyncrasy which always tried to keep his private life from the knowledge of other people was as strong when he was approaching the age of seventy as when he was a shy undergraduate at Harvard. His first marriage was a secret; his baptism took place behind locked doors; and now, having kept secret his preparations for his second marriage, he did everything possible to withhold it from public knowledge: if he could not have the doors of the church locked, he at least arranged for the service to be before daylight and in an unfamiliar church.

Hayward never visited the Eliots at the flat to which they moved at Kensington Court Gardens. Admittedly, it was extremely difficult for him to move, even in the early years of Tom's marriage to Miss Fletcher; and in the last years of the poet's life it would have been impossible for Hayward to go there at all. But neither did the Eliots ever visit him. It was as if the "hard gemlike flame" of their friendship had been nonchalantly snuffed out. Though there were still many friends (such as John Carter, Catherine Porteous, Janet Adam Smith and Noel Blakiston) to wheel him in his invalid chair, it was inevitable that he should be more and more confined to his own sitting-room, but one day he did accept an invitation to a reception at the French Embassy in honour of the retiring Ambassador, Monsieur Jean Chauvel.[6] He had not been there very long before (in his distinctly acidulous phrase) "the Eliots staged one of their appearances." Soon the two old friends were engaged in deep conversation, and Tom actually repeated to Hayward the invitation he had so often sent him over the telephone, but Hayward replied: "No, I made a special exception in this case. It is months since I have been to anybody's house, but I wanted to come and say goodbye to the Ambassador, who has been so kind to me."

"Ah," said Tom, "you have energy enough to come to the Embassy, but not enough to come to see me."

"No," was Hayward's final answer. "I have told you that I am simply going nowhere else."

"But what about all the other years when you didn't come?" Tom insisted.

If only the Eliots had visited him, and he had seen that com-

munion of heart with heart which embraced every sphere of
their married life! If only he could have seen what generosity
there was in Valerie's devotion to Tom! If only they could
have shown by what arts of sacrifice each filled the other's
life so completely! In the house of Tom's sister-in-law Theresa
I have seen a photograph in which he and his wife gaze into
the camera cheek to cheek, with an expression on their faces
that reflected more than mere contentment: it was radiance.
As I travelled about America among his friends and relations,
all told me how fully they admired her. She combined the
holiness of the heart's affection with the solicitude of the
perfect nurse.

It was a relation where each could say to the other: "cor ad
cor loquitur," a "melting of midwinter spring" (in the phrase
of Cecil Day Lewis) which not only provided Tom with an
old age of undreamed-of happiness but actually gave rise to
The Elder Statesman.

The first few pages of *The Elder Statesman* are nothing
more than a love scene in which, with a little *badinage* about
shopping and going to a restaurant, Charles Hemington and
Monica Claverton-Perry declare their mutual love. Neither is
just the one individual because besides each being there is the
new transforming reality of love itself. It transmutes the one
into the other, and all things around them seem newly created.
To the poet and his bride the play was rich in special evoca-
tions which would recall and recreate the dawning bliss which
they had come to share. But though the poet could depict his
own feelings for his bride when writing of the subtle relationship of Charles and Monica, he was also the person he had
been before they could express and declare their mutual love.

In Claverton Eliot voices the cynicism which was still his at the height of his literary success. He often asked himself what it meant and how long it would last. There had been a wealth of tribute for his seventieth birthday, most important of all, the volume of essays[7] which a young and enthusiastic admirer, Neville Braybrooke, had been preparing months in advance to coincide with the actual date of his anniversary. As Tom himself told me, it was all very gratifying and he particularly appreciated the way in which a militant agnostic like Harold Nicolson spoke with such warm gratitude of the consolations which he owed to Eliot.[8]

Although *The Elder Statesman* was staged at Edinburgh just over a month before his seventieth anniversary, he was fully aware of the tributes that were being collected in his honour, and he could not help feeling that they were rather like obituary notices. If he were to die ten years later, would there still be the same general esteem? He vaguely sensed that he no longer had the full admiration of younger people, who were beginning to think him too subtle and prim. They preferred something tougher and more down to earth, like Dylan Thomas, Robert Graves or Robert Lowell. If now, as his heart warned him, he were to leave the literary scene, having revised his critical ideas to the point where reading his earlier essays had become a painful experience for him, just where would he be?

He had always entertained a doubt whether his reputation was not absurdly exaggerated. He could well realize what a Claverton would feel as he retired from active politics to the House of Lords and read the formal tributes to one who had been a success both in business and in the House of Commons. He could put many passing reflections of his own onto the lips of Claverton as he was about to be taken to his convalescent home, not to convalesce but to reach the conclusions of a man who had gained a whole world of fame and influence, and at the same time had lost his health.

Did not Eliot show a curious nervousness at the idea that people should wish to read his own life story into his poems and plays? And yet this is what so many people were doing with this "invisible poet," as Hugh Kenner called him.[9] In truth, he was both invisible and self-revealed to the world. His poems were immensely personal. His readers were feeling into them a constant self-confession. They sensed that here was a man of warm affection, yet deeply acquainted with grief. Nevertheless, nothing in the poems and plays was photographically copied from real life. The tone of self-confession was authentic enough, but it had been overlaid with a convincing apparatus of objectivity.

The last long speech of Lord Claverton expresses the essence of Eliot's philosophy at the consummation of his days. He was at peace, he said, because he had confessed what was wrong with him and was therefore in a position to be freed from it. "If we say that we have no sin, we deceive ourselves, and the truth is not in us: but, if we confess our sins, He is faithful and just to forgive us our sins, and to cleanse us from all unrighteousness." He had at last realized the various subterfuges by which he had lapsed through life, a man successful and admired. Now at last he had come to see what love really is; it is so easy for people to think they know.

Such is the whole problem which underlies the last Eliot play. It is the necessity of finding out what we really are so that we may be loved for what we are. But what Tom Eliot was always doing was to escape into his simple self with all his little jokes and relaxations: his tea-drinking, his practical jokes, his rummy, slippery Ann and poker; and his Conan Doyle, Simeon, Wilkie Collins, and the taste for Maurice Leblanc's stories of Arséne Lupin which he shared with Graham Greene. He was not the supreme pontiff of literature. He was not the reincarnation of Shakespeare and Dante; and even if he had been, he would still have been a man of frail flesh and blood. Let him go to Jamaica with a new beach suit and a new pair of pyjamas. Let him eat his delicious meal at the Café Royal. Let him just relax and follow his own devices and find that in doing so he proved himself an exemplary husband. That was the exciting thing, and so the play ends with Lord Claverton going off to die a very different man from what he had been in time past.

Death might not have been very far off for Eliot, but with his wife beside him the prospect in every direction was secure. He and Valerie were fixed in the certainty of love at least. Thus, it was in wedded love made blissful that the now weary and disillusioned author of *The Waste Land* came to the consummation he had always desired. Nothing is more revealing, in this connection, than the play's dedication to Valerie. The impression with which it leaves us is that in these eleven lines Eliot is making an all too inadequate return for the gift of a perfect wife.

CHAPTER

19

The End of Life

O NE of the most interesting tasks in which Eliot took part
in his later years was to sit on the Commission for the
Revised Psalter of the Book of Common Prayer (1958–1963).
The chairman of this group was Dr. Donald Coggan, Bishop
of Bradford until 1961 and subsequently Archbishop of York.
Its other members were the then Bishop of Ripon, G. A.
Chase, who continued to serve on it after resigning his see in
1959; the organist of St. Paul's Cathedral, John Dykes Bower,
who was to advise his colleagues about suiting phrases to
music; G. H. Knight, Director of the Royal School of Church
Music; David Winton Thomas, Regius Professor of Hebrew at
Cambridge; C. S. Lewis, Professor of Medieval and Renaissance English at Cambridge; and Eliot.

The object of this distinguished group of men was to revise
the text of the psalms, eliminating obscurities and errors of
translation yet retaining as far as was possible the character,
style and rhythm of Bishop Coverdale's version, which four
centuries of experience had proved so suitable to Anglican

worship. For, throughout the centuries, the Prayer Book of the Church of England had preferred to retain Bishop Coverdale's translation of the psalms, rather than adopt the rendering of the Authorized Version of the Bible, completed in 1611. The Commission for the Revised Psalter never at any time intended to produce a new translation of the Hebrew texts.

This, of course, was very different from what the then Bishop of Winchester (Alwyn Williams) and others were doing in *The New English Bible*, where a fresh translation of the Bible was attempted, and has only recently been completed.

The Commission soon found that Coverdale had not been content with the Hebrew he read, but had added words and phrases of his own; nevertheless, their aim was to accord with the Coverdale tradition in both vocabulary and syntax, and they could not hope to improve on its rhythm. They sought to retain harmony and style, even at the expense of simplicity. They modernized archaisms such as "fain" for "gladly" and "leasing" for "lying." If necessary, they gave different English renderings for the same Hebrew word. Everywhere they considered what the requirements of music would be, and rejected any phrase which would be difficult to sing. They used inverted commas to denote direct speech. Recognizing how older people loved what they were used to, they were still determined never to tolerate phrases that would be meaningless or even repellent to those who did not know them.

Generally, the meeting place of the Commission was the Archbishop of Canterbury's London residence, Lambeth Palace. C. S. Lewis took a very active part in their deliberations; but Eliot seldom spoke except to plead for the retention of an old phrase. In the twenty-third Psalm generations of Englishmen had loved Coverdale's old phrase: "Though I walk through the valley of the shadow of death, I will fear no evil." The Hebrew original could not be taken to mean more than "the valley of deep darkness," but Eliot was insistent about keeping the traditional phrase, and so he was whenever a similar case occurred.

This takes us far into the pattern of Eliot's piety. As Patrick McLaughlin said to me, his had been the literary approach— and literary it always remained. It was phrases which, for him, opened the gate onto the heavenly path.

The last meeting of the Commission was held at Bishopthorpe, the seat of the Archbishop of York, in October 1963. At that time Tom and Valerie were staying, as they did every summer or fall, with her parents in Leeds, and from there she drove him over to York. All the members of the Commission stayed at Bishopthorpe, but as soon as their last meeting was over, there was Valerie with the car to drive him back to her parents' home. It was the Archbishop of York who told me this and, in fact, who gave me his general impression of Tom's attitude and appearance at that last meeting. He told me Eliot looked so frail that he might have collapsed at any moment.

It was in the middle of the work of the Commission for the Revised Psalter that *The New English Bible*, or rather the New Testament part of it, was brought out in the fall of 1961. Eliot was invited to review it in *The Sunday Telegraph*, which paid him £250 to do so (half of which, so his Vicar told me, he immediately gave to his parish church). In his review, he began by making it clear that he was not concerned with matters of doctrine or accuracy of translation, but merely with questions of style.

This review[1] is one of the most pungent things he ever

wrote. He referred to an article in *The Times Literary Supplement* quoting Dr. C. H. Dodd's statement that this version of the New Testament was intended for people who do not go to Church, for those unfamiliar with English literary tradition, and for churchgoers who care more for the meaning of the Bible than for the sound of soothing old phrases.

To Eliot, on the other hand, *The New English Bible* seemed symptomatic of the decay of the English language. If it were used for religious services, it would become an active agent of decadence: the life of sacred writing is in the music of the spoken word. He did not find much music in this version, and definitely thought of it as a change for the worse. It was intended to suit modern conditions, but Eliot asked what exactly is contemporary writing? Is it the best contemporary writers, and, if so, how are we to decide who those are? If it was meant to be colloquial, then one must decide whether it was the colloquial style of educated or uneducated people—and, if educated, to what degree of education.

He ridiculed the exchange of the word "destroy" for "extirpate," or of the well-known phrase (it has become part of the idiomatic language) "borne the burden and heat of the day" for "sweated the whole day long in the blazing sun."[2] But he fastened with his sharpest irony on the new phrase "do not feed your pearls to pigs." Why substitute this, he asked, for "neither cast ye your pearls before swine"? "Swine" is a common enough word to country people, and in town and country alike it is still used as an insult. But what was worse still was that the new phrase plainly implied that pigs were to be given pearls as pig food, which after all is the rankest nonsense. It is quite evident that pigs cannot be nourished on pearls, but they might conceivably have appreciated the sight of them.

Eliot emphasized that the Authorized Version of 1611 came from an age of the greatest literary genius, and has furnished ever since a model of English prose. It would have been unreasonable to expect a comparable achievement in the year 1962, for there were fewer great writers of English in the mid-twentieth century than in the time of Shakespeare and Ben Jonson. Nevertheless, it could legitimately have been expected that the combined work of the various distinguished scholars should be dignified, though mediocre. Yet what Eliot found himself confronted with was a translation astonishing in its pedantry, vulgarity and triviality, so much so that he was tempted to wonder what possible future there could be for the English language.

It struck the attention of countless people that *The New English Bible,* which was a tremendous success in selling three million copies almost immediately, found its rival that year in Penguin's unexpurgated edition of *Lady Chatterley's Lover,* which also sold three million copies. Did the same people read both? Or did the different publishers cater for publics as different as those who dope themselves nightly on television? The Bishop of Winchester was naturally nettled at what Eliot had said about the vulgar, the trivial and the pedantic—none of which things one quite expects from a man who had been a Fellow of All Souls, Headmaster of Winchester College, and Dean of Christ Church before taking his place on the bench of bishops. But never was Tom more ruthless than when his lash fell on the tender flesh of Anglicans who, in his view, had strayed from the right path—whether of doctrine and worship, as with the Church of South India scheme, or above all (as in this case) when it was a question of the true interpretation of words.

I agree with Tom entirely in his detestation of *The New English Bible*. I was never one of those who accepted as their first commandment: "Thou shalt worship the Lord thy Dodd, and him only shalt thou serve," any more than I accepted the second: "Thou shalt love thy Niebuhr as thyself." But I disagree with him just as strongly about the other favourite book of that season, and I would condemn his attitude towards the unexpurgated edition of *Lady Chatterley's Lover* in exactly the same terms that he applied to Bishop Williams and Dr. Dodd.

In 1961 the Crown Prosecutor indicted the publishers of *Lady Chatterley's Lover* and, thinking that to read one or two passages from the book would convince any jury of its indecency, decided not to call a single witness; whereas the defense called no less than thirty-six, including persons as distinguished as Mr. Norman St. John-Stevas, Dame Rebecca West, Professor Richard Hoggart, Dame Helen Gardner and Dr. John Robinson (at that time the universally known Bishop of Woolwich). Impressed by such evidence, the jury came out in favour of what many thought is one of the most immoral and degrading books ever to have been published in the British Isles. The theme is, of course, adultery: the adultery of a woman of title with her impotent husband's gamekeeper; as if that were not daring enough at the time, Lawrence deals with the affair in terms which until then had been consistently forbidden in books.

Lawrence's most extreme audacity, however, lay in the fact that Connie Chatterley's relationship with her husband's gamekeeper was not adultery at all—which, after all, is not a crime in the eyes of the law. In 1967 the combined Houses of Parliament passed an act permitting sexual relationships between consenting adult males; but even today the law does not allow a man to engage in unnatural vice with a woman. Thus, as the Warden of All Souls has conclusively shown,[3] the acme of the mutual passion between Connie Chatterley and Oliver Mellors was, in fact, criminal.

As for Tom's attitude, it was known only to the counsel for the defense that, if necessary, he too would appear on the side of Dame Helen. As matters turned out, however, the evidence of the first three witnesses was so compelling that he did not need to be called. How can such a readiness to rush to the aid of *Lady Chatterley's Lover* be reconciled with his particular rectitude in moral and religious matters? In my own view, Eliot regarded self-righteousness as so much worse than sexual crudity that, although he found much in both Lawrence and Yeats distasteful if not deplorable, he still preferred unveiled nakedness to the drapery of prudery. His support of *Lady Chatterley's Lover* was a counterpart to his passionate approval of *Bubu de Montparnasse, Ulysses* and a third novel which he deeply admired: *Tropic of Cancer,* by Henry Miller.

Long before his second marriage, Tom had already partially lost the use of his lungs, suffering as he was from chronic bronchitis. With time, however, his bronchitis became more serious. The air sacs of the lungs became hardened, forming fixed *bullae* which could not be emptied. The effective surface for what doctors call the gas exchange (that is to say, the oxygenation of the blood) became progressively reduced, while the alveoli of the lungs dilated. The result was that Tom suffered in a way akin to asthma. The tubes of his lungs were

indeed open, but the lungs themselves could no longer exchange the carbon dioxide in the blood for revivifying oxygen.
This condition is known as emphysema.

With every year that went by, in the last ten years or so of
his life, Tom became more and more dependent not only on
the bright sunshine of Nassau, Morocco or Barbados, but on
every type of medication which could provide his failing
organs and tissues with what nature had ceased to provide.
People have told me how, even before he married, he went
about with many different bottles of medicine: they were apt
to call him a hypochondriac.[4] But he was nothing of the kind.
He was merely following the orders of competent specialists,
whose prescriptions could offer some minimal atonement for
what his lungs were failing to obtain from the living air.

Whenever possible, therefore, Tom and Valerie would
escape from the damp chill, the fogs, frosts and snow of wintry
London to enjoy a period of invigorating sunshine, and since
his journeys usually took him in the direction of Jamaica or
the West Indies he was able to make many visits to the United
States in his declining years. Although his first wedding anniversary (10 January 1958) was spent at home, I recall that his
second was spent at Nassau, which was also his retreat for the
winter months of 1963–1964, the last occasion on which he
visited America. He was too ill to chase the sun on his sixth
wedding anniversary, but I recall that in the previous year he
was in Barbados.

In fact, every year from 1960 to 1963 took Tom back to
the United States, where he was engaged in lectures and poetry
readings. He and Valerie always stayed for a while in a hotel
at Cambridge, Massachusetts, so that they could see their
sister-in-law Theresa and other old friends. They would even

join Theresa Eliot for Christmas dinner. In New York, however, they made their home with Margot Cohn; and as they stayed with her on no less than five different occasions, she takes her own place in this memoir.

Born and brought up in Philadelphia, Marguerite (Margot) Arnauld married Louis Henry Cohn in 1930. He had gone over to France at the outbreak of the First World War, had rapidly been given French citizenship, and served on the staff of General Mangin. While in France, he met and made friends with Hilaire Belloc. When the war was over, he returned to America where he became a distinguished bookseller, the owner of House of Books Inc., dealing in manuscripts and rare editions. In due time he became Belloc's foremost bibliographer, as also of John Galsworthy, whom he introduced to Scribner's. By the time the Eliots met her, her husband was already dead and she had taken on the running of the business herself.

Margot Cohn had a special gift of sympathy and friendship which enabled her to make friends easily. Hardly had she met Tom and Valerie than she warmed their hearts by her generosity of feeling. In a short time she had offered them the use of her New York flat, but this they would only accept if she also remained in it. There they could come whenever it pleased them; it saved them an infinity of expense, and it had just the sort of easy atmosphere they appreciated.

She told me that when Tom came over for the winter of 1961–1962, the fog was so bad in New York that he had to leave her flat and go into a hospital. Another time, when their stay in New York was more prolonged, Sheila Cuddahy of Scribner's arranged for them to be made members of the River Club. Whenever they arrived for a visit, their first question was always an inquiry about her servant: "How is Marie?" They had the joy of children in buying their Christmas presents, and Valerie loved to buy Tom's beach clothes for the West Indies. What particularly delighted their hostess was the way in which Tom, like Robert Frost before him, would go to the Metropolitan Museum to read to the Young Men's Hebrew Association.

Once when Tom was ill at Mrs. Cohn's flat, he was examined by a brother-in-law of hers who was a doctor. The doctor was appalled to see how every organ in his patient's body had been affected by lung diseases. Tom was obliged to take cortisone.

Two other close American friends in the latter years of the poet's life were W. T. Levy and his mother Florence. Levy had first met Eliot in 1948, during the time he was gathering material in London for a dissertation on the Dorset poet William Barnes. Later he studied at the Union Theological Seminary, New York, and in 1953 was ordained into the Episcopalian priesthood but still continued to teach English literature at the City College of New York. Several times both before and after his marriage, Tom Eliot lunched with the Levys during visits to New York, usually after a Sunday morning service, but later he was too tired to accept their invitations and instead asked them to lunch or dine with him at the River Club. This hospitality was extended to the Levys on two occasions (2 January 1962 and 23 December 1963[5]), and William Levy has left a touching record of Tom's failing health: barely able to walk, his energies exhausted, his complexion ashen, his voice almost inaudible. After the first of these visits, Levy wondered whether he would ever see Eliot again.

With the failing of his bodily strength, religion occupied a greater and greater place in Tom's life. It is significant that William Levy himself was a clergyman of the Episcopalian Church. Back in London, the church of St. Simon's, Kentish Town, where for over twenty years he had found the solace of spiritual guidance, still remained the centre of his confessional life. But now it was Father Hillier, not Father Bacon, who was Tom's confessor. Father Hillier was quick to notice the profound change that came over Tom after his marriage: he had exchanged strain for serenity. One could see that at the first glance, and how much simpler it made the problems of his spiritual life.

As long as he had strength to do so, he made his pilgrimage to St. Simon's every two months. But in December 1962 he fell seriously ill, and was treated with continuous oxygen for five weeks at Brompton Hospital. In a letter he wrote me almost ten months after his return home,[6] he mentioned that he had been unwell ever since, was still only in the convalescent stage, but was just about to leave for a holiday of sunshine. It was now becoming impossible for him to keep up the little journeys to Kentish Town, with his intense appreciation of St. Simon's Church and his visits to Father Hillier's elegantly furnished vicarage. He then began to send a car for Father Hillier, who would come to see him at his own home in Kensington Court Gardens, arriving in the latter half of the morning, staying to lunch and being driven back again in the course of the afternoon.

The friendship between Tom and Groucho Marx was one of the special things which Mrs. Cohn told me about when I was with her in New York, and I hoped therefore that in this memoir it would be a complete novelty. But the Groucho letters were published in November 1967;[7] my reference to them must therefore be no more than those one or two strokes without which something would still be lacking in my portrait of Tom.

Kinglsey Amis has written to me that he remembers the poet standing in a long queue waiting for the autograph of Charlie Chaplin. And indeed, from the time of Marie Lloyd to that of Groucho Marx, Tom always had a profound affection for public entertainers. The friendship with Groucho began when Tom wrote him a fan letter, after which they exchanged photographs. "He is a master of nonsense," Tom told William Levy,[8] and he especially admired *A Night at the Opera*. So keen was his admiration that he even placed the photo of Groucho alongside those of Goethe, Yeats and Valéry which were always so noticeable in his office.[9] By 16 October 1963 the signature was: "Ever yours, Tom."[10] Within eight months Groucho had arrived in London, and Tom was told that a photograph of the comedian was in the newspapers with a note to say that Groucho had come to see him; this, said Tom,[11] made its due impression on the shopkeepers in the vicinity of Kensington Court Gardens, and especially on Costanzo, the greengrocer across the street.

So, on 6 June 1964, Groucho and his wife arrived at Kensington Court Gardens in a car ordered for them by their host. They found him lean and stooping, things which they naturally associated with old age and illness, and there was the charming fact that Valerie's eyes filled with adoration every time she looked at her husband. A butler served the meal, but Tom himself poured out the wine with a grace all his own. The evening had to be short because the host, dear and charming as they found him, was evidently unequal to entertaining

anybody for long. The extrovert comedian and the sophisticated poet were in immediate harmony—especially when they
discovered that they had three pleasures in common: cigars,
cats and puns.[12]

It was during the fall of 1964 that Tom paid the last of his
regular visits to the home of his parents-in-law, Mr. and Mrs.
James Fletcher of Leeds. He was never happier than in the
combined company of Valerie and her parents; and as he was
of more or less the same generation as they, she was equally
devoted in her attentions to all. The more enfeebled Tom
became, the more she adored him. It was this which made him
feel in his old age that he was happier than he had ever dreamed
he would be.

This visit to the Fletchers was the last time he went away
from his own home. The inexorable advance of emphysema
made it impossible for him to travel to the West Indies; it was
also impossible for him to receive the Medal of Freedom from
the hands of President Lyndon Johnson.[13] Clearly, he had only
a few weeks to live. The friends who visited him now were
very few in number, and none of them could stay for more
than an hour or so. To one of them he said, when asked how
he was feeling: "up and down," adding a moment later, "down
and up." And this is true of all who endure a protracted death:
one can never tell from one day to the next whether there will
be a rally. In these last months Father Jennings, who in 1957
had succeeded Eric Cheetham as Vicar of St. Stephen's, regularly came to celebrate Holy Communion at Eliot's home, now
that he even lacked the strength to attend Mass or Parochial
Church Council meetings.

On Christmas Day 1964 he was sitting by the fire when
Allen Tate came to see him for the last time. After that visit,

his strength rapidly failed and he was no more able to rise
from his bed than in those stormy days almost seven years before (1958) when he and Valerie were staying with friends of
mine in Tangiers. Then, of course, he had recovered without
much difficulty and a few days later was coming to visit me in
that delightful little palace where I was the guest of the Moroc-
can Government. But this time there was no recovery. Valerie
had to give him more and more oxygen as his breathing became
more laboured, and on 4 January 1965 the end came.

A few years later the body was cremated at Golders Green.
The tiny urn containing the ashes was later taken,[14] as he had
directed, to that corner of St. Michael's Church, East Coker,
which he himself had chosen for them; and above his remains
stands the memorial: "Of your Charity pray for the repose of
the soul of Thomas Stearns Eliot, Poet."

Exactly four weeks after the poet's death, a memorial service
was held on 4 February 1965 in Westminster Abbey,[15] which
Anthony Lewis, the London correspondent of *The New York
Times*, said was a fitting scene to commemorate the tall, spare
American who was at once a revolutionary poet and an English
traditionalist. What was especially noticeable about the gathering was the number of young people who were present, and
Frank Morley said that this showed Eliot's power of touching
many a heart. The Queen was, of course, represented, as were
the Prime Minister and President Lyndon Johnson. The oldest
person there was Ezra Pound; his mental powers were no
longer very acute but he understood that he must pay the
tribute of his presence to one who had actually called him a
better poet than himself. Among English people present were
Dame Peggy Ashcroft, Stephen Spender, Christopher Fry,

and a man of Eliot's own stature in the world of creative art, the sculptor Henry Moore.

A statement from the White House was read aloud. "The President wishes to pay tribute to a poet and playwright who had a profound impact on his times and who achieved distinction on both sides of the Atlantic." The Dean of Westminster presided. The lesson was read by Peter Du Sautoy, vice-chairman of Faber & Faber; Sir Alec Guinness, who had acted the part of Sir Henry Harcourt-Reilly in the original production of *The Cocktail Party*, read from *A Song for Simeon*, *Ash-Wednesday*, *East Coker*, *The Dry Salvages* and *Little Gidding*. Among the words he recited were: "prayer, observance, discipline, thought and action";[16] and Anthony Lewis, as he listened, felt how much they expressed of the aims of Eliot, who had often quoted Mary Queen of Scots' words at Fotheringhay: "In my end is my beginning."[17]

Two years to the day[18] after Eliot's death, yet another memorial gathering was seen in Westminster Abbey. This was in connection with the stone placed in the floor of the Abbey in his memory, and when I went to see it, I was struck by the benignity of the bust of Longfellow close by. Eliot and Longfellow: each a lover of Dante, and each so representative of his age, the two Americans whom Westminster rightly chooses to honour among England's own immortals.

Acknowledgments

Much help has been given to Robert Sencourt and myself in the tasks of writing and editing this volume. I owe a particular debt of gratitude to the family of the poet's first wife, who have elucidated and corrected many details relating to Vivienne Eliot. I am also grateful to Mrs. Henry Ware Eliot, the poet's sister-in-law; and Mrs. Eleanor Hinkley, the Hon. Mrs. Hubert Howard and Rear-Admiral Samuel Eliot Morison, U.S.N.R., F.B.A., his cousins, for information concerning his life in America and Italy. Bertrand Russell added to the memories contained in volume II of his *Autobiography*, though his relationship with Eliot and Eliot's first wife remains fairly obscure. Further assistance has been most kindly provided by Mr. Eric Alport; Mr. Kingsley Amis; Mrs. I. G. Bartholomew; Mr. T. O. Beachcroft; the late Mrs. G. K. A. Bell; Professor Quentin Bell; Sir John Betjeman; Professor Brand Blanshard; Mr. Derek Bourgeois; Mr. Neville Braybrooke; Mr. H. C. T. Briden; Professor Cleanth Brooks; Mr. E. M. Browne; Mr. D. M. M. Carey; Lord David Cecil, C.H.; Mr. Jo Chiari; Mr. James K. Clement; Mrs. Richard Cobden-Sanderson; His

Grace the Archbishop of York; Mrs. L. H. Cohn; Mrs. Aubrey Coker; Mr. W. M. Dennis; Mr. A. J. F. Doulton; Mrs. Doris Eames; the late Mr. J. Eames; Mr. K. C. Elkins; Dr. Thomas Faber; Archbishop the Lord Fisher of Lambeth, G.C.V.O.; Miss M. E. Forwood; Professor Dame Helen Gardner, F.B.A.; The Rev. J. B. Gaskell; the late Hon. Catherine Gibbs; Mr. Stanley Gillam; Mr. Graham Greene, C.H.; Mr. A. D. Hawkins; the late Mr. John Hayward; Mr. Philip Headings; Dr. J. R. L. Highfield; The Rev. F. L. Hillier; Mr. Herbert Howarth; the Rt. Rev. Dr. L. S. Hunter; the Rev. Willfred Jennings; Mr. Hugh Kenner; Mr. Cecil King; Dr. R. M. F. Kojecký; Dr. Roger Little; Dr. Patrick Lovett; Mr. Patrick McLaughlin; Mr. John Meredith; Miss Hope Mirrlees; Miss Marianne Moore; Mr. F. V. Morley; Mr. Dermot Morrah; Mr. G. R. G. Mure; the late Mrs. Mabel Nelson; the Rev. J. C. S. Mias; the Rev. Canon Donald Nicholson; Mrs. R. H. Oakley; Mrs. A. J. Parker; Mrs. I. M. Parsons; the Rt. Hon. Sir Kenneth Pickthorn, Bt.; Professor Dr. Josef Pieper; M. Roger Pierrot; Mrs. Robin Porteous; Princess Boris de Rachewiltz; Sir Alec Randall, K.C.M.G.; Mr. Maurice Reckitt; the late Sir Bruce Richmond; the Viscount Rothermere; Mrs. S. J. Russell; Mr. and Mrs. J. D. Straton-Ferrier; Mrs. William Temple; the Rev. Patrick Thompson; M. André Vagliano; Mrs. Igor Vinogradoff; the Rev. F. C. Westgarth; Mr. D. Pepys Whiteley; the Rt. Hon. Sir Henry Willink, Bt., Q.C.; Mr. B. R. Wilson; the Rev. C. P. Wright; and others who remain anonymous. But for their help, always so generously and spontaneously offered, Sencourt's narrative would have lacked something of the precision and balance demanded of any memoir.

I am grateful to the following for their kind permission to

quote copyright material: Mr. Cecil Day Lewis and Harper & Row, Publishers, Inc. for the part-stanzas from *At East Coker* printed at the head of this introduction; George Allen & Unwin Ltd. for most of the prologue to *The Autobiography of Bertrand Russell*; Mr. Richard Church for extracts from *The Voyage Home*; Eyre & Spottiswoode Ltd. for extracts from *Blasting and Bombardiering*, by the late P. Wyndham Lewis; Mrs. Nicolete Gray and the Macmillan Co. for five lines from the translation of Dante's *Purgatorio* by the late Laurence Binyon; Madame Catherine Guillaume for extracts from *Stepping Heavenward: a Record* and *Life for Life's Sake*, by the late Richard Aldington; the Trustees of the Hardy Estate and the Macmillan Co. for two years from the *Collected Poems* of the late Thomas Hardy; the Harvard University Press for an extract from *Three Philosophical Poets: Lucretius, Dante, and Goethe*, by the late George Santayana; Little, Brown and Co. Inc. for extracts from *Laughter in the Next Room*, by the late Sir Osbert Sitwell, Bt.; Rear-Admiral Samuel Eliot Morison, U.S.N.R., F.B.A. for extracts from his article *The Dry Salvages aud the Thacher Shipwreck*; Mrs. Dorothy Pound and New Directions Publishing corporation for extracts from *Drunken Helots and Mr. Eliot*, by Mr. Ezra Pound; and Mrs. (Bertha) Georgie Yeats, Mr. Michael Butler Yeats, Miss Anne Yeats and the Macmillan Co. for a stanza from the *Collected Poems* of the late W. B. Yeats.

Finally, I have a particular debt of gratitude to Mr. Graham Murrell, for some of the photographs.

D. A.

Notes

1. From *At East Coker*, in *The Whispering Roots and Other Poems*, by Cecil Day Lewis. Copyright © 1970 by Cecil Day Lewis. By permission of Harper & Row, Publishers, Inc.
2. Eliot was baptized into the Church of England on 29 June 1927; Sencourt holidayed with him in France a fortnight previously.
3. Eliot himself wrote: "Any book, any essay, any note in *Notes and Queries*, which produces a fact even of the lowest order about a work of art is a better piece of work than nine-tenths of the most pretentious critical journalism." ("The Function of Criticism," *The Criterion*, October 1923, p. 41.)
4. In a memorandum dated 30 September 1963 and attached to his will, Eliot is said to have written: "I do not wish my executors to facilitate or countenance the writing of any biography of me." Though attached to his will, this memorandum was not proved with it, however, and the first intimation of it came in a letter from Mr. Peter du Sautoy to *The Daily Telegraph* (23 July 1970).
5. B. L. Reid, *The Man from New York: John Quinn and his Friends*, Oxford 1968, p. 540.
6. Particularly *Noctes Binanianae*, written between 1933 and 1937 in conjunction with Sir Geoffrey Faber, Mr. John Hayward and Mr. Frank Morley, and privately published in 1939.
7. The text of this memoir is substantially Sencourt's own. I have sometimes added precision to the text; I have occasionally rearranged the sequence of paragraphs; and I have added the footnotes.

8. Originally Eliot's first wife was known as Vivienne, but later she preferred the abbreviated form of her Christian name. Throughout this book the spelling "Vivienne" has been adopted, for that was the name by which Eliot first knew her.

9. I owe this information to the kindness of Vivienne's brother, Maurice Haigh.

10. *Autobiography*, vol. II, London 1968, p. 56. It is a valuable insight when one realizes that the date of Eliot's marriage to Vivienne was only 26 June 1915.

11. Ibid., p. 58.

12. "A Note on the Verse of John Milton," *Essays and Studies by Members of the English Association*, 1936, pp. 32–40. Cf. *Milton*, London 1947.

13. *The Athenaeum*, 4 April 1919, pp. 136–137. *After Strange Gods*, London 1934, pp. 43–47. Cf. *Purpose*, July-December 1940, pp. 115–127, *The Poetry of W. B. Yeats*.

14. *The Use of Poetry and the Use of Criticism*, London 1933, pp. 88–98.

15. *After Strange Gods*, London 1934, pp. 47–48.

CHAPTER 1
An American Childhood

1. For more information on T. S. Eliot's family and early life, cf. H. Howarth: *Notes on Some Figures behind T. S. Eliot*, Boston 1964.

2. C. C. Eliot, "William Greenleaf Eliot, Minister, Educator," *Philanthropist*, Boston 1904.

3. *Complete Poems and Plays*, London 1969, pp. 107–108.

4. Cf. N. P. B. Braybrooke, "T. S. Eliot in the South Seas," in *T. S. Eliot: the Man and his Work* (ed. J. O. A. Tate), London 1967, pp. 382–388.

5. *Complete Poems and Plays*, London 1969, pp. 587–589.

6. London 1906.

7. I am extremely indebted to Rear Admiral S. E. Morison, U.S.N.R., F.B.A., for allowing me to quote so extensively from the text of his article "The Dry Salvages and the Thacher Shipwreck," published in *The American Neptune* in 1965 (cf. Ibid., pp. 234–235).

8. Ibid., pp. 235–236.

9. *Complete Poems and Plays*, London 1969, p. 184.

CHAPTER 2
Undergraduate Years at Harvard

1. S. E. Morison, *One Boy's Boston, 1887–1901*, Boston 1962.

2. E. N. Wharton, *Twelve Poems*, London 1926, p. 55.

3. *After Strange Gods*, London 1934, p. 40.
4. *Complete Poems and Plays*, London 1969, p. 603.
5. Ibid., pp. 54–55.
6. Ibid., pp. 13–17.
7. J. Davidson, *A Selection of his Poems*, London 1961, p. 74.
8. Ibid., pp. 72–73.
9. *Complete Poems and Plays*, London 1969, p. 596.
10. Ibid., pp. 590, 591.
11. Ibid., p. 598.
12. Ibid., p. 600.

CHAPTER 3
The Emerging Scholar

1. London 1899.
2. *Sartor Resartus*, Oxford 1913, p. 159.
3. Ibid., pp. 157–158.
4. A. W. Symons, *The Symbolist Movement in Literature*, London 1899, p. 105.
5. *Complete Poems and Plays*, London 1969, pp. 602, 603.
6. Eliot qualified for the degree of A.B. in 1909 and the initial post-graduate degree of A.M. in 1910.
7. Jean Verdenal, as Phlebas the Phoenician, has left a profound imprint on *The Waste Land*. Cf. J. Peter's thoughtful and constructive essay, "A New Interpretation of The Waste Land," *Essays in Criticism*, April 1969, pp. 140–164, and its almost equally valuable Postscript, pp. 165–175. In 1917 the volume of poems *Prufrock and Other Observations* was dedicated to Jean Verdenal.
8. C.-L. Philippe, *Bubu de Montparnasse*, Paris 1901. Philippe was also admired by Gide.
9. Cf. D. Barnes, *Nightwood*, London 1950, pp. 1–7.
10. London 1964.
11. For further information on Eliot's attitude towards F. H. Bradley, cf. *For Lancelot Andrewes*, London 1928, pp. 67–85.
12. Introduction to J. Pieper: *Leisure: the Basis of Culture*, London 1952, p. 13.
13. For a brief and clear evaluation of Eliot's thesis, cf. R. A. Wollheim, "Eliot and F. H. Bradley: an Account," in *Eliot in Perspective* (ed. G. Martin), London 1970, pp. 169–193.
14. *Knowledge and Experience in the Philosophy of F. H. Bradley*, London 1964, p. 10.
15. A. Wood, *Bertrand Russell: The Passionate Sceptic*, London 1957, p. 94.
16. Letter to Robert Sencourt, dated 22 July 1965, in the collection of Don-

ald Adamson. This letter contradicts Eliot's own statement of Russell's attitude towards himself (W. T. Levy, *Affectionately, T. S. Eliot*, New York 1968, p. 70).

17. Russell has made it plain, however, that at no time did Eliot agree with his philosophy (letter to Robert Sencourt in the collection of Donald Adamson).

18. *Complete Poems and Plays*, London 1969, p. 61.

19. Information kindly communicated by Mrs. Henry Ware Eliot.

CHAPTER 4
Eliot at Oxford

1. On 2 February 1913 Pound spoke to the St. John's College Essay Society on Dante's friend, the medieval poet and philosopher Guido Cavalcanti. Noel Stock gives a further account of this literary evening in his *Life of Ezra Pound*, London 1970, pp. 131–132. The "Mr. George" referred to on p. 132 is, in fact, Robert Sencourt, who changed his surname from George to Sencourt by deed-poll dated 17 November 1933.

2. I am deeply grateful to Eyre & Spottiswoode Ltd. for their generous permission to use extracts from the late P. Wyndham Lewis in this memoir. Cf. P. W. Lewis: *Blasting and Bombardiering*, London 1937, p. 283.

3. For Eliot's tribute to Miss Weaver, cf. *Encounter*, January 1962, p. 101.

4. Information kindly communicated by Dr. J. R. L. Highfield.

5. *Oxford University Roll of Service* (ed. E. S. Craig and W. M. Gibson), Oxford 1920, p. 79.

CHAPTER 5
The First Years of Marriage

1. Cf. P. V. B. Blanshard, "Eliot in Memory," *Yale Review*, Summer 1965, pp. 635–640.

2. 26 April 1915, a Monday, was only the second day of the Trinity Term, so presumably Eliot first met Vivienne during the Easter vacation.

3. Vivienne was born at Bury, in Lancashire, on 28 May 1888.

4. In 1915 Oxford's Trinity Term ended on 19 June. Eliot thus had a week in which to make preparations for his wedding.

5. Vivienne would not accompany Eliot to America—apparently because she was afraid of submarines (B. A. W. Russell, op. cit., vol. II, London 1968, p. 54).

6. Writing to John Quinn on 6 January 1919, Eliot explained that he chose to settle in England because it was more conducive than America to the production of literature (B. L. Reid, op. cit., p. 403).

7. However, on 1 April 1916 Eliot was apparently due to sail to America to take his viva at Harvard (ibid., p. 253, Ezra Pound to John Quinn, 16 March 1916).

8. B. A. W. Russell, op. cit., vol. II, London 1968, p. 19.

9. It is presumed that Russell dined with the newly married Eliots on 9 July 1915. Ibid., p. 54.

10. Ibid., p. 54.

11. Ibid., p. 19.

12. Lord Privy Seal 1916–1919 and 27th Earl of Crawford from 1913.

13. According to M. Holroyd (*Lytton Strachey: The Years of Achievement, 1910-1932*, London 1968, p. 364), Eliot and Strachey did not actually meet at Garsington until 12 May 1919, although they had met elsewhere some years previously.

14. B. A. W. Russell, op. cit., vol. II, London 1968, p. 25. Cf. ibid., vol. I, London 1967, p. 205: "We ceased to be lovers in 1916."

15. Ibid., vol. II, London 1968, pp. 25–26.

16. Ibid., vol. I, London 1967, p. 13. I am deeply grateful to the late Earl Russell, O.M., F.R.S., and to George Allen & Unwin Ltd. for generous permission to quote this passage.

17. Ibid., vol. II, London 1968, p. 55.

18. Ibid., p. 56.

19. Ibid., p. 58. This letter was probably written on 4 January 1916.

20. Ibid., p. 173.

21. Ibid., p. 174; T. S. Eliot to Bertrand Russell, 7 May 1925.

22. Mr. Grover Smith, editor of *Letters of Aldous Huxley* (London 1969) states that Vivienne was an ether-drinker (p. 232 n.). But this is emphatically disputed by her brother Maurice. Cf. the letter from Bertrand Russell to Robert Sencourt, dated 28 May 1968, in the collection of Donald Adamson.

23. Not five terms, as is often said. The Highgate records show that Eliot left the school in December 1916.

24. Cf. J. Betjeman, "The Usher of Highgate Junior School," in *T. S. Eliot: a Symposium*, edited by Tambimuttu and Richard March, London 1965, pp. 89–92.

25. W. T. Levy, op. cit., p. 26.

CHAPTER 6
Widening Horizons

1. Information kindly communicated by Mr. W. M. Dennis.

2. M. Holyroyd, op. cit., p. 364 n. This tour was made in or around June 1919.

3. Cf. B. L. Reid, op. cit., p. 489.

4. Ibid., p. 349–350.
5. Cf. ibid., p. 434; T. S. Eliot to John Quinn, 25 January 1920.
6. J. G. Fletcher, *Life is my Song,* Toronto 1937, p. 72.
7. Ibid., pp. 72–73.
8. P. W. Lewis, op. cit., p. 281.
9. Ibid., pp. 283–284.
10. "Drunken Helots and Mr. Eliot," *The Egoist,* June 1917, pp. 73–74, reprinted by kind permission of Dorothy Pound, Committee for Ezra Pound.
11. Cf. *The Egoist,* June 1917, p. 69.
12. Cf. J. R. Daniells, "T. S. Eliot and his Relation to T. E. Hulme," *The University of Toronto Quarterly,* April 1933, pp. 380–396.
13. Boston 1924.
14. B. L. Reid, op. cit., p. 349; T. S. Eliot to John Quinn, 4 March 1918.
15. *International Journal of Ethics,* January 1916, pp. 284–289.
16. Ibid., April 1916, pp. 426–427.
17. Ibid., October 1916, pp. 111–112.
18. Ibid., October 1916, pp. 115–117.
19. *The Monist,* October 1916, pp. 534–556, "The Development of Leibniz's Monadism"; pp. 566–576, "Leibniz's Monads and Bradley's Finite Centers."
20. *International Journal of Ethics,* July 1917, pp. 542–543.
21. Ibid., July 1917, p. 543.
22. Ibid., October 1917, pp. 137–138.
23. Cf. P. R. Headings, *T. S. Eliot,* New York 1964, pp. 31–38, 56–61, 70–95.
24. *The Egoist,* January 1918, pp. 1–2.
25. *The Egoist,* September 1918, pp. 105–106.
26. Ibid., December 1917, p. 165.
27. Bertrand Russell has denied that he directly introduced Eliot to Bloomsbury, though he admits that Eliot may have got to know some members of the Bloomsbury group through him (letter to Robert Sencourt in the collection of Donald Adamson).
28. L. S. Woolf, *Beginning Again,* London 1964, p. 244.
29. L. S. Woolf, *Downhill all the Way,* London 1967, p. 111.
30. M. Holroyd, *Lytton Strachey: The Unknown Years, 1880–1910,* London 1967, p. 404.
31. L. S. Woolf, *Beginning Again,* London 1964, p. 244.
32. In 1920.
33. F. O. S. Sitwell, *Laughter in the Next Room,* London 1949, pp. 32–33. My thanks are due to Little, Brown & Co. Inc. for their permission to quote from the American edition of Sir Osbert Sitwell's memoir.
34. Sir Osbert Sitwell succeeded to the family baronetcy in 1943.
35. On 9 December 1964.

36. E.g., *Marivaux*, spring 1919, pp. 80–85; "Some Notes on the Blank Verse of Christopher Marlowe," autumn 1919, pp. 194–199.
37. E.g. "A Brief Treatise on the Criticism of Poetry," March 1920, pp. 1–10.
38. B. Patmore, *My Friends When Young*, London 1968, p. 84.
39. Ibid., p. 85.
40. Ibid., pp. 86, 87.
41. Ibid., p. 86.
42. Ibid., p. 88.
43. Ibid., p. 90.

CHAPTER 7
James Joyce and Richard Aldington

1. Cf. L. S. Woolf, *Beginning Again*, London 1964, pp. 245–247.
2. *Horizon*, March 1941, pp. 173–175.
3. B. L. Reid, op. cit., p. 488.
4. P. W. Lewis, op. cit., pp. 270, 272–276, 286–289.
5. Eliot had spent his previous summer holiday in France—alone. Cf. M. Holroyd, *Lytton Strachey: The Years of Achievement, 1910–1932*, London 1968, p. 365.
6. P. W. Lewis, op. cit., pp. 293–294.
7. Indeed, writing on 9 May 1921 of his impression of Joyce in the previous year, Eliot informed Quinn that he liked Joyce, and found him charming (B. L. Reid, op. cit., p. 488).
8. "Ulysses, Order, and Myth," *The Dial*, November 1923, pp. 480–483.
9. There was further talk of Eliot's becoming literary editor of *The Nation and Athenaeum* in 1921 (cf. supra, p. 117), but the post was eventually filled by Leonard Woolf. Cf. M. Holroyd, *Lytton Stratchey: The Years of Achievement, 1910–1932*, London 1968, p. 352.
10. R. Aldington, *Life for Life's Sake*, London 1968, pp. 244–245. I am grateful to Madame Catherine Guillaume for allowing me to quote from her father, Richard Aldington.
11. Ibid., p. 245.
12. *Ben Jonson*.
13. R. T. Church, *The Voyage Home*, London 1964, pp. 57–59. I am grateful to Mr. Church for his kind permission to use this material.
14. R. Aldington, *Stepping Heavenward: A Record*, London 1931, pp. 28–53. I am grateful to Madame Catherine Guillaume for her kind permission to use this material.

CHAPTER 8
The Waste Land

1. Information kindly communicated by Mrs. Henry Ware Eliot.
2. Derby 1965.
3. *The Use of Poetry and the Use of Criticism*, London 1933, p. 106.
4. B. L. Reid, op. cit., p. 534; T. S. Eliot to John Quinn, 25 June 1922.
5. Ibid., p. 489, which implies that Eliot had begun to make jottings for it as early as 9 May 1921.
6. Dante Alighieri, *Purgatorio* (translated by R. L. Binyon), London 1938, p. 311. This was Eliot's favourite translation of Dante (W. T. Levy, op. cit., p. 113), and I am grateful to the Macmillan Company for allowing me to quote from it.
7. *Complete Poems and Plays*, London 1969, pp. 37–39.
8. Ibid., p. 38.
9. *Thoughts after Lambeth*, London 1931, p. 10.
10. E. A. Bennett, *Journals 1921–1928*, London 1933, p. 52; 10 September 1924.
11. *Complete Poems and Plays*, London 1969, p. 64.
12. William Shakespeare, *Antony and Cleopatra*, Act II sc. 2.
13. *Complete Poems and Plays*, London 1969, pp. 68–69.
14. Ibid., p. 66.
15. For an account of the original draft of *The Waste Land*, deposited in the Berg Collection of the New York Public Library, cf. *The Times Literary Supplement*, 7 November 1968, pp. 1, 238–9, 240. B. L. Reid op. cit., pp. 533–540, 580–581) explains how John Quinn came to acquire the original manuscript and typescript of *The Waste Land*.
16. Ibid., p. 540.
17. It was first printed in *The Criterion*, October 1922, pp. 50–64, and reprinted in America in *The Dial*, November 1922, pp. 473–485. The original volume edition appeared in 1922 in America and 1923 in England.
18. B. A. W. Russell, op. cit., vol. II, London 1968, p. 173; T. S. Eliot to Bertrand Russell, 15 October 1923.
19. Ibid., p. 58; Charlotte C. Eliot to Bertrand Russell, 23 May 1916.
20. C. C. Eliot, *Savonarola: A Dramatic Poem*, London 1926, published by Richard Cobden-Sanderson, pp. vii–xii.
21. Mrs. Eliot died on 10 September 1929, aged eighty-six.
22. It was about this time that Eliot moved to 9 Clarence Gate Gardens, Regent's Park, N.W.1.
23. With puckish humour, Eliot addressed two envelopes and a postcard to them in doggerel couplets. The originals of these addresses, dated 28 October 1932 and 7 and 8 October 1934, are in the collection of Mrs. Richard Cobden-Sanderson.

24. Under Faber & Gwyer's auspices, the magazine was first known as *The New Criterion*, then as *The Monthly Criterion* until it resumed its original name in September 1928.

25. Was this the sole reason for her retirement? After Eliot became a leading spokesman of the Church of England, following his baptism in 1927, Lady Rothermere found herself increasingly at variance with his point of view. She was also an admirer of Gide, and wished Eliot to publish extracts, in translation, from *Les Nourritures Terrestres* (1897); but this he refused to do.

26. Eliot also sought Lytton Strachey's collaboration in *The Criterion*, even suggesting an article on Macaulay, but Strachey was not to be persuaded. Cf. M. Holroyd, *Lytton Strachey: The Years of Achievement, 1910–1932*, London 1968, p. 366 n.

27. In a letter to Fr. Michael Hanbury O.S.B. dated 1 December 1954, Eliot writes appreciatively of his friendship with Thorold, whose contributions to *The Criterion* he greatly valued. (Letter in the collection of Donald Adamson.) Perhaps Thorold's best contribution was on Maine de Biran (April 1933).

28. *The Criterion*, July 1929, pp. 580–591, "The Aesthetic of Michelangelo."

29. E. A. Bennett, loc. cit.

30. *Complete Poems and Plays*, London 1969, pp. 115–126.

31. Ibid., pp. 42–43.

32. Cf. N. P. B. Braybrooke: loc. cit.

33. *Complete Poems and Plays*, London 1969, p. 121.

34. Ibid., p. 122.

35. The extant fragments of *Sweeney Agonistes* were published in *The New Criterion* (October 1926, pp. 713–718; January 1927, pp. 74–80), and afterwards in volume form in 1932.

36. This poem was not published by itself, but in *Poems 1909–1925*, where it was added to his previous volumes of poetry *Ara Vos Prec* (1920) and *The Waste Land* (1922).

37. *Complete Poems and Plays*, London 1969, p. 98.

38. Ibid., p. 84.

39. G. Santayana, *Three Philosophical Poets: Lucretius, Dante, and Goethe*, Cambridge (Massachusetts) 1910, p. 133. I am grateful to the Harvard University Press for their kind permission to quote these lines.

40. P. B. Shelley, *Complete Poetical Works*, Oxford 1952, p. 520.

41. *Complete Poems and Plays*, London 1969, p. 86.

42. *Poems 1909–1925*, London 1925, pp. 93–99.

43. C. Aiken, "T. S. Eliot," *Life*, 15 January 1965, p. 93.

CHAPTER 9
Into Publishing

1. M. Holroyd, *Lytton Strachey: The Years of Achievement, 1910–1932*, London 1968, p. 369; Virginia Woolf to Lytton Strachey, 23 February 1923.

2. Ibid., p. 366. Even Ernest Hemingway assisted the campaign (*A Moveable Feast*, London 1964, pp. 99–100). There had been a similar move in 1920: B. L. Reid, op. cit., pp. 436–437.

3. M. Holroyd, *Lytton Strachey: The Years of Achievement, 1910–1932*, London 1968, pp. 367–368.

4. E. A. Bennett, loc. cit.

5. B. A. W. Russell, op. cit., vol. II, London 1968, pp. 173–174.

6. We do not know what Russell predicted. The layout of Russell's *Autobiography* easily permits hiatuses of this sort.

7. B. A. W. Russell, op. cit., vol. II, London 1968, p. 173.

8. Ibid., p. 174.

9. Ibid., p. 173; 15 October 1923.

10. Ibid., p. 173.

11. F. V. Morley, "A Few Recollections of Eliot," in *T. S. Eliot: the Man and his Work* (ed. J. O. A. Tate), London 1967, p. 99.

12. Eliot suggests (*Geoffrey Faber, 1889–1961*, London 1961, p. 14) that Charles Whibley also had a hand in recommending him to Sir Geoffrey Faber.

13. Not without some diplomatic negotiation, however, as F. V. Morley explains (loc. cit., pp. 99–101).

14. T. S. Eliot, *Geoffrey Faber, 1889–1961*, London 1961, pp. 15–16. A. L. Rowse, *A Cornishman at Oxford*, London 1965, p. 314.

15. Andrewes was successively Bishop of Chichester, Ely and Winchester between the years 1605 and 1626. He was the most celebrated preacher of his time.

16. John Bramhall was Bishop from Derry from 1634 to 1661 and Archbishop of Armagh from 1661 to 1663.

17. *For Lancelot Andrewes: Essays on Style and Order*, London 1928.

18. "Lancelot Andrewes," *The Time Literary Supplement*, 23 September 1926.

19. "The Author of 'The Burning Babe'," *The Times Literary Supplement* 19 July 1926.

20. This article was reprinted, slightly modified, in Sencourt's *The Genius of the Vatican* (London 1935, pp. 79–92).

21. London 1926, published by Richard Cobden-Sanderson.

CHAPTER 10
A Convert to Anglicanism

1. "The Pensées of Pascal," introduction to the Everyman's Library edition of *Pascal's Pensées*, London 1931.
2. *A Sermon Preached in Magdalene College Chapel (7 March 1948)*, Cambridge 1948, p. 5.
3. H. Read, *English Stained Glass*, London 1927, reviewed by Robert Sencourt in "Storied Windows," *The Nineteenth Century*, April 1927, pp. 582–593.
4. On Francis Underhill's appointment as Dean of Rochester in 1932, the Rev. Sir Percy Maryon-Wilson Bt. became Eliot's spiritual counsellor.
5. Bishop Bell received a copy of the first edition of *Murder in the Cathedral*, containing a remarkable dedication (dated 4 June 1935) in Eliot's handwriting.
6. Letter from T. S. Eliot to Mrs. G. K. A. Bell, the only known copy of which is in the collection of Donald Adamson. The original of this letter, as of two other letters from Eliot to the Bells, was lost in February 1968.
7. For some account of Eliot's pro-Fascist inclinations at this time, cf. H. G. Nicolson, *Diaries and Letters, 1930–1939*, London 1966, p. 111; diary, 2 March 1932. Cf. Nicolson's tribute "My Words Echo," in *T. S. Eliot: A Symposium for his Seventieth Birthday* (ed. N. P. B. Braybrooke), London 1958, (republished by Garnstone Press, London 1970) pp. 34–35.

CHAPTER 11
Ash-Wednesday and Other Poems

1. *Complete Poems and Plays*, London 1969, p. 91.
2. For this detail we are indebted to Stephen Spender (J. O. A. Tate, ed., op. cit., p. 42).
3. P. Valéry, *Littérature*, Paris 1930, p. 65.
4. *Complete Poems and Plays*, London 1969, p. 310.
5. W. T. Levy, op. cit., p. 13.
6. *Complete Poems and Plays*, London 1969, p. 94.

CHAPTER 12
The Separation from Vivienne

1. R. Hodgson, *Poems*, London 1917, p. 136.
2. Queen Elizabeth II's grandmother, the Countess of Strathmore and Kinghorne, was Lady Ottoline Morrell's first cousin.
3. *Complete Poems and Plays*, London 1969, pp. 129–130.

4. Ibid., p. 105.

5. E. Caswell, *Hymns and Poems*, London 1873, p. 281.

6. After eleven years of intermittent madness, Ruskin's sanity completely deserted him ten years before his death.

7. Cf. H. M. Belgion, "Irving Babbitt and the Continent," in *T. S. Eliot: a Symposium* (Tambimuttu and Richard March, editors), London 1965, pp. 51–59.

8. Thomas Hardy, *Collected Poems*, London 1960, p. 108 (*To Life*).

9. Ibid., p. 153 (*In Tenebris*). My thanks are due to the Trustees of the Hardy Estate and the Macmillan Co. for their permission to quote from *To Life* and *In Tenebris*.

10. P. B. Shelley, op. cit., p. 673 (*To Jane*).

11. For an account of Eliot's crossing to Montreal (where he arrived on 23 October), cf. his letter to Mrs. Richard Cobden-Sanderson dated 28 October 1932.

12. *Complete Poems and Plays*, London 1969, p. 604.

13. On the limitations of Eliot's scholarship, cf. F. W. Bateson, "The Poetry of Learning," in *Eliot in Perspective* (ed. G. Martin), London 1970, pp. 31–44.

14. *Letters of Charles Eliot Norton*, London 1913, vol. II, pp. 236–237; 8 January 1896.

15. *Apology for the Countess of Pembroke*, 25 November 1932. The title concerns Sidney's sister Mary (1555–1621), wife of Henry, 2nd Earl of Pembroke.

16. *The Age of Dryden*, 2 December 1932.

17. *Wordsworth and Coleridge*, 9 December 1932.

18. *The Use of Poetry and the Use of Criticism*, London 1933, pp. 87–102.

19. Ibid., p. 106.

CHAPTER 13
33 Courtfield Road

1. Cf. F. V. Morley, loc. cit., pp. 103–107; supplemented by conversation with the late Mr. Eames.

2. H. E. Monro, *Collected Poems*, London, 1933, pp. xiii–xvi.

3. Cf. E. M. Browne, "T. S. Eliot in the Theatre," in *T. S. Eliot: the Man and his Work* (ed. J. O. A. Tate), London 1967, pp. 116–120.

4. H. W. Longfellow, op. cit., pp. 392–393.

5. W. Wordsworth, *Poetical Works*, vol. III, Oxford 1954, pp. 403–404.

6. A. Pope, *Poems*, vol. II, London 1962, p. 342.

7. In 1928–1929 Hayward contributed the following reviews to *The Criterion: Horace Walpole*, February 1928, pp. 182–184; *Sir Charles Sedley*, April 1929, pp. 540–543; *The Works of Sir Thomas Browne*, October

1929, pp. 157–162. In Hayward's engagement calendar there are entries "lunch with T.S.E." as early as 1929 (information kindly communicated by Hayward's sister, Mrs. R. H. Oakeley).

8. Reprinted with the kind permission of the Macmillan Co. from *Collected Poems* by W. B. Yeats. Copyright 1928 by the Macmillan Co., renewed 1956 by Georgie Yeats. Cf. W. B. Yeats, *Collected Poems*, London 1950, p. 219.

9. E. M. Browne, loc. cit., pp. 120–124.

CHAPTER 14
The First Plays

1. In April 1939.
2. In May 1949.
3. Letter from T. S. Eliot to Bishop G. K. A. Bell, dated 11 July 1935. The original of this letter was lost in February 1968, but a copy of the text is in the collection of Donald Adamson.
4. E. M. Browne, loc. cit., p. 124.
5. B. A. W. Russell, op. cit., vol. II, London 1968, p. 174; T. S. Eliot to Bertrand Russell, 7 May 1925.

CHAPTER 15
The War Years

1. C. Du Bos. *Approximations* (4e serie), Paris 1930, pp. 253–272.
2. Letter to T. S. Eliot dated 24 July 1944.
3. This letter, dated 3 September 1964, is reproduced by Admiral Morison in his article "The Dry Salvages and the Thacher Shipwreck" (*The American Neptune*, 1965, p. 247).
4. *The Church Looks Ahead*, London 1941, pp. 106–117: "Towards a Christian Britain."
5. *The Queen's Book of the Red Cross*, London 1939, pp. 51–52.
6. Ibid., pp. 53–54.
7. W. T. Levy, op, cit., pp. 71–72.

CHAPTER 16
Four Quartets

1. Burnt Norton House was a seat of the Earl of Harrowby. It is now a private school for maladjusted boys.
2. First published in *Collected Poems, 1909–1935*, London 1936, pp. 183–191.
3. *Bhagavad Gita* (translated by A. Besant), Madras 1924, pp. 120–121.

4. B. Pascal, *Œuvres complètes*, Paris 1954, p. 1, 313.
5. *Complete Poems and Plays*, London 1969, p. 522.

CHAPTER 17
At the Zenith

1. E. M. Browne, loc. cit., pp. 130–131.
2. Ibid., p. 130.
3. *Complete Poems and Plays*, London 1969, p. 194.
4. Much as Hayward admired Eliot's writings, he doubted whether the poet would always retain his immense reputation, as genius could hardly rest on so meagre an output. (Information kindly communicated by Mr. Cecil King.)
5. Eliot's appointment to the Order of Merit was gazetted on 1 January 1948.
6. *T. S. Eliot: A Symposium* (ed. Tambimuttu and Richard March), London 1948.
7. London 1952, with an introduction by T. S. Eliot, pp. 11–17.
8. *Gedenkschrift zur Verleihung des Hansischen Goethe-Preises 1954*, Hamburg 1955.
9. Cf. *The Book Collector*, winter 1965, Desmond Flower, pp. 452–453.
10. W. T. Levy, op. cit., p. 40; T. S. Eliot in conversation 29 June 1953.
11. London 1937.
12. E. M. Browne, loc. cit., p. 131.

CHAPTER 18
Eliot's Second Marriage

1. London 1913.
2. Indeed, even as late as 29 June 1953, when he was sixty-four, Eliot spoke of ending his days in a monastery (W. T. Levy, op. cit., p. 43).
3. According to another well-informed source, Eliot told John Hayward of his intentions on 9 January. But whether this was by word of mouth, or letter delivered after the wedding, we do not know.
4. Hayward's letters from Eliot and personal papers relating to him were bequeathed to King's College, Cambridge, with the stipulation that unpublished material should not be made available until the year 2000 to anyone other than the College Librarian.
5. Laforgue married Leah Lee on 31 December 1886 at St. Barnabas's Church, Kensington.
6. This reception was held on 26 March 1962. Eliot and Hayward met on one other occasion during the long twilight of their friendship: at Chris-

tie's auction-rooms on 22 June 1960, at the big sale of books and manuscripts in aid of the London Library.

7. *T. S. Eliot: a Symposium for his Seventieth Birthday* (ed. N. P. B.
Braybrooke), London 1958, and reprinted by Garnstone Press, London
1970.

8. H. G. Nicolson, "My Words Echo," op. cit., pp. 34–35.

9. H. Kenner, *The Invisible Poet: T. S. Eliot,* London 1960.

CHAPTER 19
The End of Life

1. It was published in *The Sunday Telegraph* on 16 December 1962, and
has been reprinted in *The New English Bible Reviewed* (ed. D. E.
Nineham), London 1965, pp. 96–101.

2. Eliot misquotes this new rendering of Matthew XX 12.

3. J. H. A. Sparrow, "Regina v. Penguin Books Ltd: an Undisclosed Element in the Case," *Encounter,* February 1962, pp. 35–43.

4. W. T. Levy (op. cit., p. 50) confirms this impression.

5. W. T. Levy, op. cit., pp. 126, 132.

6. Letter to Robert Sencourt, dated 6 November 1963, in the collection of
Donald Adamson.

7. J. H. Marx, *The Groucho Letters: Letters From and To Groucho Marx,*
London 1967.

8. W. T. Levy, op. cit., p. 140.

9. J. H. Marx, op. cit., p. 154; T. S. Eliot to Groucho Marx, April 1961.

10. Ibid., p. 160.

11. Ibid., p. 162; T. S. Eliot to Groucho Marx, 3 June 1964.

12. Ibid., pp. 162–164; Groucho Marx to Gummo Marx, 7 June 1964.

13. He was invested with this supreme civilian honour on 14 September
1964, in a ceremony at the American Embassy, London.

14. On 17 April 1965.

15. A further memorial service was held on 17 February 1965 at T. S.
Eliot's old parish church, St. Stephen's, Gloucester Road; a Requiem
Mass was celebrated and Canon V. A. Demant honoured the memory
of "the most invigorating interpreter of this age to itself." A com-
memorative tablet was unveiled in the Lady Chapel of St. Stephen's on
what would have been Eliot's eightieth birthday, 26 September 1968.

16. *Complete Poems and Plays,* London 1969, p. 190.

17. Ibid., p. 183.

18. On 4 January 1967.

Index